The Princeton Review®

T0006877

ACT® ENGLISH PREP

The Staff of The Princeton Review

PrincetonReview.com

Penguin Random House

The Princeton Review
110 E. 42nd Street, 7th Floor
New York, NY 10017
Email: editorialsupport@review.com

Published in the United States by Penguin Random House LLC,
New York.

Some of the content in *ACT English Prep* has previously
appeared in *English & Reading Workout for the ACT,* published as a trade paperback by Random House, an imprint and
division of Penguin Random House LLC, in 2019. Additionally,
some content has previously appeared in *SAT Prep*, published
as a trade paperback by Random House, an imprint and division of Penguin Random House LLC, in 2020.

ISBN: 978-0-525-57033-2
eBook ISBN: 978-0-525-57037-0
ISSN: 2691-7122

ACT is a registered trademark of ACT, Inc.

The Princeton Review is not affiliated with Princeton University.

The material in this book is up-to-date at the time of publication.
However, changes may have been instituted by the testing body
in the test after this book was published.

If there are any important late-breaking developments, changes,
or corrections to the materials in this book, we will post that
information online in the Student Tools. Register your book and
check your Student Tools to see if there are any updates posted
there.

Editor: Eleanor Green, Selena Coppock
Production Editor: Sarah Litt and Emma Parker
Production Artist: Jennifer Chapman, Jason Ullmeyer

Printed in the United States of America.

10 9 8 7 6 5 4 3 2 1

The Princeton Review Publishing Team
Rob Franek, Editor-in-Chief
David Soto, Senior Director, Data Operations
Stephen Koch, Senior Manager, Data Operations
Deborah Weber, Director of Production
Jason Ullmeyer, Production Design Manager
Jennifer Chapman, Senior Production Artist
Selena Coppock, Director of Editorial
Orion McBean, Senior Editor
Aaron Riccio, Senior Editor
Meave Shelton, Senior Editor
Chris Chimera, Editor
Patricia Murphy, Editor
Laura Rose, Editor
Alexa Schmitt Bugler, Editorial Assistant

Penguin Random House Publishing Team
Tom Russell, VP, Publisher
Alison Stoltzfus, Senior Director, Publishing
Brett Wright, Senior Editor
Emily Hoffman, Assistant Managing Editor
Ellen Reed, Production Manager
Suzanne Lee, Designer
Eugenia Lo, Publishing Assistant

Acknowledgments

Deepest gratitude to Sara Kuperstein, who was the primary author of this title.

A big thank you as well to Nicole Cosme, whose contributions helped make this title possible.

Thank you to Jess Thomas and Gabby Budzon for their contributions to this title.

Thank you to Jennifer Chapman, Sarah Litt, and Emma Parker for their time and attention to each page.

Special thanks to Adam Robinson, who conceived of and perfected the Joe Bloggs approach to standardized tests, and many of the other successful techniques used by The Princeton Review.

Amy Minster
Content Director
High School Programs

Contents

Get More (Free) Content

at **PrincetonReview.com/prep**

As easy as **1·2·3**

1 Go to PrincetonReview.com/prep or scan the **QR code** and enter the following ISBN for your book:

9780525570332

2 Answer a few simple questions to set up an exclusive Princeton Review account. *(If you already have one, you can just log in.)*

3 Enjoy access to your **FREE** content!

Once you've registered, you can...

- Find any late-breaking information released about the ACT

- Take a full-length practice ACT

- Get valuable advice about the college application process, including tips for writing a great essay and where to apply for financial aid

- If you're still choosing between colleges, use our searchable rankings of *The Best 388 Colleges* to find out more information about your dream school

- Check to see if there have been any corrections or updates to this edition

Need to report a potential **content** issue?

Contact **EditorialSupport@review.com** and include:

- full title of the book
- ISBN
- page number

Need to report a **technical** issue?

Contact **TPRStudentTech@review.com** and provide:

- your full name
- email address used to register the book
- full book title and ISBN
- Operating system (Mac/PC) and browser (Chrome, Firefox, Safari, etc.)

Look For These Icons Throughout The Book

 PROVEN TECHNIQUES

 APPLIED STRATEGIES

 OTHER REFERENCES

CONSIDERING AN ACT® PREP COURSE?

Pick the Option That's Right For You

OUR MOST POPULAR!

ACT COURSE

- 24/7 on-demand tutoring
- 36+ hours of classroom instruction
- Review and practice books

ACT TUTORING

- 18-hours of customized tutoring package
- Expert tutors matched to your goals
- Interactive score reports to track progress

ACT SELF-PACED

- 1-year access to online materials
- Practice drills for self studying

www.PrincetonReview.com | 1-800-2-REVIEW

Part I
Orientation

Chapter 1
Introduction to the English Test

WELCOME

The ACT can be an important part of college admissions. Many schools require or recommend their applicants submit either SAT or ACT scores. It's worth keeping in mind, though, that the importance of these tests will vary among the many colleges and universities in the United States. If you haven't already, make sure to research whether the ACT is required or recommended for admission to the schools you plan to apply to.

For more on admissions, see The Princeton Review's *The Best 388 Colleges* or visit our website, PrincetonReview.com.

During the COVID-19 pandemic, many schools went test-optional to account for the numerous students whose SAT and ACT tests were canceled. Some of those schools have returned to requiring test scores, while others have not yet but still may. For the most up-to-date information on the schools you are interested in, check out their admissions websites.

Even if ACT scores are optional, you may still want to submit them if you think your great ACT scores will boost your chances of acceptance. Furthermore, ACT scores are often used for scholarships, so it can be worth putting time into preparing for the test if you can save a good amount on your college education in return.

When colleges require standardized test scores, they will accept either SAT or ACT scores. The expert advice of The Princeton Review is to take whichever test you do better on and focus your efforts on preparing for that one.

Since you bought this book, we assume you've already made the decision to boost your ACT score. This book provides a strategic and efficient way to improve your scores, specifically on the English test. For a more thorough review of content and exhaustive practice, we recommend *ACT Prep* and our *ACT Practice Questions* book

FUN FACTS ABOUT THE ACT

The ACT is nothing like the tests you take in school. In your English class, you may learn grammar, but do you have to fix underlined portions of sentences? You do plenty of your own writing, but do you have to fix other people's writing?

All of the content review and strategies we teach in the following lessons are based on the specific structure and format of the ACT. Before you can beat a test, you have to know how it's built.

See The Princeton Review's companion books, *ACT Reading Prep*, *ACT Math Prep*, and *ACT Science Prep*.

Structure

The ACT is made up of four multiple-choice tests and an optional Writing test.

The five tests are always given in the same order.

English	Math	Reading	Science	Writing
45 minutes	60 minutes	35 minutes	35 minutes	40 minutes
75 questions	60 questions	40 questions	40 questions	1 Essay

Scoring

When students and schools talk about ACT scores, they mean the composite score, a range of 1–36. The composite is an average of the four multiple-choice tests, each scored on the same 1–36 scale. If you take the Writing test, you'll also receive an additional Writing score on a scale of 2–12. The Writing score is an average of four 2–12 subscores: Ideas and Analysis, Development and Support, Organization, and Language Use and Conventions. Neither the Writing test score nor the combined English plus Writing English Language Arts score affects the composite. Be sure to check ACT's website to determine whether your target schools want you to take the ACT Writing test.

Students also receive subscores in addition to their (1–36) composite ACT score. These indicators are designed to measure student performance and predict career readiness, as well as competency in STEM (Science, Technology, Engineering, Mathematics) and English Language Arts. ACT believes that these additional scores will give students better insight into their strengths and how those strengths can be harnessed for success in college and beyond. In addition to the 1–36 score for each of the tests and their composite score, students now see score breakdowns in the following categories:

- **STEM score:** This score represents students' overall performance on the math and science sections of the ACT. The goal of this score is to help students better understand their strengths in math and science and how they might use those strengths to guide their academic and career goals.

- **Progress Toward Career Readiness Indicator:** This is meant to help students understand the extent to which they are prepared for a future career. It can also help teachers guide their students toward numerous career pathways.

- **English Language Arts score:** This score measures achievement in the English, Reading, and Writing portions of the exam (for students who take all three of those sections), and it allows students to see how their performance compares with others.

- **Text Complexity Progress Indicator:** This is intended to help students determine how well they understand the kinds of complex texts they might encounter in college and whether they need to improve. This score is based on a student's performance on all of the writing passages.

There is also a section on the score report that breaks down each section into categories and tells you both how many questions there were in each category and how many of them you answered correctly. Some of these categories can be useful in helping you know what you need to study: for example, if you missed a lot of questions in the "Geometry" category, you should brush up your geometry skills. But if you did poorly in the "Integration of Knowledge and Ideas" category, it's not quite as obvious what you need to study. Don't worry about these scores, though—they're there because they align with federal academic standards and school districts that use the ACT for standardized testing for all juniors want those scores, but colleges don't typically look at them for admissions purposes.

It's All About the Composite

Whether you look at your score online or wait to get it in the mail, the biggest number on the page is always the composite. While admissions offices will certainly see the individual scores of all five tests (and their sub-scores), schools will use the composite to evaluate your application, and that's why it's the only one that matters in the end.

The composite is an average: let the full weight of that sink in. Do you need to bring up all four scores equally to raise your composite? Do you need to be a superstar on all four tests? Should you focus more on your weaknesses than your strengths? No, no, and absolutely not. The best way to improve your composite is not to shore up your weaknesses but exploit your strengths as much as possible.

> To improve your ACT score, use your strengths to lift the composite score as high as possible.

You don't need to be a rock star on all four tests. Identify two, maybe three tests, and focus on raising those scores as much as you can to raise your composite. Work on your weakest scores to keep them from pulling you down. Think of it this way: if you have only one hour to devote to practice the week before the ACT, put that hour to your best subjects.

Single-Section Tests and Superscoring

The people who write the ACT have announced their intention to allow students to take one, two, or three individual sections in a day, as opposed to needing to take the entire test. You will need to have taken a full ACT before using this option, and single-section tests will only be offered on the computer.

Unfortunately, plans to offer single-section retesting were delayed by the COVID-19 pandemic, and as of the publication of this book, a date for the rollout has not been announced. We encourage you to check the ACT website, www.act.org, for the most up-to-date information about the availability of single-section retesting when it is eventually offered.

One piece of good news is that ACT has begun Superscoring. If you take the ACT more than once, ACT will automatically take your highest English, Math, Reading, and Science scores and average them together to calculate a new "Superscore" composite.

Sounds great, right? We think it is—this gives you the opportunity to show your best ACT score to schools. Colleges and universities still have the option of whether or not to accept the Superscore, but for the schools that let you Superscore, this is all positive for you.

> Single-section testing is great, but research your goal schools' testing policies before relying on it!

Of course, you might have grabbed this book because you've already decided to focus on improving a single test for your superscore. So let's move on so we can dive in to the good stuff!

English Scores

Your English score can be one of the easiest to improve. The Reading and Science tests, for example, require skills that can be improved on, but the content you'll see in the passages is unpredictable, making it seem more difficult to prepare for those tests. The English test is much more rules-based, like the Math test. For most of the English content, if you know the rules, you can get the questions right every time, no matter what the topic of the passage is.

Time

Time is your enemy on the ACT. You have just over half a minute per question on the English test—and that's including the time it takes to read the passage. The Princeton Review's strategies are all designed to help you conquer this time crunch. In the chapters that follow, you'll learn how to use your time wisely.

STRATEGIES

You will raise your ACT score not by working harder but by working *smarter*, and a smart test-taker is a strategic test-taker. You will target specific content to review, you will apply an effective and efficient approach, and you will employ the common sense that frequently deserts many of us when we pick up a #2 pencil.

Check out these helpful Princeton Review signature strategies.

Each test on the ACT demands a different approach, and even the most universal strategies vary in their applications. In the chapters that follow, we'll discuss these terms in greater detail, customized for English.

Personal Order of Difficulty (POOD)

On other sections of the ACT, we advise students to do easier passages and easier questions first, saving the harder ones for later. Since each question is worth one point, you will get more points by doing the quicker, easier questions instead of the harder, more time-consuming questions. On the English test, however, this strategy isn't as effective. All five passages tend to be of a similar level of difficulty, so there isn't much of a reason to do them out of order. Additionally, it's not a good idea to save the harder questions for the end of the passage. Here's why: the English portion is testing you on writing skills, and part of that is the flow of ideas. Many of the harder questions require you to understand the main idea of a paragraph or passage. If you save them for last, you will have to go back and reread, and this will end up taking even more time. In addition, with 75 questions to answer in only 45 minutes, you don't want to waste time flipping back and forth. So what's a smart test-taker to do? Read and answer the questions in order so that when you come across questions that involve the author's main points and sequence of ideas, you'll have the context needed to answer them correctly.

Let's plan out a strategy to help you do this. First, let's distinguish between hard versus easy questions and time-consuming versus fast questions. The ACT English test has what we call Proofreader questions and Editor questions.

The Best Way to Bubble In

Work a page at a time, circling your answers right on the booklet. Transfer a page's worth of answers to the answer sheet at one time. It's better to stay focused on working questions rather than disrupt your concentration to find where you left off on the answer sheet. You'll be more accurate at both tasks. Do not wait until the end, however, to transfer all the answers from that test onto your answer sheet. Go a page at a time.

Proofreader questions don't actually ask a question—they just ask you to check, and possibly correct, the punctuation or grammar of an underlined portion of the text. These questions can be easy or hard, but they can always be done quickly, especially once you've learned the rules.

Editor questions take up more space on the page. They ask a question, and their answer choices are often much longer. Although these questions can also be easier or harder, no matter what, they will be more time-consuming.

Our best advice is to know the rules for the most commonly tested Proofreader topics so you can quickly get those questions right. Use the practice tests in this book to determine how rushed you feel on the English test. If, on a practice test, you have trouble getting to all the questions, try skipping some Editor questions as you go. (Skipping means you quickly bubble in your Letter of the Day and don't waste any time on the question.) This can allow you to finish the section and get to all of the quick Proofreader questions, thus earning you more points. Make a quick decision about whether each question should be done Now or Never.

Letter of the Day (LOTD)

Just because you don't *work* a question doesn't mean you don't *answer* it. There is no penalty for wrong answers on the ACT, so you should never leave any blanks on your answer sheet. When you guess on Never questions, pick your favorite two-letter combo of answers and stick with it. For example, always choose A/F or C/H. If you're consistent, you're statistically more likely to pick up more points.

Note: If you are taking the ACT on a computer, all of the questions will have answer choices A, B, C, D (or A, B, C, D, E on the Math test). On the paper-and-pencil ACT, every other question will have answer choices F, G, H, J (or F, G, H, J, K on the Math test).

Process of Elimination (POE)

Because the ACT is a multiple-choice test, using Process of Elimination, or POE, is hugely helpful. *You do not always need to know the right answer, as long as you know that the other options are not correct.* This is especially important on the English test. When you read an underlined portion that you know is incorrect, you may be tempted to correct it yourself. However, try to avoid this strategy. The ACT may not correct the sentence in the same way you want to correct it, and worse yet, there may be answers that do make your preferred correction but make other mistakes that you might not notice. It's always best to use POE with the answers that are there, rather than to come up with your own corrections. Furthermore, sometimes you may not notice that a sentence has an error. The answer choices can help you realize what rule the question is testing and whether it actually does have a mistake. Do not wait to look at the answers until you are ready to pick one—look at them right away. You'll find that this actually saves you time and improves your accuracy.

Pacing

The ACT may be designed for you to run out of time, but you shouldn't rush through it as fast as possible. All you'll do is make careless errors on easy questions you should get right and spend way too much time on difficult ones you're unlikely to get right.

To hit your target score, you have to know how many raw points you need. (Your raw score is simply the number of questions you answered correctly in that section of the ACT.) Your goals and strategies depend on the test and your own individual strengths.

On each test of the ACT, the number of correct answers converts to a scaled score of 1–36. ACT works hard to adjust the scale of each test at each administration as necessary to make all scaled scores comparable, smoothing out any differences in level of difficulty across test dates. There is thus no truth to any one test date being "easier" than the others, but you can expect to see slight variations in the scale from test to test.

This is the scale from the 2021-2022 free test ACT makes available at www.act.org. We're going to use it to explain how to pick a target score and pace yourself.

Proven Techniques
Familiarize yourself with these Princeton Review techniques before you dive into the practice drills.

English Pacing

Scale Score	Raw Score	Scale Score	Raw Score	Scale Score	Raw Score
36	72-75	24	53-55	12	23-24
35	70-71	23	51-52	11	19-22
34	68-69	22	48-50	10	16-18
33	67	21	45-47	9	13-15
32	66	20	42-44	8	11-12
31	65	19	40-41	7	9-10
30	64	18	38-39	6	7-8
29	62-63	17	36-37	5	6
28	61	16	33-35	4	4-5
27	60	15	30-32	3	3
26	58-59	14	27-29	2	2
25	56-57	13	25-26	1	0-1

For English, there is no order of difficulty of the passages or the questions. The most important thing is to finish, finding all the Now questions you can throughout the whole test and skipping over (LOTD) the Never questions as you go.

If you have not already, research some schools you may apply to and find out their average ACT scores. Use that to determine your target composite score. Then, determine your target score for each section. If you are stronger in one area, aim to score above your goal composite in that area. This will balance out a weaker area that may be below your goal composite.

Whatever your goal for English is, the chart on the previous page shows you the approximate number of questions you need for your target score. In theory, you could just do that number of questions, get them all right, and be good to go! However, that obviously isn't the safest or most realistic approach. We recommend that you aim to attempt about 10% more questions than the number of questions that you would need to get right for your target score, as a buffer. As an example, if you are aiming for a 25, we would recommend that you attempt 62–64 questions. This means you would be skipping 11–13 questions, which is about 2–3 per passage. By skipping a couple of the more time-consuming Editor questions on each passage (and using LOTD!), you give yourself a bit more time to ensure you get the 56-57 questions you need correct. Be careful, though—this only works if you have the tools you need to get the other questions right. Learn the rules before attempting this strategy.

Of course, if you are aiming to score above a 30, you will have to attempt (and get right!) almost all of the questions. This book will provide all you need, no matter what your target score is. You might be weaker in English or have a limited amount of time and simply want to master the biggest topics. Conversely, you might already do well on the English test, in which case, you may want to improve on some of the harder or more obscure topics. This book will provide you with the tools to accomplish any of these goals.

Be Flexible

The worst mistake a test-taker can make is to waste good time on bad questions. You read a question, don't understand it, so you read it again. And again. If you stare at it really hard, you know you're going to just *see* it. And you can't move on, because really, after spending all that time, it would be a waste not to keep at it, right? Actually, that way of thinking couldn't be more wrong.

You can't let one tough question drag you down. Instead, the best way to improve your ACT score is to follow our advice.

1. Use the techniques and strategies in the lessons to work efficiently and accurately through all your Now questions.
2. Know your Never questions, and use your LOTD.
3. Know when to move on. Use POE and guess from what's left.

Now, let's move on to the lessons and learn the best way to approach the content.

Chapter 2
How to Approach the ACT Online Test

In this chapter, you'll learn what to expect on the ACT Online Test, including how to apply its computer-based features and our strategies to the question types in each section—English, Math, Reading, Science, and Writing.

If your ACT will be pencil-and-paper, skip this chapter.

At the time of this book's printing, the option to take the ACT online at a testing center was postponed. ACT also plans to offer at-home online testing, although an exact rollout date has not yet been announced. For up-to-date news on both options, check the ACT website.

WHAT IS THE ACT ONLINE TEST?

The ACT Online Test is the ACT that you take on a computer, rather than with a pencil and paper. Despite the name, you can't take the ACT from the comfort of your own home; instead, you'll have to go to a testing center (possibly your high school) and take the test on one of the center's computers.

The ACT Online Test has the same overall structure, timing, and number of questions as the pencil-and-paper ACT. The scoring, score range, and scoring method are also the same. If the ACT Online Test is basically the same as the pencil-and-paper ACT, who would take the ACT Online Test?

WHO TAKES THE ACT ONLINE TEST?

ACT has been offering versions of the ACT on computer since about 2016. The first students to take the ACT on the computer were students taking the test at school. Schools and school districts decided whether to give the test on the computer.

As of September 2018, all students taking the ACT outside of the United States take the test on a computer (except for those students with accommodations requiring the use of a traditional pencil-and-paper test).

ACT has indicated that eventually students in the United States will have the option of taking the ACT Online Test instead of the traditional pencil-and-paper version. Students choosing this option will get their scores in about two to three business days (e.g., take the test on Saturday, have your score the next Wednesday). However, at the time of this printing, no specific timeline was available.

Single-Section Retesting is an incredible option for students. However, colleges still have the option to accept or not accept these new scores. Research your target schools early so you know your options!

Single-Section Retesting

If you are happy with the score you receive from a single test administration, you will still have the option to send just that score to colleges. If your score in one section is not as high as you'd like, you will eventually have a chance to correct that. Students who have already taken the full ACT may choose to take one, two, or three sections again using Single-Section Retesting. ACT will then produce a "superscore" consisting of your best results in all tests (English, Math, Reading, Science, and Writing (if you took it)). Note that not all colleges accept a superscored ACT, so do your research before taking advantage of this option.

ACT ONLINE TEST FEATURES

So, besides the obvious fact that it's taken on a computer, what are the differences between taking the ACT on the computer and taking it on paper? Let's start with what you can't do on the ACT Online Test. You can't "write" on the screen in a freehand way. You're limited in how you're able to mark the answer choices, and each question appears on its own screen (so you can't see multiple questions at one glance). You will also be given a small "whiteboard" and dry erase pen with which to make notes and do work.

So, what features does the ACT Online Test have?

- Timer
    - You can hide the timer by clicking on it.
    - There is a 5-minute warning toward the end of each test. There is no audible signal at the 5-minute warning, only a small indicator in the upper-right corner of the screen.
- Nav tool
    - You can use this tool to navigate directly to any question in the section.
    - The Nav tool blocks the current question when opened.
    - It also shows what questions you have flagged and/or left blank.
    - You can flag questions in this menu.
- Question numbers at the bottom of the screen
    - You can click on these numbers to navigate directly to any question in the section.
    - These numbers also indicate whether a question has been flagged and/or left blank.
- Flag tool
    - You can flag a question on the question screen itself or by using the Nav tool.
    - Flagging a question has no effect besides marking the question for your own purposes.
- Answer Eliminator
    - Answer choices can be "crossed-off" on-screen.
    - An answer choice that's been eliminated cannot be chosen and must be "un-crossed-off" first by clicking the answer choice.
- Magnifier
    - You can use this to magnify specific parts of the screen.
- Line Mask
    - This tool covers part of the screen. There is an adjustable window you can use to limit what you can see.
    - This is an excellent tool if you need an aid to help you focus on specific parts of the text or figure.
    - However, not everyone will find this tool useful, so do not feel obligated to use it!
    - Note that you cannot highlight the text in the window of the Line Mask.
- Answer Mask
    - This tool hides the answer choices of a question.
    - Answers can be revealed one at a time.
- Screen Zoom
    - This tool changes the zoom of the entire screen (as opposed to the magnifier, which magnifies only one part of the screen).
    - Your screen zoom setting will remain the same from question to question.
- Highlighter
    - You can use this tool to highlight parts of passage text, question text, or answer text.
    - You cannot highlight within figures.
    - If you highlight in a passage with multiple questions, your highlights will only show up on that question. (In other words, if you highlight, for example, question 1 of a Reading passage, questions 2–10 of that same passage will not show those highlights.)
    - Turning off the highlighter tool removes your highlights.

- Shortcuts:

Keybind	Function	Keybind	Function
Ctrl + H	Toggle Help	Ctrl + Enter	Answer Question
Ctrl + F	Flag Item	Alt + M	Toggle Magnifier
Ctrl + I	Item Navigation	Alt + H	Toggle Highlighter
Alt + P	Previous Question	Alt + E	Toggle Answer Eliminator
Alt + N	Next Question	Alt + A	Toggle Answer Masking
A-E or 1-5	Select Alternative	Alt + L	Toggle Line Masking

- The Writing test is typed, rather than written by hand.

You will also be given a small "whiteboard" and dry erase pen with which to make notes and do work.

HOW TO APPROACH THE ACT ONLINE TEST

The strategies mentioned in this chapter are thoroughly discussed in our comprehensive guide, *ACT Prep*, so be sure to pick up a copy of that book if you have not already done so. These approaches were created in reference to the pencil-and-paper format, but they still apply to the ACT Online Test with some adjustments. This chapter assumes your familiarity with these strategies and will show you how to make the best use of them given the tools available in the computer-based format.

You will also want to incorporate some computer-based practice into your prep plan. ACT's website has practice sections for each of the four multiple-choice parts of the test and for the essay. We recommend that you do those sections toward the end of your preparation (and close to your test date) to give yourself an opportunity to practice what you've learned on a platform similar to the one you'll be using on the day of the test.

> **Remember!**
> Your goal is to get the best possible score on the ACT. ACT's goal is to assign a number to you that (supposedly) means something to colleges. Focus on your goal!

If you are planning to take the ACT online, you should practice as if you're doing all your work on the computer, even when you're working in a physical book. Use a highlighter, but don't use the highlighter on any figures (as the ACT Online Test won't let you do so). Use your pencil to eliminate answer choices and have a separate sheet of paper or a whiteboard to do any work you need to do, instead of writing on the problem itself.

Also, remember that our approaches work. Don't get misled by ACT's instructions on the day of the test—their way of approaching the test won't give you the best results!

Overall

Your Personal Order of Difficulty (POOD) and Pacing goals will be the same on the ACT Online Test as on the pencil-and-paper version. Because it is easy to change your answers, put in your Letter of the Day (LOTD) when skipping a Later or Never question. Use the Flag tool on the Later questions so you can jump back easily (using either the navigation bar at the bottom of the screen or the Nav tool).

Process of Elimination (POE) is still a vital approach. On both the paper-and-pencil ACT and the ACT Online Test, there are more wrong answers than correct ones. Eliminating one you know are wrong helps you to save time, avoid trap answers, and make a better guess if you have to. On the ACT Online Test, you cannot write on the test, but you can use the Highlighter tool. Turn on these tools (and the Line Mask, if desired) at the beginning of the English section and use them throughout.

ENGLISH

The Basic Approaches to both Proofreader and Editor questions are the same on the computerized and the paper versions of the ACT. When you decide to skip a question to come back to it Later (for example, a question asking for the introduction to the topic of the passage before you've read any part of the passage), flag the question so you can easily jump back to it before moving on to the next passage. When you have five minutes remaining, flag your current question and use the Nav tool to make sure you've put in your LOTD for any questions that you haven't done, then return to your spot and work until time runs out.

For a comprehensive review of all sections of the ACT and the strategies mentioned throughout this chapter, check out our book, *ACT Prep*.

When you work Proofreader questions, you can use the Highlighter tool to help you focus on the key parts of the text. Let's see an example:

    Sneaking down the corridor, the agent, taking

care not to alert the guards, spotting the locked door.

  A. NO CHANGE
  B. spot
  C. are spotting
  D. spots

Use the tools available to help you focus on the key portions of the text. Practice with a highlighter when you're working on paper (instead of underlining with your pencil).

Here's How to Crack It

Verbs are changing in the answer choices, so the question is testing subject/verb agreement. The verb must be consistent with the subject. *The agent* is the subject; highlight it:

    Sneaking down the corridor, the agent, taking

care not to alert the guards, spotting the locked door.

  A. NO CHANGE
  B. spot
  C. are spotting
  D. spots

The agent is singular, so the verb must be singular. Eliminate (B) and (C), as both are plural. *Spotting* cannot be the main verb of a sentence, so eliminate (A). The correct answer is (D).

Similarly, the Highlighter tool is helpful on Editor questions. Use the tool on both the passage and the question to help you focus on the relevant parts of each.

As it's name suggests, the Indian fantail is not native to North America. In fact, its establishment here was quite accidental. In 1926, the San Diego Zoo acquired four pythons from India for its reptile exhibit. The long trip from India required, that, the pythons be provided with food for the journey, and a group of unfortunate fantails was shipped for just that purpose. Two lucky fantails survived, and their beautiful appearance caused the San Diego Zoo to keep and breed them for the public to see. Eventually, some of the animals escaped captivity and developed populations in the wild, all thanks to those two birds!

Given that all the choices are true, which one provides the most relevant and specific information at this point in the essay?

- A. NO CHANGE
- B. and they have quite an appetite.
- C. because no one wanted them to starve.
- D. and they are quite picky in what they'll eat.

Here's How to Crack It

The question asks for the *most relevant and specific information*. Highlight those words in the question. The first sentence of the paragraph focuses on the *Indian fantail*, and the sentence after the underlined portion discusses *(t)wo lucky fantails*. The final sentence discusses *the animals* that escaped. Highlight these words in the paragraph.

Your screen should look like this:

As it's name suggests, the Indian fantail is not native to North America. In fact, its establishment here was quite accidental. In 1926, the San Diego Zoo acquired four pythons from India for its reptile exhibit. The long trip from India required, that, the pythons be provided with food for the journey, and a group of unfortunate fantails was shipped for just that purpose. Two lucky fantails survived, and their beautiful appearance caused the San Diego Zoo to keep and breed them for the public to see. Eventually, some of the animals escaped captivity and developed populations in the wild, all thanks to those two birds!

Given that all the choices are true, which one provides the most relevant and specific information at this point in the essay?

- A. NO CHANGE
- B. and they have quite an appetite.
- C. because no one wanted them to starve.
- D. and they are quite picky in what they'll eat.

Use POE, focusing on whether the choice is consistent with the highlights in the passage. The sentence as written discusses *a group of unfortunate fantails*; keep (A). Choices (B), (C), and (D) do not talk about the Indian fantail; instead, they focus on the pythons. This is inconsistent with the goal of the sentence and the content of the paragraph; eliminate those answers. The correct answer is (A).

Finally, you can't write in the passage, so you'll need to approach the Vertical Line Test slightly differently. On the paper-and-pencil ACT, you would use this strategy for questions about punctuation, drawing a vertical line where the punctuation breaks up the ideas in the text. On the computerized ACT, you should use the whiteboard to handle these questions.

I'm not searching for a ghost or yeti, my phantom is the Indian fantail. These beautiful creatures are members of the pigeon family, but you could not tell that by looking at them.

   ○ **A.** NO CHANGE
   ○ **B.** yeti: my phantom
   ○ **C.** yeti my phantom
   ○ **D.** yeti, since this

Here's How to Crack It

Punctuation is changing in the answer choices, so the question is testing STOP and GO punctuation. There is Half-Stop punctuation in (B), so use the Vertical Line Test. You cannot draw a line in the text, so draw a "t" on your whiteboard, with "yeti" in the bottom-left and "my" in the bottom-right:

Read each part of the sentence and determine whether it is complete or incomplete. *I'm not searching for a ghost or yeti* is a complete idea; write "C" in the upper-left of the "t." *My phantom is the Indian fantail* is also a complete idea; write "C" (for "complete") in the upper-right of the "t." Your board should look like this:

Eliminate any answer that cannot link two complete ideas. Both (A) and (C) use GO punctuation, which cannot link complete ideas; eliminate (A) and (C). Choice (D) adds *since*, which makes the idea to the right of the line incomplete. However, *since* is used to show time or causation, which does not work in the context of the sentence. Eliminate (D). The correct answer is (B).

MATH

First off, you'll still need to bring your calculator to the ACT Online Test—which is a good thing! You're already comfortable with your personal calculator, so there will be one less thing to worry about on the day of the test.

> **Write it down!**
> It is tempting to do all your work in your head. Don't fall into this trap! It's easier to make mistakes when you're not writing down your work, and you'll often have to "go back" if you don't have something written down. Use your whiteboard!

When choosing questions to do Later, flag the question so you can easily navigate back to it after doing your Now questions. Do put in your LOTD when doing so; you don't want to accidently leave a question blank! When you get the five-minute warning, finish the question you're working on, flag it (so you can find your spot easily), then put in your LOTD for every unanswered question. Then you can go back to working until time runs out.

Use the Highlighter tool to highlight what the question is actually asking, especially in Word Problems. Of course, you'll want to use your whiteboard when working the steps of a math problem (don't do the work in your head!).

ACT Online Geometry Basic Approach

Because you can't write on the screen, the Basic Approach for Geometry questions needs a few slight tweaks:

1. Draw the figure on your whiteboard (copy if it's provided; draw it yourself otherwise). If the figure would be better drawn differently from the way ACT has drawn it (for instance, a similar triangles question), redraw the figure in a way that will help you answer the question.

2. Label the figure you drew on your whiteboard with the information from both ACT's figure and the question.

3. Write down any formulas you need and fill in the information you know.

Let's see how that works on a question.

In the figure below, triangle *ABC* is similar to triangle *DEF*. What is the length of *EF* ?

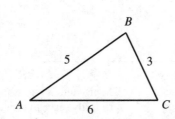
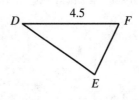

- A. 1.5
- B. 2.25
- C. 3
- D. 4
- E. 4.5

Here's How to Crack It

The question asks for the length of *EF*, so highlight that in the question. Follow the Geometry Basic Approach. Start by drawing the figure on your whiteboard. Because the triangles are similar, redraw triangle *DEF* to be oriented the same way as *ABC*. Label your figure with the given information.

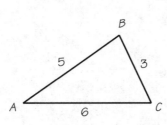
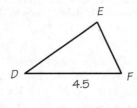

Write down the equation you need and fill in the necessary information. *AC* corresponds to *DF*, and *BC* corresponds to *EF*. Set up a proportion: $\dfrac{AC}{DF} = \dfrac{BC}{EF}$. Fill in the information from your figure: $\dfrac{6}{4.5} = \dfrac{3}{x}$, where *x* is equal to *EF*. Cross-multiply to get $6x = 3(4.5)$, or $6x = 13.5$. Divide both sides by 6 to get $x = 2.25$. The correct answer is (B).

READING

First off, there are a few differences between the pencil-and-paper ACT and the ACT Online Test. In the ACT Online Test, there are no line references; rather, the relevant part of the text is highlighted. The passage will also "jump" to the highlighted text if it's off the screen when you go to that question. This may disorient you at first: be prepared for this to happen.

Let's see an example.

...protested every step. We could still run, but, Hook worried, for how long? In a cross-country race, only a team's top five runners score, and we weren't those five. Our job was to finish ahead of as many of our rival teams' top fives as we could.

Leah was a senior that year, my freshman year. All season, she'd been counting down to this last race, praying her body wouldn't say *No*. She and I joked that we needed to go to the Knee Store and pick out new knees, ones that wouldn't crack and pop and burn all the time. It was hard to watch a teammate in that much pain, but Leah was a trooper, never slacking from workouts, never stopping to walk, never losing sight of the next person in front of her to catch.

The crack of the starter's pistol sent us surging out of that little crop of trees and onto the race course. I hollered, "See you at the Knee Store!" Behind me, she laughed.

The pack stayed tight through the first quarter-mile, and I was surrounded by so many bodies I couldn't think. I just ran, putting one foot in front of the other, trying not to fall. Trying to look beyond the jostling mass surrounding me, I could barely...

The narrator's references to the Knee Store primarily serve to suggest that:

- **A.** Leah wishes to buy better knee supports.
- **B.** the narrator and Leah use humor to cope with their pain.
- **C.** the narrator desires to learn more about her injury.
- **D.** Leah's injuries, unlike the narrator's, have become unbearable.

> Reading on a computer screen can be disorienting. Practice by reading articles or other passages on the computer when possible.

Here's How to Crack It

The question asks what the *references to the Knee Store...suggest*. The references to the *Knee Store* are highlighted in the text. Note that the text has shifted down to the highlighted portions. The window indicates that Leah and the narrator *joked that we needed to go to the Knee Store*. Leah *laughed* after the narrator referred to the Knee Store. Therefore, the answer should be consistent with joking and laughing. Choice (A) takes the reference too literally; eliminate (A). "Humor" is consistent with the text's references to *joked* and *laughed*; keep (B). There's no indication of the narrator's goal to *learn more about her injury*, nor does the text support the idea that Leah's injuries *have become unbearable*, eliminate (C) and (D). The correct answer is (B).

When you have five minutes remaining, flag your current question and use the Nav tool to make sure you've put in your LOTD for any questions that you haven't done. Then return to your spot and work until time runs out. If you've just started or finished a passage, click through the questions to look for Easy to Find questions in the remaining time, and don't forget to put in your LOTD for any question you don't answer!

The biggest difference between the ACT Online Test and the paper-and-pencil ACT is that you can only see one question on the screen at a time. Rather than looking over the questions at a glance, you must click from question to question. This feature means that the Reading Basic Approach (covered below) needs to be modified in order to be as time efficient as possible.

ACT Online Reading Basic Approach

1. **Preview**
   Read only the blurb—do not go through and map the questions. Instead, write the question numbers on your whiteboard to prepare to Work the Passage.

2. **Work the Passage**
   This step is *even more* optional on the ACT Online Test than on the pencil-and-paper ACT. You haven't mapped the questions, and your highlights only show up on one question. If you do decide to Work the Passage, ensure that you're getting through the passage in 2–3 minutes. More likely, you'll find it best to just skip this step and move on to the questions after reading the blurb and setting up your whiteboard.

   > You don't get points for reading—only for answering questions correctly. Determine whether Working the Passage helps you answer questions correctly and quickly.

3. **Select and Understand a Question**
   When Selecting a Question, if a question is Easy to Find (a portion of the text is highlighted or you Worked the Passage and know where in the passage the content you need is), do it Now. Understand the question, then move on to Step 4. If the question is not Easy to Find (in other words, you don't immediately know where in the passage to go), write down the question's lead words on your whiteboard next to the question number. Include EXCEPT/LEAST/NOT if the question includes those words. If there are no lead words, flag the question.

   After you do all the questions with highlights, then Work the Passage, scanning actively for your lead words. Once you find a lead word, do the corresponding question. After answering the questions with lead words, finish with the flagged questions.

4. **Read What You Need**
   Find the 5–10 lines you need to answer the question. Remember that only the quotation will be highlighted—the answer is not necessarily highlighted. You must read the lines before and after the highlighted portion to ensure that you find the correct answer to the question. If you find the Line Mask tool helpful, use it to frame your window.

5. **Predict the Correct Answer**

   As you read, look for evidence for the answer to the question in your window and highlight it using the highlighter tool. (You can highlight text that ACT has already highlighted—the color will change to "your" highlighting color.) As always, base your prediction on the words in the passage as much as possible.

6. **Use POE**

   Use the Answer Eliminator tool to narrow the answer choices down to one answer. If the question is an EXCEPT/LEAST/NOT question, instead write ABCD on your whiteboard and mark each answer T or F for True or False (or Y or N for Yes or No) and choose the odd one out.

Dual Reading Approach

The questions for Dual Reading passages are grouped with the questions about Passage A, then those about Passage B, then those about both passages. Each question should be labeled with an indicator for the passage the question refers to. Work each passage separately, answering all the Passage A questions you plan to answer before moving onto the Passage B questions.

You should also write down the Golden Thread of each passage on your whiteboard—either after Working the Passage or after finishing the questions on that passage. That will aid you in answering the questions about both passages.

SCIENCE

The overall approach to the Science test is the same on the ACT Online Test as it is on the traditional pencil-and-paper version. There are a few small adjustments to make, but the overall strategy remains the same.

The Flag tool is very important when identifying Later passages and questions. On a Later passage, flag the first question, then put your LOTD for every question on the passage. Make a note on your whiteboard of the first question in the passage so you can easily jump back to the passage.

When working a Now passage, you may still encounter a Later question. For these stand-alone Later questions, flag the question but don't put in your LOTD. When you get to the end of a passage, check the bar at the bottom of the screen to make sure you have answered every question up to that point.

Science Basic Approach

There are a few small changes to the Science approach when taking the ACT Online Test.

1. **Work the Figures**

   You can't highlight the figures. Experiment with taking quick notes about the variables, units, and trends on your whiteboard and determine whether it helps you find the needed information quickly.

2. **Work the Questions**
   Highlight the words and phrases from the figures in the question to help guide you to the relevant information.

3. **Work the Answers**
   Use the Answer Eliminator tool to work POE on answer choices with multiple parts.

Let's look at an example.

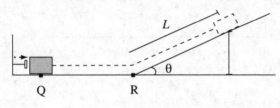

A block is placed on a frictionless horizontal surface at point Q. The block is pushed with a plunger and given initial velocity v along the horizontal surface. At point R, the block slides up a ramp with coefficient of friction f to a maximum distance L along the ramp. The distance between points Q and R is 1.0 m.

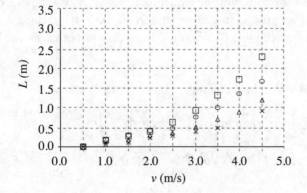

Figure 1

Figure 2, below, shows how L varies with v for different f on a ramp with $\theta = 20°$. Figure 3 (on the following page) shows how L varies with v for different θ on a ramp with $f = 0.1$.

Key	
Marker	f
□	0.15
○	0.30
△	0.60
×	0.90

Figure 2

> **Scrolling Passages**
> Most passages in Science will require scrolling down to see all the figures. Look for a scroll bar for every passage!

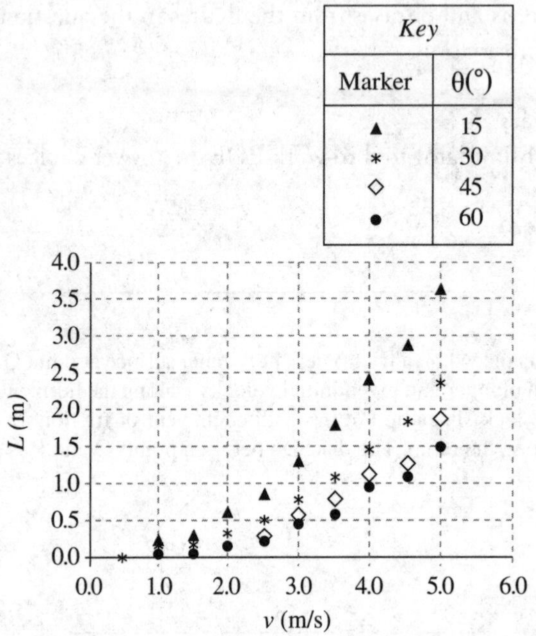

Key	
Marker	θ(°)
▲	15
∗	30
◇	45
●	60

Figure 3

If $f = 0.90$ for the sliding block and $v = 5.5$ m/s, L will most likely be closest to which of the following?

- A. 0.3 m
- B. 0.7 m
- C. 1.5 m
- D. 3.0 m

Here's How to Crack It

Start by Working the Figures. Figure 1 shows the points Q and R and variables L and θ, but there are no numbers or trends. Figure 2 shows a direct relationship between L (m) and v (m/s); mark this on your whiteboard. Furthermore, the legend gives values of f; as f increases, L decreases. Mark these relationships on your whiteboard. Figure 3 also shows a direct relationship between L (m) and v (m/s); the legend, however, gives θ (°). As θ increases, L decreases. Put these on your whiteboard as well. Note that Figures 2 and 3 show both L and v; Figure 2 has f, whereas Figure 3 has θ.

Your whiteboard should look like the following:

Figure 2: L (m) ↑ v (m/s) ↑ and f ↑ L ↓

Figure 3: L (m) ↑ v (m/s) ↑ and θ ↑ L ↓

The question refers to the variables f, v, and L; highlight those variables. Figure 2 has all three variables. The highest value of v given in the figure is 4.5, so start there and use the trend to make a prediction about a v of 5.5. At $v = 4.5$ and $f = 0.90$, L is approximately 0.9. The trend is increasing, so a v of 5.5 must result in an L value of greater than 0.9; eliminate (A) and (B).

An *L* value of 3.0 would be higher than any value already in Figure 2, and extending the trend for the line created by the $f = 0.90$ marks would not result in *L* increasing to 3.0 by the time *v* reaches 5.5; eliminate (D). Although you can't physically extend the line because it's on a computer screen, it may be a good idea to use your finger to trace where you would draw on the screen. The correct answer is (C).

You'll still approach the passage that's all or mostly text as if it is a Reading passage. Unlike in Reading, you will want to Map the Questions during the Preview step, as there will not be a group of questions about each passage like there is in the Dual Reading passage. Instead, the questions will not be asked in any particular order, so use your whiteboard to map out which scientist(s) or experiment(s) each question refers to. As with the other sections, at the five-minute warning, flag your question, put in your LOTD on any unanswered question, then keep working until time runs out.

WRITING

As you have probably guessed, you'll be typing the Writing test on the ACT Online Test. But before we get to writing the essay, there are a few minor points to note about the format of this test on the computer.

First, you won't be able to highlight when Working the Prompt or Perspectives, so be sure to write notes on your whiteboard. Second, ACT has given the prompt and perspectives on one screen, then repeated them on the screen that contains a text box. Feel free to do your work on the screen within the text box. If you're used to making your essay outlines on a computer, you can use the text box to do so here, as long as you remember to delete any notes before the section comes to an end.

When writing the essay, all the same points apply to both the pencil-and-paper and online tests (have a clear thesis, make and organize your arguments in a way that is easy to follow, etc.). When you have 5 minutes left, quickly type up a conclusion paragraph (if you haven't already), then go back and finish up your body paragraph ideas. It's more important to have a conclusion than it is to have perfect body paragraphs. Finally, spend a minute or two at the end to quickly fix any obvious typos or grammatical issues.

When you practice the Writing test at home, type your essay in a word processing program instead of writing it by hand. Be sure to turn off spell check, as the ACT does not provide it, so you don't want to rely on it.

That's it! Everything you've learned for the pencil-and-paper ACT can be applied to the ACT Online Test with a few small tweaks. You've got this!

Part II
English Basics

Chapter 3
The ACT
English Test

The English test is not a grammar test. It's also not a test of how well you write. In fact, it tests your editing skills: your ability to fix errors in grammar and punctuation and to improve the organization and style of five different passages. In this chapter, you'll learn the basic strategy of how to crack the passages.

FUN FACTS ABOUT THE ENGLISH TEST

Before we dive into the details of the content and strategy, let's review what the English test looks like. Remember, the five tests on the ACT are always given in the same order, and English is always first.

There are five prose passages on topics ranging from historical essays to personal narratives. Each passage is typically accompanied by 15 questions for a total of 75 questions that you must answer in 45 minutes. Portions of each passage are underlined, and you must decide whether these are correct as written or one of the other answers would fix or improve the selection. Other questions will ask you to add, cut, or reorder text, while still others will ask you to evaluate the passage as a whole.

WRITING

While the idea of English grammar makes most of us think of persnickety, picky rules long since outdated, English is actually a dynamic, adaptive language. We add new vocabulary all the time, and we let common usage influence and change many rules. Pick up a handful of style books and you'll find very few rules that everyone agrees upon. This is actually good news when studying for the ACT: you're unlikely to see questions testing the most obscure or most disputed rules.

The 4 Cs: Complete, Consistent, Clear, and Concise

ACT test writers will never make you name a particular error. But with 75 questions, they can certainly test a lot of different rules—and yes, that's leaving out the obscure and debated rules. You would drive yourself crazy if you tried to learn, just for the ACT, all of the grammar you never knew in the first place. You're much better off with a common-sense approach. That's where the 4 Cs come in.

Good writing should be in *complete* sentences; everything should be *consistent*; the meaning should be *clear*. The best answer, free of any errors, will be the most *concise*.

Grammar Review

The 4 Cs make sense of the rules you should specifically study. Focus your efforts on heavily tested topics that you can identify and know (or can learn) how to fix. Can't identify what the question is testing? Apply the 4 Cs.

In this book, you will learn how to crack the most heavily-tested and straightforward topics. If you already do well on the English test and are aiming for a top score, you'll also find a review of some of the trickier topics. But first, you need to know how to crack the test and apply our 5-step Basic Approach.

HOW TO CRACK THE ENGLISH TEST

The Passages

As always on the ACT, time is your enemy. With only 45 minutes to review 5 passages and answer 75 questions, you can't read a passage in its entirety and then go back to do the questions. For each passage, work the questions as you make your way through the passage. Read from the beginning until you get to an underlined selection, work that question, and then resume reading until the next underlined portion and the next question.

The Questions

Not all questions are created equal. In fact, ACT divides the questions on the English test into three categories: Production of Writing, Knowledge of Language, and Conventions of Standard English. These designations will mean very little to you when you're taking the test. Each question is worth the same number of points, after all, and you'll crack most of the questions the same way, regardless of what ACT calls them. Many of the Production of Writing questions, however, are those on organization and style, and these Editor questions can take longer to answer than other questions do. Since there is no order of difficulty of the passages or of the questions, all that matters is that you identify your *Now* and *Never* questions and make sure you finish.

The Basic Approach

While some of the Production of Writing questions come with *actual* questions, the majority of the 75 questions are Proofreader questions that provide only 4 answer choices and little direction of what to do. So allow us to tell you *exactly* what to do.

Step 1: Identify the Topic

For each underlined portion, read to the end of the sentence and then look at the answers. The answers are your clues to identifying what the question is testing. Take a look at the following example.

While innovations in the mass production of steel were an important element in the rise of skyscrapers, elevators are equally responsible for the dramatic heights of modern cities skylines.
                                          1

1. **A.** NO CHANGE
   B. cities' skyline's.
   C. cities' skylines.
   D. city's skylines'.

Do any of the words change? No. What is the only thing that does change? Apostrophes. So what must be the topic of the question? Apostrophes.

Always identify the topic of the question first. Pay attention to what changes versus what stays the same in the answers.

Step 2: Use POE

To go from good to great on ACT English, you can't just fix the sentence in your head and then look for the answer choice that matches your idea of the correct sentence. Instead, once you've identified what's changing in the answer choices, use POE to eliminate the answers you know are wrong.

For question 1, no apostrophe is needed on *skylines*, since nothing belongs to the *skylines*; eliminate (B) and (D). The difference between (A) and (C) is whether there's an apostrophe on *cities*. The *skylines* belong to the *cities*, so *cities* needs an apostrophe: choose (C). (If you're not quite sure about the apostrophe rules, don't worry—you'll learn more about them in the next chapter).

If you tried to fix this sentence in your head, you might have missed the extra apostrophe in (D) and gotten the question wrong. Using POE on every English question (instead of just when you're stuck or unsure) will help you consistently choose the correct answer. Always start by eliminating the answers you know are wrong, and then compare the choices that are left.

Step 3: Use the Context

Even though you may struggle with time on the English test, you can't skip the non-underlined text in between questions in order to save yourself a few seconds. Take a look at this next question.

> Because rudimentary elevators have been around
> <u>2</u>
> at least since the 4th century BCE, what we would
> consider "modern" passenger elevators were not
> common until the late 19th century.

2. **F.** NO CHANGE
   G. Considering that
   H. Although
   J. Now that

Don't forget to apply the first two steps. The transition word is changing in the answers. Transitions must be *consistent* with the ideas in the sentence. How do you know which transition to use? Read the entire sentence for the full context. The first part of the sentence says that elevators have been around for a long time. The second one says they haven't been around all that long. These ideas contrast with one another, so eliminate all answers that don't indicate a contrast between ideas. Only (H) indicates a contrast, so that's the answer.

Always finish reading the sentence before attacking the question, and don't skip the non-underlined portions between questions. The non-underlined text provides the context you need.

Step 4: Trust Your Ear, But Verify

Your ear can be good at raising the alarm for outright errors and clunky, awkward phrasing. You should, however, always verify what your ear signals. Steps 1 and 2 will help with that: use the answers to identify the topic, and use POE heavily. It's also important to be careful of errors your ear *won't* catch. Using the answers to identify the topic will save you there as well.

Try the following question.

The Otis Elevator Company was the first to

install their product, a passenger elevator with a
    <u>   </u>
    3

safety brake that kept passengers from plummeting

to their deaths if a cable broke, in a New York

building in 1874.

3. A. NO CHANGE
   B. they're
   C. it's
   D. its

That sounds fine as-is, right? But before you circle NO CHANGE and go on your merry way, look at the answers to identify the topic and confirm there is no error. Only the pronoun changes, so the question is testing pronouns. *Their* is a plural pronoun, but it refers to the *Otis Elevator Company,* which is singular. Cross off (A) and (B) because both contain plural pronouns. Since you need a possessive pronoun, cross off (C) as well. Choice (D) is the correct answer.

> Need a pronoun refresher? Check out Chapter 8!

Step 5: Don't Fix What Isn't Broken

Take a look at the following question.

Elisha Otis, the inventor of the safety

mechanism, demonstrated the device in dramatic

fashion at the New York World's Fair in 1854

<u>by having the ropes cut on a makeshift elevator in</u>
                     4

<u>which he was riding.</u>
  4

4. F. NO CHANGE
   G. when, to the amazement of the crowd, the ropes of the elevator, which Otis was riding in, were cut.
   H. when he cut the makeshift elevator in which he was riding.
   J. by means of having the ropes, which were those belonging to the makeshift elevator in which he was riding, completely severed.

Start with Step 1, and identify the topic. *Everything* seems to be changing in the answers for question 4: what the question is testing isn't obvious at all. You can't confirm what you can't identify, so leave "NO CHANGE," and apply the 4 Cs.

Does one of the answers fix something you missed?

Does one of the answers make the sentence better by making it more concise?

If the answer to both questions is *No* for the other three answers the correct answer is (F), NO CHANGE. NO CHANGE *is* a legitimate answer choice. Don't make the mistake of assuming that all questions have an error that you just can't spot. If you use the five steps of our Basic Approach, you'll catch errors your ear would miss, and you'll confidently choose NO CHANGE when it's the correct answer.

WHAT'S IT TESTING? DRILLS

Directions: In each of the following questions, you are given only a list of answer choices. Compare the answer choices, and identify the ACT concept being tested. Choose from the following list and write your answer next to each question: *apostrophes, concise, pronouns, punctuation, verbs, transitions.*

Drill 1

1. A. shine
   B. shines
   C. shined
   D. is shining

2. F. critical reputation
   G. reputation among critics and writers
   H. being known as having repute among critics
   J. reputation among critical people

3. A. depth but a
   B. depth. A
   C. depth; a
   D. depth, a

4. F. uncles
   G. uncles'
   H. uncle's
   J. uncles's

5. A. frowned each
   B. frowned. Each
   C. frowned—each
   D. frowned; each

6. F. whose
    G. ours
    H. its
    J. who's

7. A. dog, but it's actually really smart.
    B. dog.
    C. dog, and it's sort of smart.
    D. dog—no bones about it.

8. F. but
    G. that
    H. because
    J. although

9. A. words, by
    B. words by
    C. words. By
    D. words if by

10. Which of the following alternatives to the underlined portion would NOT be acceptable?

    F. though
    G. because
    H. since
    J. for

Drill 2

1. A. will have gone
    B. would go
    C. have gone
    D. will be going

2. F. Montclair, where there is a theater called the Wellmont.
    G. Montclair, where the Wellmont is a popular theater.
    H. Montclair, a suburb of New York City.
    J. Montclair.

3. A. however,
    B. nevertheless,
    C. that is to say,
    D. therefore,

4. F. one's
    G. him
    H. one
    J. he

5. A. children's,
    B. childrens,
    C. childrens's,
    D. childrens',

6. F. needs
   G. needed
   H. is needing
   J. have been needing

7. Which of the following alternatives to the underlined portion would NOT be acceptable?

   A. fences. Before doing this, the builders
   B. fences, before which, they
   C. fences. The builders soon
   D. fences; next they

8. Which of the following alternatives to the underlined portion would NOT be acceptable?

   F. Because
   G. Although
   H. Even though
   J. While

9. F. variation,
   G. variation because,
   H. variation:
   J. variation

10. F. arisen
    G. arosen
    H. arised
    J. arise

WHAT'S IT TESTING? DRILL EXPLANATIONS

Drill 1

1. verbs
2. concise
3. punctuation
4. apostrophes
5. punctuation
6. pronouns
7. concise
8. transitions
9. punctuation
10. transitions

Drill 2

1. verbs
2. concise
3. transitions
4. pronouns
5. apostrophes
6. verbs
7. punctuation
8. transitions
9. punctuation
10. verbs

Summary

o   Identify what the question is testing by identifying changes in the answer choices.

o   Use POE heavily.

o   Don't skip the non-underlined text: use it for context.

o   Trust your ear, but verify with the rules.

o   NO CHANGE is a legitimate answer choice, but use the rules and consider each answer before choosing NO CHANGE.

o   Good writing should be *Complete, Consistent, Clear,* and *Concise.*

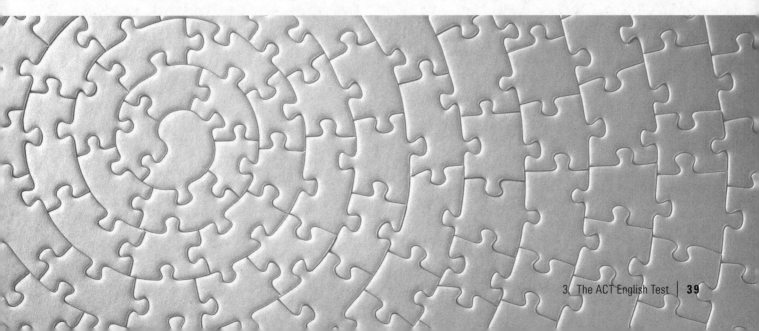

Part III
Maximum
Impact Topics

PREVIEW

It can be overwhelming to consider all the different grammar, punctuation, and style topics that are tested on the ACT. This is especially true if English is a weaker area for you or if you only have a short time to work on it before taking the real ACT. This section of the book will give you a thorough review of some of the ACT English topics that are both frequently tested and rules-based. Studying these topics will help you improve your score the most in the shortest amount of time. You will also learn strategies that will help you get the questions right more quickly even if you know some of the rules already.

In another context, you might have heard the phrase, "The only rule is there are no rules." The English test is the exact opposite. But that's good news for you. Once you learn the rules that are tested, you will be able to answer a great deal of English questions correctly—and quickly. Many students assume that grammar and punctuation are just a matter of what "seems" right or "sounds good." There are some areas of English writing in which rules are debated, and of course some published authors even break grammar and punctuation rules as a stylistic choice, but the ACT sticks to a reliable set of rules. You will never see a Proofreader question that cannot be supported by the rules. Learn them!

Chapter 4
Punctuation

There are two basic types of punctuation questions on the ACT: apostrophes and connecting ideas. Apostrophes are pretty simple, so let's start there.

APOSTROPHES

Apostrophes make your writing more concise. They have two uses: possession and contraction.

Possession

To show possession with singular nouns, add *'s*, and with regular plural nouns, add just the apostrophe. For tricky plurals that do not end in *s,* add *'s.*

Consider the following examples.

> *The career of Elisha = Elisha's career*
> *The actions of the boys = the boys' actions*
> *The voices of the people = the people's voices*

To show possession with pronouns, never use apostrophes. Use the appropriate possessive pronoun.

> ***His*** *invention*
> ***Their*** *fear*
> ***Its*** *legacy*

Contractions

Whenever you see a pronoun with an apostrophe, it's (it is) a contraction, which means the apostrophe takes the place of at least one letter.

Consider the following examples.

> *It is an important innovation. =* ***It's*** *an important innovation.*
> *They are dangerous. =* ***They're*** *dangerous.*
> *Who is responsible? =* ***Who's*** *responsible?*

Because these particular contractions sound the same as some possessive pronouns, these questions can be tricky on the ACT. You can't use your ear: you have to know the above rules.

Try a question.

Tall buildings meant that passenger elevators

became necessary and people had to overcome

they're fears of elevators.
<u>   </u>
             1.

1. A. NO CHANGE
B. their fear's
C. they're fear's
D. their fears

Here's How to Crack It

Step 1 identifies apostrophes as the topic. Use Step 2, POE, to eliminate wrong answers. *They're* is the same as *they are,* which doesn't make sense in the sentence, so eliminate (A) and (C). Nothing belongs to *fears,* so no apostrophe is needed there, either; eliminate (B). The correct answer is (D).

Apostrophe questions are almost like freebies, if you know these basic rules, because these questions can usually be done very quickly. The second half of this chapter contains some drills to help ensure that you get these questions right every time.

CONNECTING IDEAS

Many punctuation questions will ask you for the punctuation mark that correctly connects two ideas. You may remember from the English Basics section of this book that the first of the 4 Cs is *Complete.* These punctuation questions deal with complete sentences. For the ACT, you will need to know the differences between types of punctuation, such as commas and semi-colons, and be able to choose which is appropriate in a given sentence. Luckily, this topic, too, is very dependent on rules. Once you master our strategy and the three punctuation categories, you will be able to quickly get these questions right every time. Let's dive in!

Complete and Incomplete Ideas

In order to decide what type of punctuation is needed to connect ideas in a sentence, you must be able to identify whether the ideas being connected are complete or incomplete. A complete idea can stand on its own. It might be its own sentence, or it might be part of a longer sentence, but it's allowed to be by itself. Here are some examples.

> *The view is beautiful.*
> *Look at that sunset!*
> *How high is the summit?*
> *I gazed at the majestic mountains before me.*

As you can see, commands and questions can be complete ideas. However, they are rarely tested on the ACT. Most complete ideas on the ACT will be statements. In general, a complete idea must have a subject and a verb. Sometimes it needs more than that. Consider the following idea:

> *The tour guide told us we will need*

This idea has a subject (*tour guide*) and a verb (*told*), but it's missing the rest of the idea—what *we will need*. Therefore, this idea is incomplete. An incomplete idea could also be missing the subject, verb, or both, as in the examples below.

> *Bought hiking boots*
> *To get to the top of the mountain*
> *The people in our group*

In addition, some transition words and conjunctions can make an idea incomplete even when it has a subject and a verb. Consider the following statement.

> *We began to descend into the canyon*

The idea above is complete. It has a subject (*we*) and a verb (*began*). However, look what happens when we add some transition words.

> *Because we began to descend into the canyon*
> *When we began to descend into the canyon*
> *But we began to descend into the canyon*
> *As we began to descend into the canyon*

All of the ideas above are incomplete. Even though each has a subject and a verb, the word at the beginning makes each idea incomplete. We will come back to this idea of words and complete sentences in Part IV, as some of the more challenging—and less common—questions test sentence structure.

Now that we have established the difference between complete and incomplete ideas, let's take a look at the different types of punctuation that can connect two ideas.

Stop Punctuation

Imagine that there are two big trucks heading toward each other at an intersection with no stop sign or traffic lights. What will happen? They will crash into each other. You can think of those two trucks as two complete ideas. If you try to put two complete ideas together without anything to stop them, they will crash together, which is no good. To prevent them from crashing together, you can use what we call Stop punctuation.

> ## Stop Punctuation
>
> Period (.) Semicolon (;) Question mark (?) Exclamation mark (!)
> comma + FANBOYS

All of the punctuation marks in the box above are Stop punctuation, and they ONLY link two complete ideas. These punctuation marks can never link anything involving an incomplete idea. This is the first important rule for connecting punctuation.

Question marks and exclamation marks are rarely tested on the ACT, but the other three types of Stop punctuation are common. FANBOYS stands for **F**or, **A**nd, **N**or, **B**ut, **O**r, **Y**et, **S**o. A comma followed by one of these FANBOYS words is Stop punctuation. However, it's very important to understand that just a comma or just a FANBOYS word is not Stop punctuation.

Let's see how this works in a question.

———————————— ◯ ————————————

　　The earliest elevators consisted of a platform or

a box hoisted by a <u>cable before</u> the invention of the
　　　　　　　　　　　2

steam engine, most were lifted by people or animals

pulling the cable.

2. **F.** NO CHANGE
　 G. cable. Before
　 H. cable but before
　 J. cable, before

Here's How to Crack It

Start with Step 1 of the basic approach. Punctuation is changing in the answers, and choice (G) has Stop punctuation. Whenever you see Stop punctuation in the underlined portion or in the answer choices, use what we call the Vertical Line Test. Draw a vertical line where the Stop punctuation appears, and determine whether the ideas before and after the line are complete or incomplete.

　　The earliest elevators consisted of a platform or

a box hoisted by a <u>cable│before</u> the invention of the
　　　　　　　　　　　2

steam engine, most were lifted by people or animals

pulling the cable.

2. **F.** NO CHANGE
　 G. cable. Before
　 H. cable but before
　 J. cable, before

The earliest elevators consisted of a platform or a box hoisted by a cable is a complete idea. *Before the invention of the steam engine, most were lifted by people or animals pulling the cable* is also a complete idea. Remember, complete ideas need to be stopped so they don't crash together. Answer choice (F) uses no punctuation at all, which is not Stop punctuation, so eliminate it. Choice (G) is Stop punctuation, which links two complete ideas, so keep it. Choice (H) uses a FANBOYS word without a comma, which isn't Stop punctuation, so eliminate (H). Choice (J) uses a comma alone, which isn't Stop punctuation, so eliminate it. Choice (G) is the only answer that keeps the complete ideas from crashing together—it's Stop punctuation. Choice (G) is the correct answer.

In the previous question, it would also have been fine if the answer had a semicolon or a comma plus FANBOYS, as both can also link two complete ideas. You will not have to choose between a semicolon and a period on the ACT because they work in exactly the same way. The same is true for the comma plus FANBOYS, with the caution that it is dependent on whether the FANBOYS word correctly matches the meaning of the sentence.

Otis worked for a bedstead company, where his duties included moving heavy equipment.
3

3. A. NO CHANGE
   B. company; where
   C. company. Where
   D. company, and where

Here's How to Crack It

First determine what's changing in the answers: punctuation. Stop punctuation appears in several answer choices, so use the Vertical Line Test. Draw the line between *company* and *where*. The first part of the sentence, *Otis worked for a bedstead company*, is a complete idea. The second part of the sentence, *where his duties included moving heavy equipment*, is an incomplete idea. Therefore, Stop punctuation cannot be used to connect these ideas because Stop punctuation only links two complete ideas. Identify which answers contain Stop punctuation: (B), (C), and (D). Eliminate them. Only (A) does not have Stop punctuation, so it is the correct answer.

Go Punctuation

In the last question, the correct answer was a comma by itself. You know that that's not Stop punctuation, but what type of punctuation is it? We call it Go punctuation.

> Go punctuation
>
> Comma (,) or No punctuation

As you can see in the box, Go punctuation is very simple. It can be either a comma or no punctuation at all. The important rule to remember here is that Go punctuation can link anything EXCEPT two complete ideas. This means it can connect a complete and incomplete idea, in either order, or two incomplete ideas that together make one complete idea.

Whereas the various types of Stop punctuation are generally interchangeable, the types of Go punctuation are not. Sometimes a comma is necessary, and sometimes it is not. On the ACT, you often will not have to make that decision, but if you do have the choice between a comma and no punctuation, consider whether there is a shift in ideas. If the two ideas form one thought, do not use a comma, but if there is a shift in ideas or a pause, then a comma should typically be used.

After seeing one too many elevator cables

snap; Otis invented the "safety hoist" to protect his
4
equipment.

4. **F.**   NO CHANGE
    G.   snap.
    H.   snap
    J.   snap,

> Sometimes a complete and an incomplete idea (in either order) need a comma as Go punctuation, whereas two incomplete ideas never use a comma as Go punctuation—that combination won't have punctuation at all.

Here's How to Crack It

Stop and Go punctuation are changing in the answer choices, so draw a vertical line between *snap* and *Otis*. The first part of the sentence, *After seeing one too many elevator cables snap*, is an incomplete idea. The second part of the sentence, *Otis invented the "safety hoist" to protect his equipment*, is a complete idea. To link an incomplete idea to a complete idea, Go punctuation is needed. Eliminate (F) and (G) because they are both Stop punctuation. Now consider whether there is a reason to include a comma. There is a shift in ideas or a pause, so the sentence does need a comma. Eliminate (H). The correct answer is (J).

Half-Stop Punctuation

You may be wondering about a couple of other punctuation marks that we haven't discussed yet. The colon and the long dash make up our last category: Half-Stop punctuation.

> Half-Stop Punctuation
>
> Colon (:) and Dash (—)

Here is the rule for Half-Stop punctuation: the first part of the sentence must be a complete idea. The second part can be either complete or incomplete. That's why we call it Half-Stop! It can work like Stop punctuation (Complete + Complete), but it can also be used in the Complete + Incomplete combination. That might seem like a tricky rule to remember, but the good news is that we've now covered all the punctuation marks you will see on the ACT. Once you learn the rules for Stop, Go, and Half-Stop, you will have the tools you need to get these punctuation questions right every time.

In a demonstration of Otis's invention, the rope

holding a platform Otis was standing on was cut.

The platform only fell a few inches before <u>stopping,</u>

<u>the safety mechanism</u> had worked.

5. **A.** NO CHANGE
   B. stopping: the safety mechanism
   C. stopping the safety mechanism
   D. stopping. The safety mechanism,

Use the Vertical Line Test whenever you see Stop or Half-Stop punctuation in the underlined portion or the answer choices.

Here's How to Crack It

Half-Stop and Stop punctuation appear in the answer choices, so use the Vertical Line Test. Draw the line between *stopping* and *the*. The first part of the sentence, *The platform only fell a few inches before stopping*, is a complete idea. *The safety mechanism had worked* is also a complete idea. Therefore, either Stop or Half-Stop punctuation is needed. Eliminate (A) because a comma by itself is Go punctuation. Keep (B) because a colon is Half-Stop punctuation. Eliminate (C) because no punctuation is Go punctuation. Choice (D) has Stop punctuation, but it has a comma after *mechanism* that isn't correct because *The safety mechanism had worked* is a single thought that shouldn't have a comma within it. Eliminate (D). The correct answer is (B).

What about lists?
You may be most familiar with colons used before a list, which you will sometimes see on the ACT. The important rule to remember is that, on the ACT, the idea before the colon *MUST* be complete! Otherwise, a colon may not be used.

In case you're wondering, a period or semicolon would also work in the previous example. However, the ACT would not have asked you to choose between one of those and a colon in this case because they work equally well. This is why it's so important not to correct the sentence in your head and to look for that correction. Most students probably would not choose to use a colon in the example above, but it is 100% correct. Although many students might like to use a period in that example, (D) is a trap because it creates a different error. Always use POE and compare the answer choices.

One more thing to note about Half-Stop punctuation is that it can only be used when the second part of the sentence provides a related list, explanation, or definition. For example, the colon in the question above works because the idea after the colon explains the idea before it: the platform stopped because the safety mechanism worked. If the second part of the sentence does not relate to the first part in one of the ways above, the colon or dash isn't correct.

Comma Rules

In question 5, (D) was incorrect because it had a comma that didn't belong between the subject and the verb. On the ACT, there are only four reasons to use a comma (we've already covered two). If you can't cite one of these reasons, then don't pick an answer that contains a comma. Let's take a look at what the four reasons are.

#1—Stop punctuation. A comma **with a FANBOYS word** can be used to link two complete ideas.

#2—Go punctuation. A comma by itself is sometimes used to link an incomplete idea and a complete idea in either order.

#3—Lists. In a list of three or more things, there should be a comma after every item in the list, including before the word *and* or *or*. Let's see an example.

These days, elevators have multiple safety features, including extra cables, several different braking systems and, shock absorbers.
₆

6. **F.** NO CHANGE
   G. braking, systems, and shock
   H. braking systems, and shock
   J. braking systems, and shock,

Here's How to Crack It

Identify what's changing in the answer choices: commas. Consider whether there is a reason to use a comma here. The sentence contains a list of three things, so there should be a comma after each item in the list. The second item is *several different braking systems*. Eliminate (F) because it does not have a comma after that item. Choice (G) has a comma after *braking*, but *braking systems* is one idea, so there is no reason to put a comma in between the words. Eliminate (G). Choice (J) adds a comma after *shock*, but *shock absorbers* is one idea, so there shouldn't be a comma in between the words. Eliminate (J). The correct answer is (H).

> If you see a comma with *and* or *or*, check whether you have a list of three or more things. If there is such a list, don't do the Vertical Line Test—it's a different type of comma. If there isn't a list, though, use the Vertical Line Test because a comma with FANBOYS is Stop punctuation.

Occasionally you will see a variation of this rule tested, in which a comma goes between two or more adjectives that describe a noun. Here's an example.

I petted the cat's soft, shiny fur.

Because the fur is both "soft" and "shiny," a comma is needed in between the adjectives.

The strange electronic device fascinated me.

Here, a comma would not be used, because you wouldn't say that the device is "strange and electronic." If you see a question testing commas used like this, try substituting the word *and* for the comma and see whether it makes sense. If it does, use a comma.

Now let's take a look at the final comma rule.

#4—Separating unnecessary information. As you may know, when you want to share information that is not critical to the meaning of the sentence, you may put that information in parentheses. Two commas, or two dashes, can work the same way. Here are some examples.

In my city, people are looking for healthier (and tastier) alternatives to fast food.

In my city, people are looking for healthier—and tastier—alternatives to fast food.

In my city, people are looking for healthier, and tastier, alternatives to fast food.

> A single dash is Half-Stop punctuation. Two dashes separate unnecessary information. If you see a dash in the underlined portion or answers, double check whether there is another dash somewhere in the sentence. If there is, don't do the Vertical Line Test.

All of these examples are correct. Two parentheses, two dashes, and two commas are not always interchangeable, but they work similarly to separate information that is not absolutely required for the meaning of the sentence. The most important thing to remember here with commas is that this rule requires a comma before AND after the unnecessary phrase. When you know this rule is being tested, you can start by eliminating any options that only have a comma before or only have a comma after a particular phrase.

The safety hoist consisted of a spring mechanism, held in place by the tension of, being lifted, that automatically snapped open if the tension was released.

7. **A.** NO CHANGE
   B. of being lifted that
   C. of being lifted, that
   D. of being lifted that,

Here's How to Crack It

First identify what's changing in the answers: commas. Next, consider whether there is a reason to use a comma in any place that one occurs in the answers. There's no Stop punctuation, and there's no list. Check for unnecessary information. Notice that there is a comma earlier in the sentence, which must be before an unnecessary phrase since there is no other explanation for the comma. There must then be another comma after the phrase. Eliminate (B) because it doesn't have a second comma. Now consider where the end of the phrase is. The phrase *that automatically snapped open* describes the *spring mechanism*, so the phrase in between is unnecessary: *held in place by the tension of being lifted*. Eliminate (D) because it does not have a comma after *lifted*. Choice (A) has a comma after *lifted*, but it also has a comma after *of* that should not be there because *of being lifted* is one idea. Eliminate (A). The correct answer is (C).

These questions highlight the importance of reading the whole sentence. Seeing whether there is a comma, dash, or single parenthesis before an unnecessary phrase is crucial to determining what must come after the phrase, or vice versa.

That's all for comma rules! If you can't cite one of those four reasons to use a comma, don't use one. Here are some more example questions to practice those rules.

The sides of the elevator <u>shaft, had beams</u>
₈
<u>attached to it,</u> that the jaws of the safety spring
₈
would catch on when the tension was released.

8. **F.** NO CHANGE
   G. shaft, had beams attached to it
   H. shaft had beams attached to it
   J. shaft had beams, attached to it,

Here's How to Crack It

Commas are changing in the answer choices, so consider the four reasons to use a comma. There's no Stop punctuation in the answers, and there isn't a list of 3 or more. *The sides of the elevator shaft had beams attached to it* is one idea without any unnecessary information, so there's no reason for a comma within that phrase. Eliminate (F) and (G). Choice (J) puts commas around *attached to it*, suggesting that that phrase is unnecessary, but *attached to it* is necessary, so there should not be commas around it. Eliminate (J). The correct answer is (H). Remember, don't use a comma if there isn't a good reason to do so.

The safety device revolutionized the reliability

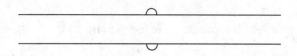

of <u>elevators, but, it</u> did not become widely used until
₉
buildings taller than 10 stories became common.

9. **A.** NO CHANGE
   B. elevators but
   C. elevators,
   D. elevators, but

Here's How to Crack It

Commas are changing in the answer choices, so consider the four reasons to use a comma. Notice that there is also a FANBOYS word: *but*. A comma with FANBOYS is Stop punctuation, so use the Vertical Line Test. Because the word *but* is part of the Stop punctuation, draw two lines around the FANBOYS word and consider the ideas before and after. The first part of the sentence, *The safety device revolutionized the reliability of elevators*, is a complete idea. The second part of the sentence, *it did not become widely used until buildings taller than 10 stories became common*, is also a complete idea. To connect two complete ideas, Stop or Half-Stop punctuation is needed. Eliminate (B) and (C) because a comma alone and no punctuation are both Go punctuation. Choices (A) and (D) both have a comma with FANBOYS, but (A) has an extra comma after *but* that isn't needed. Eliminate (A). The correct answer is (D).

PUNCTUATION DRILLS

Apostrophes Drill 1

In the following sentences, cross out any apostrophes that don't belong. If a word is spelled or used incorrectly because of an apostrophe error, write the correct word in the margin.

1. My arteries' seemed to get more and more clogged with every trip to the donut shop.

2. The pie was delicious when I first made it, but it's not so great anymore.

3. I absolutely did not expect them to be here on time, but they're they are.

4. If this device needs them, then why are there no battery's included?

5. I know the car seems out of her price range, but I'm pretty sure it's hers'.

6. It was time to go back to class, but the teacher didn't want to interrupt the children's game.

7. Do you have any idea who's letter this is?

8. Thank you so much for the cookies. Their delicious.

9. There's no dog in the world whose as much fun as ours'.

10. The politician ran on the idea that he was the people's candidate.

Apostrophes Drill 2

In the following sentences, add any apostrophes that are missing. If a word is spelled or used incorrectly because of an apostrophe error, write the correct word in the margin.

1. I need to start exercising more if I want to improve my arteries health.

2. St. Louis seems close to Chicago, but its actually five hours away by car.

3. I prefer red grapes, but there never available at the grocery store.

4. Because of all the corrosion, I cannot read the part where it lists this batteries charge.

5. There are two hamburgers here: one is his, and the other is hers.

6. The childrens treehouse was marked with a sign that said, "No Girls Allowed."

7. I cannot tell whose on the phone: I do not recognize the voice.

8. Were going to the concert later, so were trying to relearn some of the lyrics.

9. I think I see your car across the street, and ours is over there.

10. I thought the singer was terrible, and I had no idea why he was chosen as the peoples choice.

Apostrophes Drill 3

Choose the correct word from the parentheses.

1. My parents didn't give us permission, but (we're/were) going anyway.

2. I don't want to start a movie now: (it's/its) almost midnight!

3. My (adversary's/adversaries) favorite team was losing, and I was delighted at his agony.

4. (Who's/Whose) child is this, and (who's/whose) responsible for him?

5. My wallet feels full right now, but most of the bills are (one's/ones).

6. The cat guarded (it's/its) toy, as if to suggest, "(It's/Its) mine."

7. These (dictionary's/dictionaries) seem identical to me, so I'm not sure which one to get.

8. I thought my essay was pretty good, but (her's/hers) was much better.

9. Were you the one looking for the lost sunglasses? (They're/There) over (they're/there).

10. You can say (it's/its) (society's/societies) fault all you want: I still insist (it's/its) (your's/yours).

FIX THE APOSTROPHE DRILLS

Directions: In each of the following sentences, one word is used incorrectly. Find the incorrect word and rewrite it correctly.

Drill 1

1. Butterflies' are known in France as *papillons*.

2. There are so many citation style's that I'm not sure which to use.

3. Most goalies save percentage is above 90 percent.

4. Let's go see whose inside.

5. A stories style is more important to me than its plot.

6. I usually don't like them, but these potatoes preparation has made them really exceptional.

7. Because of all the young parents, there are so many baby's in Hoboken.

8. I'm not sure what it mean's, but there's a big envelope from Harvard at home.

9. My band's version of the song is pretty good, but theirs' is much better.

10. Whose ski's are these?

Drill 2

1. The first song from the album was the bands biggest hit.

2. The Harlem Globetrotters are fun to watch even if there not the best basketball players.

3. I forgot to take my contact's out last night, and now my eyes are burning.

4. F. Scott Fitzgerald was one of the best writers of the twenties'.

5. Cristiano Ronaldo is one of soccers biggest stars.

6. To write, one needs a little bit of money and a room of ones own.

7. In the proper season, there's nothing more delicious than raspberries'.

8. Because I've listened to so many, I can't remember all the sermons contents.

9. The restaurant serves everything, but it's specialty is Greek food.

10. I swear he has sent me a thousand texts' today.

Drill 3

1. Its' a real shame that people don't read more.

2. A religious communities presence does a lot to shape the character of a town.

3. In Latin, the meaning of a word depends a lot on that words declension.

4. Each of the questions' has its own particular slant on the concept.

5. They have a variety of purposes, but the drills main one is to test your knowledge of apostrophes.

6. I can't keep track of all the medicine's my grandmother takes.

7. Sushi would be much more popular if it's rawness weren't so weird to people.

8. If you like that place's pancakes, you should definitely try our's.

9. My English teachers love of grammar is a total mystery to me.

10. Someone must've left the door open and let all these fly's in.

FIX THE STOP/GO PUNCTUATION DRILLS

Directions: For each question, choose the sentence that uses Stop/Go punctuation correctly.

Drill 1

1. A. I know I will be a successful warrior for I will never back down.

    B. I know I will be a successful warrior, for I will never back down.

2. F. This is a brand new suit, so you should wear it for a job interview or something.

    G. This is a brand new suit so you should wear it for a job interview or something.

3. A. He just goes to the mall and walks around.

    B. He just goes to the mall, and walks around.

4. F. I know it's childish, yet I can't fully let go of my rocking horse.

    G. I know it's childish yet I can't fully let go of my rocking horse.

5. A. Do you want to hang on to your old baseball cards or just throw them all away?

    B. Do you want to hang on to your old baseball cards, or just throw them all away?

6. F. I've never eaten at a Hardee's, nor do I ever intend to.

    G. I've never eaten at a Hardee's nor do I ever intend to.

7. A. James said he would come to my party but in the end said he couldn't.

    B. James said he would come to my party, but in the end said he couldn't.

8. F. Mario Lemieux stopped playing hockey for a reason few could understand at the time.

    G. Mario Lemieux stopped playing hockey, for a reason few could understand at he time.

9. A. He has neither rhyme nor reason for anything he does.

    B. He has neither rhyme, nor reason for anything he does.

10. F. Your love letter contains too many grammatical mistakes, so I think we should break up.

    G. Your love letter contains too many grammatical mistakes so I think we should break up.

Drill 2

1. A. Please don't look at my iTunes playlist. It's so embarrassing.

    B. Please don't look at my iTunes playlist, it's so embarrassing.

2. F. It seems like I only care about politics when: there's some big election going on.

    G. It seems like I only care about politics when there's some big election going on.

3. A. The Flyers are going to win the Cup this year, the team's goalie is one of the best in the league!

    B. The Flyers are going to win the Cup this year; the team's goalie is one of the best in the league!

4. F. Although it's a huge honor to get an academic book published, the books often sell only 200 or 300 copies.

    G. Although it's a huge honor to get an academic book published. The books often sell only 200 or 300 copies.

5. A. I'm not sure why I love furniture shopping so much: maybe it's because I feel like Ikea is a playground!

    B. I'm not sure why I love furniture shopping so much maybe it's because I feel like Ikea is a playground.

6. F. Humanities departments all over the country changed in the 1970s; when French literary theory became popular.

    G. Humanities departments all over the country changed in the 1970s when French literary theory became popular.

7. A. Every time I go to a squash match, I make sure to take my lucky bandana and an extra racquet.

    B. Every time I go to a squash match, I make sure to take: my lucky bandana and an extra racquet.

8. F. My favorite app is probably Duolingo.

   G. My favorite app is probably: Duolingo.

9. A. Colin Kaepernick is a talented athlete, NFL blacklisting notwithstanding.

   B. Colin Kaepernick is a talented athlete; NFL blacklisting notwithstanding.

Drill 3

1. A. If you see Ravneet, tell him I said hi.

   B. If you see Ravneet: tell him I said hi.

2. F. The doctor told me I should eat more kale. Whatever that is.

   G. The doctor told me I should eat more kale, whatever that is.

3. A. I've lost a lot of weight on the grapefruit diet although I'm pretty sick of grapefruit.

   B. I've lost a lot of weight on the grapefruit diet; although I'm pretty sick of grapefruit.

4. F. It seems like things just keep getting worse: there was more crime in the city this year than last year.

   G. It seems like things just keep getting worse, there was more crime in the city this year than last year.

5. A. My favorite Beatle is Paul; Nathaniel's favorite is John.

   B. My favorite Beatle is Paul, Nathaniel's favorite is John.

6. F. First, she published a poem in *The Atlantic*. Then, she published a whole book of poems.

   G. First, she published a poem in *The Atlantic*, then, she published a whole book of poems.

7. A. When I learned that flourless chocolate cake was gluten-free, I didn't feel so bad about my gluten allergy.

   B. When I learned that flourless chocolate cake was gluten-free. I didn't feel so bad about my gluten allergy.

8. F. Many adults suffer from a Vitamin D deficiency because they don't get enough sunlight.

   G. Many adults suffer from a Vitamin D deficiency; because they don't get enough sunlight.

9. A. The Senator from Pennsylvania, took the whole legislature by storm.

   B. The Senator from Pennsylvania took the whole legislature by storm.

10. F. I don't like protein bars either, but I much prefer them to raw eggs.

   G. I don't like protein bars either but I much prefer them to raw eggs.

FIX THE COMMA DRILLS
Directions: For each question, choose the option that uses commas correctly.

Drill 1

1. A. Going for broke, Scottie shot the ball from half court.

   B. Going for broke Scottie shot the ball from half court.

2. F. A class, on literary theory, can be really interesting for non-English majors.

   G. A class on literary theory can be really interesting for non-English majors.

3. A. I got an A in math, English, and physics.

   B. I got an A in math, English and physics.

4. F. The most populous cities in New Jersey are Newark, Jersey City, Paterson and Elizabeth.

   G. The most populous cities in New Jersey are Newark, Jersey City, Paterson, and Elizabeth.

5. A. Either the Flyers, the Penguins or the Rangers will win the Atlantic Division this year.

   B. Either the Flyers, the Penguins, or the Rangers will win the Atlantic Division this year.

6. F. A filmmaker, particularly one who has gone to film school, should be well-versed in the editing process.

   G. A filmmaker particularly one who has gone to film school should be well-versed in the editing process.

7. A. Heeding the weather report Jonathan remembered to take his umbrella.

    B. Heeding the weather report, Jonathan remembered to take his umbrella.

8. F. It's hard to say who the greatest living American writer is, but I'd say it's a four-way tie among Michael Chabon, Judy Blume, Alice Walker, and Thomas Pynchon.

    G. It's hard to say who the greatest living American writer is, but I'd say it's a four-way tie among Michael Chabon, Judy Blume, Alice Walker and Thomas Pynchon.

9. A. Facebook Chat, an earlier version of Messenger, isn't as popular as it once was.

    B. Facebook Chat an earlier version of Messenger isn't as popular as it once was.

10. F. I couldn't afford to go to the furniture store, so I checked Craigslist a yard sale, and a garage sale.

    G. I couldn't afford to go to the furniture store, so I checked Craigslist, a yard sale, and a garage sale.

Drill 2

1. A. There are three ways to tell time in my room: my wristwatch, my pocketwatch, and my old grandfather clock.

    B. There are three ways to tell time in my room: my wristwatch my pocketwatch, and my old grandfather clock.

2. F. The name Syd Barrett, Pink Floyd's original singer, is now known only to the band's superfans.

    G. The name, Syd Barrett, Pink Floyd's original singer is now known only to the band's superfans.

3. A. I'm going to see a concert tonight at the Bowery Ballroom, one of New York's most notorious nightclubs.

    B. I'm going to see a concert tonight at the Bowery Ballroom one of New York's most notorious nightclubs.

4. F. Turkish bread contains only four ingredients: water, flour, salt, and sesame.

    G. Turkish bread contains only four ingredients: water, flour, salt and sesame.

5. A. Head to the nearest exit if you hear the fire alarm go off.

    B. Head to the nearest exit, if you hear the fire alarm go off.

6. F. Eric Clapton, Jeff Beck and Jimmy Page were all members of the Yardbirds at one point or another.

   G. Eric Clapton, Jeff Beck, and Jimmy Page were all members of the Yardbirds at one point or another.

7. A. Every time I go to the store, I have to buy a candy bar.

   B. Every time, I go to the store, I have to buy a candy bar.

8. F. Actually the new conditioner made her hair much shinier.

   G. Actually, the new conditioner made her hair much shinier.

9. A. The best time to see a hockey game is Saturday afternoon.

   B. The best time, to see a hockey game, is Saturday afternoon.

10. F. Whenever I'm at the airport, I'm always amazed that FedEx, UPS's main competitor, has such huge jets.

    G. Whenever I'm at the airport, I'm always amazed that FedEx UPS's main competitor has such huge jets.

Drill 3

1. A. *The Atlantic Monthly* does a fiction issue every summer.

   B. *The Atlantic Monthly* does a fiction issue, every summer.

2. F. Colleen's cuticles were especially dry, so the nail technician suggested lotion, ointment, or Vaseline.

   G. Colleen's cuticles were especially dry, so the nail technician suggested lotion, ointment or Vaseline.

3. A. No matter which song you like best you have to admit the Beatles have a lot of great songs.

   B. No matter which song you like best, you have to admit the Beatles have a lot of great songs.

4. F. Originally opened in 1871 Grand Central Station is one of the most impressive train stations in the world.

   G. Originally opened in 1871, Grand Central Station is one of the most impressive train stations in the world.

5. A. Uncertain why it mattered so much, Sally studied hard for the ACT.

   B. Uncertain why it mattered so much Sally studied hard for the ACT.

6. F. Named for the shape of its wings, the comma butterfly is found mainly in the temperate areas in Europe and Asia.

   G. Named for the shape of its wings the comma butterfly is found mainly in the temperate areas in Europe and Asia.

7. A. I need to take my dirty clothes to the laundromat the one on the corner.

   B. I need to take my dirty clothes to the laundromat, the one on the corner.

8. F. The south, of France, is beautiful this time of year.

   G. The south of France is beautiful this time of year.

9. A. I couldn't decide between Honey-Nut Cheerios, Raisin Bran, Golden Grahams and Apple Jacks, so I bought all four.

   B. I couldn't decide between Honey-Nut Cheerios, Raisin Bran, Golden Grahams, and Apple Jacks, so I bought all four.

10. F. In any case, brushing your teeth three times a day isn't such a bad thing.

    G. In any case brushing your teeth three times a day isn't such a bad thing.

Commas Drill 1

In the following sentences, cross out the commas IF they are unnecessary or incorrectly placed. Some sentences have more than one comma error, and some sentences are correct as written.

1. The book, you're reading right now, looks really interesting.

2. I always meant to study more for the ACT, but I just couldn't find the time.

3. Jack loved to listen to music, and to play games on his new iPhone, which he had purchased the day before.

4. Every time, I go on Twitter, there's always something interesting next to something really annoying.

5. When I see an action movie, I love the explosions, but not the romantic subplot.

6. Every, single time I work out I feel like I'm going to puke.

7. The Flyers won the game in overtime, but they should have won it earlier.

8. My grandparents used to listen, to the radio, but now they just watch TV.

9. Of all the cities, I've visited, my favorites are probably Paris, France, and San Francisco, California.

10. Squash is not well known in the United States, yet it is one of the most popular sports, in Egypt.

11. Next time I go to the store, I'm going to get peanut butter, jelly, and, bread.

12. It seemed like the characters' treatment of their dog in the movie was exceedingly, inhumane, and hurtful.

13. On sunny summer days, history, museums don't seem so appealing.

14. Jazz, whether you like that style of music or not, was one of the most important cultural movements of the twentieth century.

15. Sometimes, when Americans, who love Chinese food, go to China, they find, ironically, that they don't like the food.

Commas Drill 2

Add commas if necessary. If you add commas, state why you need them.

1. We'd like to hire you for the job and we hope you can start Monday.

   Why?

   _____

2. If you'd like to lose weight try eating better drinking more water and exercising regularly.

   Why?

   _____

3. The Philadelphia Phillies my favorite baseball team won the World Series in 2008.

   Why?

   _____

4. We took a scary drive on a dark stormy night.

   Why?

   _____

5. When used properly commas can really help to improve the clarity of a sentence.

Why?

_____

6. The lecturer's style was a little dull but so informative.

Why?

_____

7. I don't typically like Thai food yet I must admit I could drink Thai iced teas all day long.

Why?

_____

8. Some people still buy CDs but most have switched to digital music mainly for the convenience.

Why?

_____

9. I prefer a walk in the park to a walk around a city block.

Why?

_____

10. Around here you're out of luck if you won't buy your groceries at A&P Shop-Rite or Pathmark.

Why?

_____

11. The author Philip Roth wrote some of my favorite books.

Why?

_____

12. Sometimes I think plums the red ones especially are the best fruits in the world.

Why?

_____

13. Ice hockey is a fun challenging sport and it's great to watch.

Why?

_____

14. I don't think I could go five minutes without checking my e-mail or updating my Facebook status.

Why?

_____

15. When I was in college I had nothing but time but not anymore now that I'm working.

Why?

_____

PUNCTUATION DRILL ANSWERS

Apostrophes Drill 1

1. My arteries⁁ seemed to get more and more clogged with every trip to the donut shop.
2. The pie was delicious when I first made it, but it's not so great anymore.
3. I absolutely did not expect them to be here on time, but ~~they're~~ ^{there} they are.
4. If this device needs them, then why are there no ~~battery's~~ ^{batteries} included?
5. I know the car seems out of her price range, but I'm pretty sure it's hers⁁.
6. It was time to go back to class, but the teacher didn't want to interrupt the children's game.
7. Do you have any idea ~~who's~~ ^{whose} letter this is?
8. Thank you so much for the cookies. ~~Their~~ ^{They're} delicious.
9. There's no dog in the world ~~whose~~ ^{who's} as much fun as ours⁁.
10. The politician ran on the idea that he was the people's candidate.

Apostrophes Drill 2

1. I need to start exercising more if I want to improve my **arteries'** health.
2. St. Louis seems close to Chicago, but **it's** actually five hours away by car.
3. I prefer red grapes, but **they're** never available at the grocery store.
4. Because of all the corrosion, I cannot read the part where it lists this **battery's** charge.
5. There are two hamburgers here: one is his, and the other is hers.
6. The **children's** treehouse was marked with a sign that said, "No Girls Allowed."
7. I cannot tell **who's** on the phone: I do not recognize the voice.
8. **We're** going to the concert later, so **we're** trying to relearn some of the lyrics.
9. I think I see your car across the street, and ours is over there.
10. I thought the singer was terrible, and I had no idea why he was chosen as the **people's** choice.

Apostrophes Drill 3

1. My parents didn't give us permission, but **we're** going anyway.
2. I don't want to start a movie now: **it's** almost midnight!
3. My **adversary's** favorite team was losing, and I was delighted at his agony.
4. **Whose** child is this, and **who's** responsible for him?
5. My wallet feels full right now, but most of the bills are **ones**.
6. The cat guarded **its** toy, as if to suggest, "**It's** mine."
7. These **dictionaries** seem identical to me, so I'm not sure which one to get.
8. I thought my essay was pretty good, but **hers** was much better.
9. Were you the one looking for the lost sunglasses? **They're** over **there**.
10. You can say **it's society's** fault all you want: I still insist **it's yours**.

FIX THE APOSTROPHE DRILLS ANSWERS

Drill 1

1. Butterflies
2. styles
3. goalies'
4. who's
5. story's
6. potatoes'
7. babies
8. means
9. theirs
10. skis

Drill 2

1. band's
2. they're
3. contacts
4. twenties
5. soccer's
6. one's
7. raspberries

8. sermons'

9. its

10. texts

Drill 3

1. It's

2. community's

3. word's

4. questions

5. drills'

6. medicines

7. its

8. ours

9. teacher's

10. flies

STOP/GO DRILLS ANSWERS

Drill 1

1. B

2. F

3. A

4. F

5. A

6. F

7. A

8. F

9. A

10. F

Drill 2

1. A
2. G
3. B
4. F
5. A
6. G
7. A
8. F
9. A

Drill 3

1. A
2. G
3. A
4. F
5. A
6. F
7. A
8. F
9. B
10. F

FIX THE COMMA DRILLS ANSWERS

Drill 1

1. A
2. G
3. A
4. G
5. B

6. F
7. B
8. F
9. A
10. G

Drill 2

1. A
2. F
3. A
4. F
5. A
6. G
7. A
8. G
9. A
10. F

Drill 3

1. A
2. F
3. B
4. G
5. A
6. F
7. B
8. G
9. B
10. F

Commas Drill 1

1. The book/ you're reading right now/ looks really interesting.
2. I always meant to study more for the ACT, but I just couldn't find the time.
3. Jack loved to listen to music/ and to play games on his new iPhone, which he had purchased the day before.
4. Every time/ I go on Twitter, there's always something interesting next to something really annoying.
5. When I see an action movie, I love the explosions/ but not the romantic subplot.
6. Every/ single time I work out I feel like I'm going to puke.
7. The Flyers won the game in overtime, but they should have won it earlier.
8. My grandparents used to listen/ to the radio, but now they just watch TV.
9. Of all the cities/ I've visited, my favorites are probably Paris, France, and San Francisco, California.
10. Squash is not well known in the United States, yet it is one of the most popular sports/ in Egypt.
11. Next time I go to the store, I'm going to get peanut butter, jelly, and/ bread.
12. It seemed like the characters' treatment of their dog in the movie was exceedingly/ inhumane/ and hurtful.
13. On sunny summer days, history/ museums don't seem so appealing.
14. Jazz, whether you like that style of music or not, was one of the most important cultural movements of the twentieth century.
15. Sometimes, when Americans/ who love Chinese food/ go to China, they find, ironically, that they don't like the food.

Commas Drill 2

1. We'd like to hire you for the job, and we hope you can start Monday.

   Why? Stop.

2. If you'd like to lose weight, try eating better, drinking more water, and exercising regularly.

   Why? Go, List.

3. The Philadelphia Phillies, my favorite baseball team, won the World Series in 2008.

   Why? Unnecessary information

4. We took a scary drive on a dark, stormy night.

   Why? List.

5. When used properly, commas can really help to improve the clarity of a sentence.

   Why? Go.

6. The lecturer's style was a little dull but so informative.

    Why? No commas necessary.

7. I don't typically like Thai food,↓ yet I must admit I could drink Thai iced teas all day long.

    Why? Stop.

8. Some people still buy CDs,↓ but most have switched to digital music,↓ mainly for the convenience.

    Why? Stop, Go.

9. I prefer a walk in the park to a walk around a city block.

    Why? No commas necessary.

10. Around here,↓ you're out of luck if you won't buy your groceries at A&P,↓ Shop-Rite,↓ or Pathmark.

    Why? Go, List.

11. The author Philip Roth wrote some of my favorite books.

    Why? No commas necessary.

12. Sometimes I think plums,↓ the red ones especially,↓ are the best fruits in the world.

    Why? Unnecessary information

13. Ice hockey is a fun,↓ challenging sport,↓ and it's great to watch.

    Why? List, Stop.

14. I don't think I could go five minutes without checking my e-mail or updating my Facebook status.

    Why? No commas necessary.

15. When I was in college,↓ I had nothing but time but not anymore now that I'm working.

    Why? Go.

Summary

o   Use an apostrophe with nouns to show possession. Use an apostrophe with pronouns to make a contraction. Be careful of your ear with contractions, since some possessive pronouns sound the same as pronouns with contractions.

o   Stop punctuation only links complete ideas. Half-Stop punctuation requires the sentence to start with a complete idea, but the second part can be either complete or incomplete. Go punctuation can link anything except two complete ideas.

o   Use the Vertical Line Test whenever you see Stop or Half-Stop punctuation in the underlined portion or answer choices.

o   There are only four reasons to use a comma on the ACT. Name the reason to use a comma, or don't use one if there isn't a good reason.

Chapter 5
Purpose Questions

EDITOR QUESTIONS

As you may recall, we classify ACT English questions as being either Proofreader or Editor questions. So far, we have only looked at Proofreader questions, which tend to be faster to answer. Editor questions actually ask a question, so the questions themselves are longer, and they often require you to read more. Since these questions often concern main ideas, you may have to read an entire paragraph for one question. You'll also see Editor questions that involve the main idea of the entire passage.

The most important thing for Editor questions is to notice that you are being asked a question. If you go straight to the answers, you may find yourself getting a question wrong by choosing an answer that you personally like but that doesn't not answer what the question is asking. Always notice when there is a question and make sure to consider what the question is asking when using POE.

As we discussed in the beginning of this book, you may decide to skip some of those longer questions. They will take more time, and you don't want to miss out on some of the easier and faster questions at the end of the section by running out of time. In this section, though, we're going to focus on one of the most common types of Editor questions: those that ask you to fulfill a particular purpose. These questions are not as time-consuming, since they rarely require you to read more than the one sentence (and as you'll see, you can often get the answer without reading the sentence at all), so they are another good maximum impact topic.

———————○———————

The fact that few buildings were over ten stories in the early nineteenth century undercut any demand for passenger elevators, and many people were also scared to ride in them.
10

10. Which choice provides the most specific reason that people were reluctant to ride in passenger elevators?

F. NO CHANGE
G. people didn't like them and rarely rode in them.
H. concerns about safety prevented all but the most daring from riding in them.
J. people weren't used to them, either.

Here's How to Crack It

Identify the purpose of the proposed text. The question asks which choice *provides the most specific reason that people were reluctant to ride in passenger elevators.* Your job is to find the answer choice that is *Consistent* with that purpose. Only (H) gives a specific reason: *concerns about safety.* Eliminate (F), (G), and (J). Choice (H) is the correct answer.

———————○———————

The example above is what you can expect to see from this type of question. It's a good idea to underline the purpose stated in the question. You MUST pick the answer that fulfills this purpose. Generally, all of the answers will contain correct punctuation and grammar, so you won't have to worry about identifying errors. Instead, consider the meaning of each answer. There will likely be more than one option that makes sense or sounds good in the sentence. The key is to pick the option that does what the question is asking—whether you personally like that option or not.

Take a look at a couple of examples.

The world's first modern passenger elevator was installed in a New York building in 1874. This is partly because of the invention of metal-framed buildings in the late nineteenth century, which allowed for buildings that were far taller than <u>had previously been possible.</u>
11

11. The writer wants to emphasize that the invention of metal-framed buildings allowed structures to be taller than ever before. Which choice best accomplishes that goal?

   A. NO CHANGE
   B. those in other parts of the world.
   C. wood and brick buildings.
   D. people had expected.

Here's How to Crack It

Underline the purpose stated in the question: *emphasize that the invention of metal-framed buildings allowed structures to be taller than ever before.* Check each answer choice to see whether it suggests that the new buildings were *taller than ever before.* Choice (A) indicates that it previously hadn't been possible to build such tall buildings, which is consistent with *taller than ever before.* Keep it. Choice (B) doesn't relate to the idea of *taller than ever before*, so eliminate it. Choice (C) requires the assumption that *wood and brick buildings* were the only type of buildings available before, which the sentence does not indicate, so eliminate (C). Choice (D) references what *people expected*, which doesn't provide a comparison to previous types of buildings. Eliminate (D). The correct answer is (A).

<u>Tall buildings</u> created a demand for elevators that
12
could safely transport people.

12. Which choice provides the clearest and most specific description of the size of the buildings that contained the first elevators?

   F. NO CHANGE
   G. Buildings of twenty stories and more
   H. Extremely high buildings
   J. Buildings with many offices

Here's How to Crack It

Underline the purpose stated in the question: *the clearest and most specific description of the size of buildings that contained the first elevators*. Choices (F) and (H) do not specifically state how tall or high the buildings were, so eliminate them. Choice (J) uses a vague word, *many*, and references only the number of *offices*, not the *size* of the buildings, so eliminate it. Choice (G) gives a specific indication of how tall the buildings were, so keep it. The correct answer is (G).

As you might start to notice, you do not always need to understand the full sentence in order to answer these. That isn't to say that you shouldn't read the sentence, but stay focused on the purpose in the question. It is not about what sounds good or even what is consistent with the ideas in the sentence or paragraph. It's also not about whether the answer choice is short or long, unless the question explicitly asks you to choose an option that is concise. The only thing that matters is whether the answer choice fulfills the purpose stated in the question. Try it out on the following drills.

PURPOSE QUESTION DRILLS

Drill 1

Find the correct answer using only the information given in the question. We've written out choice (A)/(F) so that you know what the NO CHANGE option is. We've also underlined the key words in the question. Make sure to choose an option that fulfills that purpose.

1. Which of the following choices would most effectively communicate the parents' <u>skeptical attitude</u> toward the narrator's plans?
   A. Enthusiastically,
   B. Distracted by other tasks,
   C. Because they were older,
   D. Despite their clear doubts,

2. Which of the following begins this paragraph and conveys the <u>importance of this album</u>?
   F. The Mars Volta's debut album was just like the debut albums of many other bands: underappreciated.
   G. It's hard to choose a single Mars Volta album to represent the band's huge range.
   H. The Mars Volta's debut album showed that a band could write complex, unique music but still sell records.
   J. There was a time when it seemed like progressive rock would never reach the major labels again.

3. Given that all the choices are true, which one best develops the paragraph's focus on the place of radio in Welles's career?
    A. Welles's voice performances over the airwaves well outnumber his appearances in film.
    B. Though he is best known for film, Welles was initially a famed director in the theater.
    C. Welles performed in thousands of radio broadcasts, but many of them are lost today.
    D. Many Americans considered radio their main news source during the Second World War, and Welles was no exception.

4. Given that all the choices are true, which one would most clearly suggest the song-writing collaboration between Lennon and McCartney?
    F. listened to the song.
    G. liked the song more than he thought he would.
    H. thought about the song a lot the next day.
    J. heard one part of the song, then added his own.

5. Given that all the choices are true, which one is most relevant to the writer's intention to help readers hear the sound produced by the car horn?
    A. almost like two trumpets playing dissonant notes.
    B. as if the driver were honking in a panic.
    C. like the horn on one of the other cars in the traffic jam.
    D. just like a horn I remembered hearing on the road in Italy.

6. The writer wants to emphasize that geologists are now conducting a more thorough study of the age of the bryozoan fossils. Which choice best accomplishes that goal?
    F. starting to consider
    G. looking into at times
    H. thinking a little about
    J. digging deeper into

7. Which choice most clearly indicates viewers' reaction to Diller's comedic talent?
    A. delighted
    B. performed for
    C. appeared in front of
    D. attempted to humor

8. Which choice most effectively emphasizes that Copeland is graceful?
    F. walked
    G. went
    H. glided
    J. meandered

9. The writer wants to emphasize the idea that climbing the mountain is a difficult and dangerous feat. Which choice best accomplishes that goal?
    A. hike up the tall hill
    B. effortlessly scale the peak
    C. wander around the slopes
    D. traverse the formidable heights

10. Which choice most <u>clearly and concisely</u> indicates that Carson wanted cities to <u>improve their environmental laws</u>?
    F. act.
    G. act to protect the earth.
    H. perform actions that would protect the earth.
    J. consider the planet.

Drill 2

This time, underline the key words in the question yourself.

1. Which choice most vividly supports the idea in the rest of the sentence?
    A. as stated by experts,
    B. called "underwater ballrooms,"
    C. accordingly,
    D. on that day,

2. Which choice most strongly conveys that Chen developed significant animosity toward the group?
    F. wasn't always a fan of
    G. spent much time with
    H. started to despise
    J. began a relationship with

3. Which of the following best contrasts with the idea in the first part of the sentence?
    A. as we can all agree.
    B. and there is little doubt as to its accuracy.
    C. which is simple to understand.
    D. though some people are unconvinced.

4. Which of the following best emphasizes that Glass played a prominent role in the development of the program?
    F. worked tirelessly as a leader in
    G. took part in
    H. helped with
    J. spent several months working on

5. Which choice best indicates when the book was written?
    A. in the fall of 1984, when the author had just completed medical school.
    B. with over 800 pages and dozens of anatomical drawings.
    C. in a way that impressed most of those who reviewed it.
    D. to provide a resource that was at the time not available.

6. The writer wants to end this sentence by suggesting that children in particular may enjoy the museum. Which choice best accomplishes that goal?
   F. ready to visit the museum?
   G. what more could a kid ask for?
   H. what makes kids like to be silly?
   J. it's not your average museum, is it?

7. Which choice most strongly and specifically suggests that the introduction of the polio vaccine was a turning point in the history of medicine?
   A. transformed things.
   B. affected the field of medicine.
   C. was a breakthrough medical innovation.
   D. helped many people.

8. Which choice best specifies the types of plays the troupe performs?
   F. stuff
   G. performances
   H. nineteenth-century comedies
   J. older works

9. Which choice best illustrates the vibrancy the author exhibited when describing her trip?
   A. told
   B. gushed
   C. communicated
   D. shared

10. The writer wants to begin this paragraph by emphasizing the importance of the technology mentioned in the previous paragraph. Which choice best accomplishes this goal?
    F. Manufactured by a company located in California,
    G. Composed primarily of steel and plastic,
    H. Proven effective by medical trials,
    J. Expected to save thousands of lives,

PURPOSE QUESTION DRILL ANSWERS AND EXPLANATIONS

Drill 1

1. **D** *Skeptical* means "doubting." Choices (A), (B), and (C) do not match with "doubting," but (D) does.

2. **H** The answer choice needs to express that the album was *important*. Choice (F) states the opposite, that it was *underappreciated*. Choices (G) and (J) don't provide any information about the album at all. Choice (H) states that the album was *complex* and *unique* and that it sold well, so this matches the purpose stated in the question.

3. **A** First, the answer must relate to *radio*. Choice (B) can be eliminated because it doesn't mention radio. Choices (C) and (D) downplay the role of radio in Welles's career, which is the opposite of the purpose stated in the question. Only (A) mentions the significance of radio in his career by stating that he did more radio performances than film performances.

4. **J** The question asks for an answer that relates to *collaboration*. Choices (F), (G), and (H) don't reference anybody working together. Choice (J) suggests that the song was written by two different people, so this fulfills the purpose in the question.

5. **A** The answer choice must help readers *hear the sound*, so it must be specific about what the horn sounded like. Choices (B), (C), and (D) don't provide specific details on the sound of the horn that would help the reader. Choice (A) does so by describing the horn's sound using a reference that the reader might be able to imagine hearing.

6. **J** The answer must show that geologists are being *more thorough*. Choices (F), (G), and (H) show only mild interest, and they don't draw a comparison. Choice (J) uses the comparison word *deeper* to show *more thorough* research.

7. **A** The question asks for the choice that shows *viewers' reaction*. Choice (A) indicates that the viewers were delighted, so that fulfills the purpose in the question. Choices (B), (C), and (D) do not indicate how the viewers reacted to the performance, merely that they viewed it.

8. **H** Look for a word that implies being *graceful*. The word *glided* means "moved in a graceful manner," so it is the correct answer.

9. **D** The question asks for a phrase that implies something *difficult and dangerous*. Choices (A) and (C) are neutral toward the climb, and (B) is the opposite of what the question asks because it says *effortlessly*. For (D), *traverse* implies a challenge, and *formidable* means "daunting" or "challenging," so this matches with *difficult and dangerous*.

10. **G** The answer needs to involve improving *environmental laws*, and it also needs to be *clear and concise*. Choice (F) is concise, but it doesn't indicate what type of actions should be taken. Choice (H) relates to improving environmental laws, but it's overly wordy compared to (G), and the question specifically asks for a *concise* option. Choice (J) is too weak because it doesn't relate to improving laws the way that *act* does.

Drill 2

1. **B** The question asks for something that is *vivid*, meaning it provides the reader with a visual image. Only (B) brings to mind an image.

2. **H** The answer choice must indicate *significant animosity*. *Animosity* means "dislike." Choices (G) and (J) don't mention anything related to "dislike." Choice (F) matches with "dislike," but it's too mild to convey *significant animosity*. *Despise* means "strongly dislike," so (H) is a good match.

3. **D** The question asks for a *contrast*. Choice (A) has no contrast words. Choice (B) has the word *doubt*, but *little doubt as to its accuracy* lends support to the previous point, as does the word *and*. Choice (C) doesn't bring up a contrast. Choice (D) has a contrast word, *though*, and suggests that whatever was stated in the first portion of the sentence has some people *unconvinced*, which indicates a contrast.

4. **F** The question asks for an answer that relates to *a prominent role in the development of the program*. Choices (G), (H), and (J) all indicate that the subject was involved in development, but only choice (F) indicates *a prominent role* through the use of the words *tirelessly* and *leader*.

5. **A** The correct answer must indicate *when the book was written*. Choices (B), (C), and (D) don't provide any time-related information. Choice (A) indicates *when the book was written*.

6. **G** The question asks what choice would suggest that *children in particular may enjoy the museum*. Choices (F) and (J) don't mention children at all. Choice (H) mentions children, but it doesn't tie back to any information about the museum. Choice (G) mentions *a kid*, and the question *what more could a kid ask for?* indicates that the museum has everything a kid could want, which suggests that it appeals to children.

7. **C** The question asks for an answer choice that relates to *a turning point in the history of medicine*. Choices (B) and (D) are too weak because *a turning point* means more than just affecting or helping. Choice (A) is too vague because it doesn't mention medicine. Choice (C) is specific and uses the words *breakthrough* and *innovation* to indicate *a turning point*.

8. **H** The correct answer must *specify the types of plays*. Choice (F) is too vague. Choice (G) is slightly more specific, but it doesn't indicate the *types of plays*. Choice (J) is not as specific as (H) because (H) mentions the specific century and what genre of *works* are performed.

9. **B** The question asks for an answer choice that illustrates *vibrancy*, or "excitement." Choices (A), (C), and (D) are merely factual. The word *gushed* means "telling in an excited way," so (B) matches *vibrancy*.

10. **J** The question asks for an answer that emphasizes *the importance of the technology*. Choices (F) and (G) merely provide facts—they don't relate to the technology's *importance*. Choice (H) is not a good match because something that is *proven effective* is not necessarily *important*. Choice (J) shows that the technology is *important* because it will *save lives*.

Summary

o   Notice when you are being asked a question on the ACT English test.

o   Underline the task of the question.

o   Use Process of Elimination to determine whether each answer does what the question is asking you to do.

o   Focus on the purpose stated in the question, not on how much you personally like an answer choice or believe it to be true.

Chapter 6
Concision

CONCISION

A common topic that is frequently and regularly tested on the questions of the English section of the ACT is concision. Did you catch that? Concision means being concise—not using more words than are necessary as well as not repeating the same idea. In the first sentence of this paragraph, for instance, you might have noticed that we wrote *common*, *frequently*, and *regularly*, which all convey the same idea. If this sentence were part of a concision question on the ACT, you would want to pick an answer choice that uses only one of those words. These questions can be easy when you know how to spot them because the answer is often the shortest one. The trick, however, is recognizing when concision is being tested—on other types of questions, you should never assume the shortest option is right.

There are two main ways concision is tested on the ACT. The first is through sentences that are redundant. Take a look at the following examples.

> *I take my daily vitamins every day.*

> *At first, the investigator was initially looking into the suspect's best friend.*

> *After putting the child in a small room with a puppy, the researchers watched the child play, taking note of any negative interactions with the puppy that were apparent to them while the child played with the dog.*

All of the previous sentences had redundancy—they used different words to say the same thing. *Daily* means the same thing as *every day*, *At first* means the same thing as *initially*, and *that were apparent to them while the child played with the dog* isn't needed because the sentence already indicated that information.

You may also see sentences that repeat information from a previous sentence. Redundancy questions demonstrate why it's important to do the English questions in order and read in between the underlined portions. Otherwise, you might not realize that some of the words are redundant with what was previously stated.

A second type of concision question involves consistency with a paragraph or the passage. Take a look at the following example.

The style of Ukrainian Petrykivka painting originated several hundred years ago, likely from murals in homes. The traditional art typically consists of colorful floral patterns, frequently featuring three flowers in the center. The background is traditionally white, and artists use a distinctive brush technique with four different strokes. Throughout the art world, there are dozens of different brush strokes artists can choose from.

1 Petrykivka painting is two-dimensional and may have abstract elements.

1. The writer is considering deleting the preceding sentence. Should the sentence be kept or deleted?
   A. Kept, because it introduces a modern perspective to the paragraph.
   B. Kept, because it contrasts the strokes of Petrykivka artists with those of artists in general.
   C. Deleted, because it adds information that is not relevant to the paragraph's introduction of Petrykivka art's characteristics.
   D. Deleted, because it takes away from the paragraph's focus on various types of Ukrainian art.

Here's How to Crack It

Since the question asks whether a sentence should be kept or deleted, read the paragraph to see whether the sentence is consistent with its main idea. All of the other sentences in the paragraph discuss the particular style of Petrykivka painting. This sentence provides information about brush strokes in art as a whole. While this information might be interesting, it does not belong in this paragraph, since this paragraph is focused on the specifics of Petrykivka art. Eliminate (A) and (B) because the sentence should be deleted. Choice (C) is supported by the paragraph, so keep it. Choice (D) does not provide a correct reason to delete the sentence because the paragraph is focused on only one type of Ukrainian art, not *various types*. Eliminate (D). The correct answer is (C).

For questions that ask whether a word, phrase, or sentence should be kept or deleted, or added or not added, consider whether the information is consistent with the topic of the paragraph. Sometimes there is a good reason to keep or add a phrase or sentence. If the information makes the meaning of the sentence or paragraph clearer, then it should be there. If not, then it should be deleted or not added. Remember that it's all about what ACT likes, not what you like. ACT likes for its passages to be concise. If there isn't a good reason to include the information, don't include it, even if you think the information is interesting. In fact, when you see an answer like (C) above that essentially says the sentence should be deleted because it's not relevant to the topic of the paragraph, that answer is almost always correct.

Here's another example of how concision is commonly tested.

While Petrykivka painting started as wall art, it is used today for various purposes. In some cases, artists produce paintings to decorate walls, but this style is now commonly used to decorate a variety of household objects. Plates, vases, and decorative boxes are all items that artists frequently paint in the Petrykivka style. <u>For example, these</u> painted objects are often made of wood.

2.
2. **F.** NO CHANGE
   G. However, these
   H. These
   J. Anyway, these

Here's How to Crack It

Transitions are changing in the answers, but note that (H) eliminates the transition entirely. Read the paragraph and determine whether a transition is needed. The previous sentence lists several objects that are commonly painted *in the Petrykivka style*. This sentence provides more information on those objects. This isn't a contrasting relationship, so eliminate (G) and (J), which are both opposite-direction transitions. Choice (F) is same-direction, but this sentence isn't an example of the previous sentence. Eliminate (F). The correct answer is (H).

When you see transitions changing and one answer choice doesn't have a transition at all, that option is usually correct! That doesn't mean you should automatically pick it—of course, in some cases removing the transition could make the sentence incomplete or not flow correctly with the previous sentence. But pay attention to that pattern in the answers. When the pattern appears, the question is likely testing concision.

Redundancy can sometimes be tricky to spot. If you didn't notice those redundancy errors immediately, don't worry. Now that you know this topic is frequently tested on the ACT, you can practice learning how to spot it. Here are some other clues that you may be dealing with a concision question.

1. DELETE the underlined portion is an answer choice. Never automatically choose the option to DELETE. However, if you notice that all three of the other options basically say the same thing in different ways, or all three contain information that was previously stated, DELETE is most likely the answer. Keep in mind that not all questions with a DELETE option test concision. For instance, a question with answer choices like *which, of which, which was,* and DELETE is likely testing sentence structure, not concision.

2. The number of words in the answer choices changes. If you notice some longer answers and some shorter answers, all with similar meanings, the question is likely testing concision. However, do not automatically pick the shortest one. Sometimes more words are needed to make the meaning clear or make the sentence complete.

Here are some examples of answer choices only (no sentences) that are likely testing concision. These questions would normally have the words NO CHANGE for choice (A), with the option for (A) underlined in the text. Instead of NO CHANGE, for this exercise, we've made choice (A) what the underlined portion would be.

1. A. seen from the car window.
    B. which she saw while she was driving.
    C. that were visible on the road.
    D. DELETE the underlined portion and end the sentence with a period.

Choices (A), (B), and (C) all say essentially the same thing, so check whether this information is already implied earlier in the sentence or in the previous sentence. If so, (D) is the answer.

2. F. However, with
    G. In addition, with
    H. With
    J. For example, with

The option to take away a transition word is almost always right. Check the sentence with the surrounding sentences to see whether a transition word is necessary. If one is not needed, (H) is your answer.

3. A. a priceless piece of art.
    B. a piece of art that is extremely valuable and was acquired.
    C. an extremely valuable, priceless, recently sold piece of art.
    D. a piece of art that was recently purchased by a buyer for a large sum.

These answers have one concise option and three wordy options. Check whether the sentence already indicates that the art was *acquired*, *sold*, or *purchased*. Most likely it does, and if so (B), (C), and (D) are redundant. Choice (A) is the concise option.

4. F. in the city of Savannah.
    G. in the eighteenth century.
    H. signaling the beginning of a new trend.
    J. DELETE the underlined portion and end the sentence with a period.

All of these options say something completely different, so this question isn't testing grammar. Most likely it's testing concision, and, most likely, (F), (G), and (H) all repeat different ideas from the sentence. But, as always, double check that that is the case.

5. A. definite issues that, surely, must have influenced voters
    B. issues that voters were almost certainly influenced by
    C. issues that surely influenced voters
    D. issues that certainly had a definite influence on voters

Notice the three long answers and one short answer. Choices (A) and (D) are repetitive because they each use two words with the same meaning. When comparing (B) to (C), (B) is longer and uses passive voice, whereas (C) is more direct and concise. Without even reading the sentence, it's a safe bet that the answer is (C).

Passive Voice?
Active voice is when the subject of the sentence is the actor ("The hero defeated the villain."). Passive voice provides the same meaning but makes the recipient of the action the subject ("The villain was defeated by the hero."). The ACT prefers active voice—it's more direct and concise.

CONCISION DRILLS

Drill 1

Each of the following sentences has a redundancy. Correct the sentence by crossing off a redundant word or phrase.

1. Using her hands, the bus driver manually opened the stuck window.
2. Spinning in circles, the boy whirled carelessly about the playground.
3. I could not stand the constant and repeating sound of the smoke detector chirping.
4. Putting puzzle pieces together one by one, Mia enjoys catching up on her favorite TV shows, doing a jigsaw puzzle while she watches.
5. The new Indian restaurant offers a variety of options for diners who come to eat there.
6. The library allows patrons to borrow and check out books for three weeks.
7. Researchers found that a second dose of vitamin-infused water revived the plants, bringing them back to life.
8. Anthony likes riding his bike, but despite enjoying riding it he doesn't like riding in the rain.
9. After I submitted my first draft, my teacher asked me to resubmit my essay again because it had gotten lost.
10. When you take your test, it is important that you remember to bring a sharpened pencil on test day.
11. Every year, members of the club must pay an annual activities fee.
12. Next, we will then proceed to the auditorium for a seminar on budgeting.

Drill 2

Choose the sentence that is both clear and concise. Remember that the shorter option is not always correct—sometimes more words are needed to make the meaning clear.

1. A. The museum is what sometimes could be considered to be a treasure trove of art.
   B. The museum could be considered a treasure trove of art.

2. A. The painting is a reminder of a time when they suffered from them.
   B. The painting is a reminder of a time when they suffered from famine and drought.

3. A. The professor wanted to study the new medication's effect on diabetes patients.
   B. The professor was wanting to study the new medication's effect on diabetes patients.

4. A. As for the slim chance of a kid becoming a famous actor as a child, the odds aren't great.
   B. As for becoming a famous actor as a child, the odds aren't great.

5. A. The smell of freshly baked pretzels in the lobby lured me, along with several of my coworkers, out of my cubicle.
   B. The smell of freshly baked pretzels in the lobby lured me, along with several of my coworkers, out of my cubicle and toward the scent.

6. A. Past Nobel Peace Prize honorees include Malala Yousafzai, Abiy Ahmed, and Nadia Murad, among other winners.
   B. Past Nobel Peace Prize honorees include Malala Yousafzai, Abiy Ahmed, and Nadia Murad.

7. A. The artist was pleased to see people interacting with his art installation in Griffith Park.
   B. The artist was pleased to see people interacting with his art installation in Griffith Park, the park being where his art installation was located.

8. A. For my birthday, I received *The Comprehensive Northern Italian Cookbook*, and I immediately perused the large book.
   B. For my birthday, I received *The Comprehensive Northern Italian Cookbook*, and I immediately perused the large book, which contained recipes.

9. A. Many of the donors, Nicole Kidman and Elton John, expressed their concerns for people and animals affected by the fires.
   B. Many of the donors, including such celebrities as Nicole Kidman and Elton John, expressed their concerns for people and animals affected by the fires.

10. A. Such a large prize like that doesn't seem fair to give to just one person.
    B. Such a large prize doesn't seem fair to give to just one person.

CONCISION DRILL ANSWERS AND EXPLANATIONS

Drill 1

1. *Using her hands* is redundant with *manually*, so cross off either one.
2. Cross off *spinning in circles* because it's redundant with *whirling*.
3. Cross off either *constant* or *repeating*, along with *and*, because the two words mean roughly the same thing.
4. Cross off *putting puzzle pieces together one by one* because that information is stated later in the sentence.
5. Cross off *who come to eat there* because the word *diners* already means "people who come to eat there."
6. Cross off either *borrow* or *check out*, along with *and*, because the words mean roughly the same thing.
7. Cross off *bringing them back to life* because *revived* means "bringing back to life."
8. Cross off *despite enjoying riding it* because that information is already stated in the beginning of the sentence.
9. Cross off *again* because *resubmit* already means "submit again."
10. *When you take your test* is redundant with *on test day*, so cross off either one.
11. *Every year* is redundant with *annual*, so cross off either one.
12. *Next* is redundant with *then*, so cross off either one.

Drill 2

1. **B** Choice (A) is overly wordy.
2. **B** Choice (B) is longer, but it's more precise. Assuming that the sentence before explains who *they* are, it's still not correct to put *they* and *them* in the same sentence if the two pronouns refer to two different things: *they* presumably refers to a previously mentioned group of people, but *them* refers to *famine and drought*.
3. **A** Choice (A) is more concise. It's generally best to use a more direct verb like *want* rather than an *-ing* form.
4. **B** Choice (A) is redundant because the sentence says *the odds aren't great*, so it's not necessary to also say *slim chance*. Furthermore, it isn't necessary to say *as a child* when the subject is already *a kid*.
5. **A** Choice (B) is redundant because the word *lured* already implies that the narrator was going toward the location of the pretzels.
6. **B** The word *includes* implies that the following list is incomplete and that there are others. Therefore, (A) is redundant because it says *among other winners*, which is already suggested.
7. **A** The sentence already indicates that the art was installed *in Griffith Park*, so (B) is redundant because it states that idea again.
8. **A** The title of the book states that it is a cookbook, and all cookbooks contain recipes. Thus, (B) is redundant.
9. **B** Choice (A) is shorter, but the sentence does not make sense. Two people cannot be *many of the donors*. The word *including* makes it clear that these are just two of *many* donors, and the phrase *such celebrities* makes it clear why these two people are mentioned in the sentence.
10. **B** The word *such* already means "like that," so (A) is redundant.

Summary

- Watch out for concision questions, as this topic is regularly tested.

- If the number of words changes in the answers or if you see the option to DELETE, that's a good clue that concision is being tested.

- Do not automatically pick the shortest option. Sometimes more words are needed to make the sentence Complete, Clear, or Consistent.

- Always read in between the questions and do the questions in order so that you can identify when information was already stated and should not be repeated.

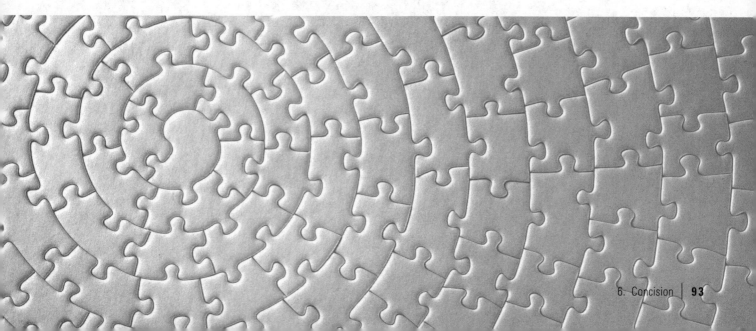

Chapter 7
Transitions

TRANSITIONS

A final, commonly tested topic on the ACT is transitions. In the previous chapter, you saw that the option to take away the transition is usually correct. When all four options have a transition, though, you'll have to identify which one best fits within the flow of ideas. A transition connects two ideas, so you must decide how the two ideas need to be connected. The most common transitions on the ACT can be categorized as "same-direction" or "opposite-direction." Same-direction transitions connect two ideas that agree, and opposite-direction transitions connect two ideas that disagree. The following are the most common transitions on the ACT and include examples of how each one may be used.

Same-Direction Transitions

Accordingly—used when the second idea is a result of the first idea

> *Our accountant's sudden departure left our company with no way to pay our clients. Accordingly, in order to make payroll, we had to hire a temporary accountant.*

Additionally/in addition—used when the second idea adds more information to the first idea

> *The proposed law would harm local beaver populations near the highway. In addition, an endangered plant species could be threatened.*

As a result—used when the second idea is a result of the first idea

> *My teacher was out sick for five days. As a result, our test had to be postponed.*

Besides—used when the second idea reinforces the first idea

> *I don't feel like going to school today. Besides, we aren't doing anything important.*

For example/for instance—used when the second idea is an example of the first idea

> *Some people dispute the validity of the study. For example, Dr. Annika Raza has criticized the researchers' method for measuring patients' pain levels.*

Similarly/likewise—used to compare two different things that have something in common

> *Art therapy can help children and adults recover from past and present traumas. Similarly, music therapy may help those struggling with mental distress.*

Therefore/thus—used to draw a conclusion based on previously provided evidence

> *Analysis of the painting showed that it had been completed in 1885 and that it was originally owned by a friend of Van Gogh's. Therefore, it is likely that the painting was in fact painted by Van Gogh.*

Opposite-Direction Transitions

Conversely—used to illustrate the reverse of the first idea

Scientists discovered that the rats who discovered how to receive food by pressing the button were able to navigate the maze in under a minute. Conversely, those rats who did not press the button took over a minute to complete the maze.

However—used when the second idea is an exception to or contradiction of the first idea

Most young people think that credit cards have always been around. However, this isn't the case: credit cards are a relatively recent invention.

Instead—used when the second idea contradicts the first

Butler's editor was expecting to receive only a few chapters of the book. Instead, she found a 600-page manuscript in her inbox.

Nevertheless/nonetheless—used to show disregard of the first idea

The sky was overcast, and the dark clouds threatened rain. Nonetheless, we took our chances and headed to the beach, hoping the forecast would change.

Otherwise—used to explain circumstances in which the first idea isn't fulfilled

If you have received your instructions, go ahead and start on your project. Otherwise, wait here for directions.

Still—used to soften the first idea by providing contrasting information

The criticisms of Levitt and Dubner's book are plentiful. Still, the authors make some new and compelling arguments.

TRANSITIONS BASIC APPROACH

Whenever you see transitions changing in the answer choices, be sure to look at the sentence before the transition. The key to transition questions is the relationship between the sentence with the underlined portion and the sentence before it. Consider how the two ideas are related. If you can determine that they either agree or disagree, that can help you to use POE. Then, consider which specific transition works best. As you can see in the examples above, some transitions like *for example* and *for instance* are fully interchangeable, while others, like *nevertheless* and *however* may go the same direction but are mostly used in different contexts.

Here are a couple of example questions, followed by some drills for more practice on transitions.

After reading an article about the poor state of her town's bridge, Jesslyn decided to organize in support of repairing or replacing the worn-out infrastructure. Similarly, she wasn't sure how to start getting involved in her community.

1. A. NO CHANGE
   B. In addition,
   C. For example,
   D. However,

Here's How to Crack It

Start by determining what's changing in the answers: transitions. Then consider the relationship between this sentence and the one before. The previous sentence tells what Jesslyn *decided* to do. This sentence explains that she *wasn't sure how to start*. This is a contrasting relationship, so eliminate any same-direction transitions: (A), (B), and (C). Choice (D) is the only opposite-direction transition. The correct answer is (D).

She distributed pamphlets to local businesses and organizations to let them know about an upcoming town meeting. Instead, to recruit supporters in local government, she set up meetings with a number of committee members.

2. F. NO CHANGE
   G. Then,
   H. Therefore,
   J. Actually,

Here's How to Crack It

Transitions are changing in the answers, so consider the relationship between the sentence before and this sentence. The sentence before mentions one thing the subject did. This sentence explains another action. The ideas agree, so eliminate (F) and (J) because they are both opposite-direction transitions. Now consider the difference between *then* and *therefore*. *Then* can be used to refer to an action that happened after another one, so keep (G). *Therefore* draws a conclusion based on the previous information, which isn't the relationship here. Eliminate (H). The correct answer is (G).

TRANSITION DRILLS

Choose which transition in the parentheses is a better fit in the pair of sentences.

Drill 1

1. Studies show that wealth yields diminishing returns on happiness. (However/In addition), this is only true once someone has reached a comfortable level of income.

2. Personal computers became mainstream in the 1980s. (In contrast/Subsequently), the internet was developed and made available for broad use in the 1990s.

3. Children who are homeless may be lacking basic necessities like food. (Besides/Accordingly), schools can provide free breakfast and lunch to support these students.

4. After high school you may decide to go straight to a four-year college. (Otherwise/Nevertheless), you can start at a community college to fulfill general requirements and then transfer to a university to finish your degree.

5. As a rule, cats aren't considered to be social creatures. (Accordingly/However), many cats love to cuddle and sit in people's laps.

6. You have probably heard of Taylor Swift. (However/Indeed), she is one of the highest-grossing music artists of the past decade.

7. My co-worker decided to blow off a meeting with an important client. (As a result/Instead), he was fired.

8. My car broke down over the weekend. (Therefore/Nonetheless), I wasn't able to go to the school dance.

9. Some colleges offer yoga classes, which can help students learn to reduce their stress. (For example/Similarly), other schools offer meditation clubs.

10. The computer program is not functioning correctly at the moment. (Besides/Therefore), we will not be able to complete the project by the deadline.

Drill 2

1. The piano piece seems simple at first glance because it does not have many sharps or flats. (Nevertheless/In addition), it cannot be played by a beginner because it must be played extremely fast.

2. The team observed that the worms that were fed a diet rich in vitamin C were more energetic. (However/Thus), the scientists argue, supplementing soil with vitamin C can make vermiculture more effective.

3. Gorillas have demonstrated that they are able to communicate to some extent through sign language. (Still/Likewise), studies have shown that birds can ask and answer questions.

4. The team hoped that the mission would uncover clues about the city's past. As the work progressed, (then/though), the archaeologists learned more about the city's recent history than its past.

5. In recent years, Americans have become used to the idea of conserving water in the home. (For instance/Instead), people might take shorter showers, purchase water-saving dishwashers, or even remove grass from their lawns.

6. The study showed a clear relationship between the consumption of lead and poor learning outcomes in children. (As a result/Conversely), legislators passed a law banning lead paint that could be eaten by children.

7. The cheetah is the fastest land animal on earth. (For example/In fact), it can run at a speed of up to 75 miles per hour.

8. According to researchers, students who read for pleasure for 30 minutes per day scored higher on tests of English language skills than did students who did not read. (Furthermore/However), the reading students were more successful in assessments of focus and attention span.

9. One way to avoid the pollution caused by burning gasoline is to purchase an electric vehicle. (Clearly/Conversely), consumers can buy a hydrogen fuel cell car, a type of vehicle that is starting to become commercially available.

10. The first artificially intelligent robots aren't likely to appear before 2050, according to most scientists. (Simply put/Nonetheless), you won't have a robo-butler anytime soon.

TRANSITION DRILL ANSWERS AND EXPLANATIONS

Drill 1

1. **However**   The word *only* indicates that the second sentence goes against the first sentence.

2. **Subsequently**   The two sentences describe a series of events. *Subsequently* means "next" or "then."

3. **Accordingly**   *Besides* is used to add on to a previous point. That isn't the relationship here. *Accordingly* means "based on this information."

4. **Otherwise**   The second sentence presents an alternative, which is the correct use of *otherwise*.

5. **However**   The two sentences disagree because the first one says cats aren't *social*, but the second sentence says that many *love to sit in people's laps*. *Accordingly* is a same-direction transition.

6. **Indeed**   The second sentence reinforces the first, so a same-direction transition is needed. *However* is opposite-direction.

7. **As a result**   The second sentence explains what happened because of the first sentence, which is the correct use of *as a result*. *Instead* is an opposite-direction transition.

8. **Therefore**   The second sentence explains something that happened as a result of the first sentence, which means the ideas agree. *Nonetheless* is an opposite-direction transition.

9. **Similarly**   The sentences offer two different situations that have something in common, which is the correct use of *similarly*. *For example* requires the second sentence to be an example of the first, which isn't the case here.

10. **Therefore**   *Besides* is similar to "in addition," which isn't the relationship here. The second sentence describes the result of the first sentence.

Drill 2

1. **Nevertheless**   The sentences draw a contrast between *seems simple* and *cannot be played by a beginner*. *Nevertheless* is an opposite-direction transition, while *in addition* is not.

2. **Thus**   The second sentence offers a conclusion based on evidence in the first sentence, which is the correct use of *thus*. *However* is an opposite-direction transition.

3. **Likewise**   The sentences offer two different situations that have something in common, which is the correct use of *likewise*. *Still* is an opposite-direction transition.

4. **Though**   The two sentences illustrate a contrast between the expected findings of the *past* and the actual findings of *recent history*. *Then* is a same-direction transition.

5. **For instance**   The second sentence is an example of the first, which is the correct use of *for instance*. *Instead* is an opposite-direction transition.

6. **As a result**   The two sentences agree because the second one is an outcome due to the information in the first sentence. *Conversely* is an opposite-direction transition.

7. **In fact**   The second sentence is not an example of the first, so *for example* is not the correct transition. *In fact* can be used to provide supporting details, as it does here.

8. **Furthermore**   The two sentences agree. The first one explains a benefit of reading, and the second sentence provides a second benefit. *However* is an opposite-direction transition. *Furthermore* is used for an additional point, which is the relationship here.

9. **Conversely**   *Clearly* is used for a conclusion that is evident based on data. This isn't the relationship here. The second sentence provides an alternative to the first sentence, so *conversely* is a correct transition.

10. **Simply put**   The second sentence restates the first sentence using fewer words. This makes *simply put* a good match. *Nonetheless* doesn't work because the second sentence doesn't contrast with the first.

Summary

- ○ Know whether the common transitions are same-direction or opposite-direction.

- ○ Always read the sentence before the one with the underlined portion and determine its relationship to the sentence with the underlined portion.

- ○ Use Process of Elimination to determine which option is the best fit.

Part IV
Advanced Topics

PREVIEW

In Part III, we explored some of the most commonly tested, easiest-to-spot, and most rule-based types of questions on the ACT English test. If you have already mastered those topics, Part IV includes five more topics that you can expect to see on the test. These topics may be a bit less common and a bit more challenging. If you are aiming for a top English score, you will want to master these topics.

Chapter 8
Tricky Verbs
and Pronouns

SUBJECT-VERB AGREEMENT

A number of ACT questions require you to identify the subject and verb of a sentence. One such topic is subject-verb agreement. As you already know, a sentence's subject and verb must agree, as shown in the examples below.

The detective walks to the station.

The detectives walk to the station.

When a singular noun (*detective*) is used, a singular verb (*walks*) must be used. When a plural noun (*detectives*) is used, a plural verb (*walk*) must be used. You probably won't have much trouble identifying whether a noun like *detective* is singular or plural, as most plural nouns add an -*s* or -*es* to the end of their singular forms. Whether a noun or verb is singular or plural is called "number."

> Some nouns—like *child*, *tooth*, and *woman*—are tricky because their plural forms do not end in -*s*: *child* becomes *children*, *tooth* becomes *teeth*, and *woman* becomes *women*.

While plural nouns can usually be identified by their -*s* or -*es* endings, verbs do not follow the same rules as nouns. As you can see above, the verb with the -*s* (*walks*) is the singular one. If you want to know whether a verb is singular or plural, try placing the pronouns *it* and *they* before the verb, one at a time. For instance, if you are not sure whether *tries* is singular or plural, think to yourself: *it tries* or *they tries*? *It tries* is the correct phrase, so *tries* is singular because it agrees with a singular pronoun. Generally, singular verbs end in -*s*, and plural verbs do not.

This concept may seem simple, but the ACT loves to test it in tricky ways. Consider the following example:

Going to the beach with my friends are one of my favorite activities.

Going to the beach with my friends is one of my favorite activities.

What's the subject of the sentence? The test writers want you to (incorrectly) think that the subject is *friends*. If *friends* were the subject, the correct subject-verb pair would be *friends are*, as in the first example sentence above. However, this suggests that *friends are one of my favorite activities*. This doesn't make sense because *friends* themselves aren't an *activity*. Ask yourself: what is the author's *favorite activity*? *Going to the beach with friends*. This whole phrase is the complete subject, but the one-word subject is *going*. It might seem odd that *going* could be the subject because it seems like a verb. However, a verb can act like a noun and be the subject of the sentence in some cases (as in the simpler example *Swimming is fun*). *Going*, as a noun, is singular—all -*ing* verbs functioning as nouns are singular. Alternatively, you might recognize that *going to the beach with my friends* is just *one* of the author's favorite activities. This makes the subject singular as well. In either case, the second sentence is correct and the first one is wrong, since *are* is plural and *is* is singular. To recap, a singular verb must accompany a singular subject.

You might notice that the subject (*going*) is separated from the verb (*is*) in the example above. This is what the ACT loves to do to try to trick you. The more distance there is between the subject and verb, the more likely it is that you'll forget what the actual subject was and make a mistake. Often you will see *prepositional phrases* in between the subject and the verb.

Prepositional phrases are those that include prepositions: little directional words like *of*, *in*, *for*, *with*, *by*, and *from*. These example sentences contain two prepositional phrases between the subject and verb: *to the beach* and *with my friends*. You may also see phrases that don't involve prepositions but perform a similar function. Regardless, when you are checking a sentence for subject-verb agreement, it may be helpful to cross off the phrases that separate the subject and verb. You will get more practice with this in the drills that follow this lesson.

VERB TENSE
Consider the following examples.

The detective walks to the station.

The detective walked to the station.

The detective will walk to the station.

You probably noticed that these sentences differ in tense. *Walks* is present tense, *walked* is past tense, and *will walk* is future tense. When you see verb tense changing in the answer choices, look for a clue in the sentence that will indicate what tense is needed. For instance, the word *yesterday* is a good indication that a past tense verb should be used.

Verbs in simple tenses, like the three shown above, are generally straightforward to recognize and apply. Students tend to struggle more with two other tenses: the present perfect and the past perfect. These tenses require more than one word. Each uses a past participle and a helping verb.

The present perfect tense always uses the helping verb *have* or *has* before the past participle of the verb:

She has studied for the ACT every day for the last month.

I have been there before.

The present perfect tense indicates an action that started in the past and continues into the present or an action that happened repeatedly or at an indefinite time in the past. The past participle of a regular verb is the same as the verb's simple past tense form (*She studied, she has studied*), but for irregular verbs there is a difference (*I went there, I have been there*). However, on the ACT all that will matter in most questions is identifying the correct tense, so look for *has* or *have* to spot the present perfect tense.

The past perfect tense always uses the helping verb *had* before the past participle of a verb:

She had studied for the ACT every day up until the test date.

I had been there before, so I decided to stay home.

The past perfect tense indicates an action that started in the past and has ended, or an action that happened in the past but before something else that was also in the past. In the first example, she stopped studying on the day of the test. In the second example, *decided* is already in past tense. Even before making the decision *to stay home*, the narrator *had been there before*. The past perfect tense indicates that this previous visit happened prior to the time the story takes place. In the drills that follow this lesson, you will get more practice with verb tense. For now, here's an example of how this topic could be tested on the ACT.

———————————————○———————————————

A classic novel by Isabel Allende, *The House of the Spirits* <u>exemplifies</u> the genre of magical realism.

₁

1. **A.** NO CHANGE
   B. are exemplifying
   C. have exemplified
   D. exemplify

> Many verb questions, like this one, only require you to correctly match the subject and verb in order to eliminate the three wrong answers. For that reason, it's generally best to start by finding the subject rather than by determining the correct tense.

Here's How to Crack It

Verbs are changing in the answer choices, so consider the topics of tense and number. First identify the subject of the sentence: *The House of the Spirits*, which according to the sentence is *a novel*. This makes the subject singular, since it is just one book (Tricky ACT! Just because it ends in *-s* doesn't mean it's plural). Eliminate any answer choices that are plural: (B), (C), and (D). The correct answer is (A).

———————————————○———————————————

PRONOUNS

A pronoun is a word that stands in for a noun, and it must agree with the noun it is supposed to refer back to. Here is an example:

> *The dog buried their bone.*

The pronoun *their* presumably refers to *the dog*, but *dog* is singular. Thus, the sentence is incorrect. A singular pronoun must be used to make the sentence correct:

> *The dog buried its bone.*

The most common way the ACT makes this topic tricky is through the use of collective nouns such as *family*, *company*, *team*, and *country*. Even though each refers to a group of multiple people, the words themselves are singular. For example, you would say *my family is*, not *my family are*. This is a good way to test whether a noun is singular or plural: try saying the noun with the verbs *is* and *are*, and you'll probably be able to tell which one is correct from how the phrase sounds.

Another way pronouns may be tested is in terms of pronoun case. Pronouns can be identified not only in terms of singular or plural but also in terms of their case. Even if you aren't familiar with this term, you are certainly familiar with the concept. For example, you would say "Give the book to me," not "Give the book to I." The pronoun *me* is in the object case. The object case is correct for this sentence, since I am the receiver of the action, not the one doing the action. The pronoun *I* is in the subject case, and it is used when I am the one doing the action. The following chart shows you the different cases of pronouns.

	Subject Pronoun	Object Pronoun	Possessive Pronoun
What It Does	replaces the noun doing the action	replaces the noun receiving the action	replaces the noun that is showing ownership
	I	me	my / mine
	you	you	your / yours
	he	him	his
	she	her	her / hers
	it	it	its
	we	us	our / ours
	they	them	their / theirs

Worth Noting

In the real world, you will often hear the pronoun "they" used to refer to a person whose gender is unknown or who does not wish to be identified with either male or female pronouns. This is because the English language does not have a gender-neutral singular pronoun. Many people agree that "they" is a fine substitute, but keep in mind that for the purposes of the ACT, "they" should only be used when referring to more than one person or thing.

Have you ever had anyone correct you by telling you to say, for example, "my friend and I" instead of "my friend and me"? Sometimes this correction makes people assume that the correct phrase is always the one that includes *I*. However, this isn't true. It all depends on how the pronouns are used in the sentence. Consider the following examples.

My friend and I are going to the movies.

My dad drove my friend and me to the movies.

Both of those sentences are correct. In the first sentence, you and your friend are the subject, so use the subject pronoun *I*. In the second sentence, you and your friend are the object: the ones being driven, not the ones doing the driving. Thus, the object pronoun *me* should be used. When in doubt, cross off every part of the subject or object phrase except for the pronoun. If you cross off *my friend and*, it's easy to see whether *I* or *me* should be used.

The pronoun case topic that many students struggle with the most is *who* versus *whom*. *Who* is a subject pronoun and should be used when it describes the person doing the action, just like *I, he, she,* or *they*. *Whom* is an object pronoun and should be used when it describes the person receiving the action, just like *me, him, her,* or *them*. One good trick for determining whether *who* or *whom* is needed is to replace the pronoun with *he* or *him*, which sound a bit like *who* and *whom*. Here are some examples.

I went to the movies with Amelia, who is my best friend.

I went to the movies with Amelia, whom everyone likes.

In the first example, *who* is the subject of the second part of the sentence. It goes with the verb *is*. You could replace *who* with *she* to say *she is my best friend*. You wouldn't say *her is my best friend*, so the object pronoun *whom* would be incorrect.

In the second example, *whom* is the object of the second part of the sentence. The subject is *everyone* and the verb is *likes*. Amelia is not the person doing the "liking" but rather the one being liked. This makes her the object of this part of the sentence, so the object pronoun *whom* is used. You can also try substituting with *she* and *her*, but you have to turn the sentence around a bit to do so. You would say *everyone likes her*, not *everyone likes she*, so the object pronoun is the correct one.

Here's an example of an ACT pronoun question.

When I finished reading it, I called my brother,

<u>whom had given me the book for my birthday.</u>
<u>   2   </u>

2. **F.** NO CHANGE
   G. who had given me
   H. who had given myself
   J. whom had given myself

Here's How to Crack It

Pronouns change in the answers, starting with *who* versus *whom*. Consider whether the subject or object pronoun is needed. The verb *had given* needs a subject, so the subject pronoun *who* is needed. You can also substitute "he" into the second part of the sentence: "he" had given the book, not "him" had given the book, so the subject pronoun is correct. Eliminate (F) and (J), which contain the object pronoun *whom*. Next, consider the difference between *me* and *myself*. *Myself* is a reflexive pronoun, which means it is used when it refers back to the main pronoun in the sentence. Here, the second part of the sentence is about the brother, not the narrator, so *myself* is not correct. The object pronoun *me* is correct because the narrator is the one receiving the book, so *me* is the object in this part of the sentence, rather than the subject. Eliminate (H). The correct answer is (G).

TRICKY VERBS AND PRONOUNS DRILLS

Subjects and Verbs Drills

Directions: Circle the subject and underline the verb in each sentence. Watch out for phrases in between the subject and verb.

Drill 1

1. My dad's favorite team used to be the Indianapolis Colts.

2. Ten years is not such a long time.

3. Dashiell Hammett was one of the first detective writers.

4. How long has this band been popular?

5. Matt started his own wine company a few years ago.

6. Buying a new car can be intimidating because it's so expensive.

7. Anna will know where she's moving as soon as she receives her acceptance letters.

8. Nothing I've ever seen can compare to this new movie.

9. The stories on *The Daily Show* are funniest around election time.

10. We'll leave as soon as we're done packing all our things.

Drill 2

1. The tissues in the box are almost gone.

2. Tamara is studying for her test.

3. Running outside on cold days can make you sick.

4. The release of the commission's findings was timed carefully.

5. The students in the class have chosen to stay after school.

6. After a loss, the players on the visiting team leave the field quickly.

7. The article in the newspaper was about the proposed soda tax.

8. Going on a trip with your school band is something not everyone has experienced.

9. The girl who ordered waffles, a biscuit, and scrambled eggs is sitting over there.

10. An art therapist does not need to have a Ph.D.

Tense Drill

Directions: Choose the verb that is in the correct tense based on the clue(s) in each sentence.

1. I (am/was/will be) well prepared to take the ACT right now.

2. She (takes/took/will take) three AP classes next year.

3. They (have read/had read) at least 50 pages every day this month.

4. Before you took the ACT, you (have taken/had taken) several practice tests.

5. He (send/sent/will send) his ACT scores to eight schools the last time he took the test.

6. Every time my teacher asks a question, he (waits/waited/had waited) thirty seconds before calling on someone.

7. Since she (had biked/has biked) thirty miles already, she chose to take the bus home.

8. If your meeting (will run/ran/had run) late, please let me know.

9. Yesterday they (had gone/went) to see a concert.

10. I (have/had) never seen an alligator before, but I hope I will today.

SUPPLY THE PRONOUN DRILLS

Directions: Fill in the correct pronoun. Choose from the following list: *I, me, you, he, him, she, her, it, we, us, they, them, who, whom.*

Drill 1

1. Once he calls me, John and _____ will go eat.

2. It was his birthday, so I got _____ an iTunes gift card.

3. She won the award, for _____ was the best violinist.

4. I have two tickets to the concert, but I can't get anyone to go with _____.

5. _____ among you let the dogs out?

6. She and _____ sister are going to open a shop.

7. It is said that we all have at least one novel within _____.

8. My brother would be a better squash player if _____ were only a little more patient.

9. _____ told us it wasn't possible, but we proved them wrong.

10. The American Airlines Center in Dallas is a great arena: _____ has so many great food options!

Drill 2

1. Beyonce's new song isn't great, but I can't stop listening to _____.

2. The owners haven't listed the price on the "For Sale" sign, so you should ask _____.

3. _____ didn't have any idea where to buy our new couch.

4. If only _____ had bought Microsoft stock early on, Melissa and I would be rich now.

5. Willa Cather won the Pulitzer Prize for *One of Ours*, but _____ didn't consider it one of her own best novels.

6. Bob Dylan's songs are so powerful because they speak to all of _____.

7. No, not that girl, the one to the left of _____.

8. You bought a Snuggie? For _____?

9. My uncle got the promotion even though _____ doesn't do much work.

10. I know Justin Bieber is very popular, but I don't much like _____.

Drill 3 (who/whom set)

1. Not one of us _____ owns a dog has any problem with cats.

2. I'm going to sue the guy _____ sold me this defective banana tree.

3. _____ are you going to invite to your retirement party?

4. _____ is your roommate this year?

5. They say you can be whoever you want when you go to college, but I'm not sure _____ I am now.

6. You wrote, "From me to you." From you to _____?

7. _____ did you vote for in the last election?

8. _____ was your preferred candidate last year?

9. My grandmother, _____ is Swiss, makes incredible Christmas cookies.

10. I've always been curious _____ figured out that plantains are edible.

TRICKY VERBS AND PRONOUNS DRILL ANSWERS

Subjects and Verbs Drill 1

1. team; used

2. years; is

3. Dashiell Hammett; was

4. band; has been (You may need to turn a question into a statement to identify the subject and verb.)

5. Matt; started

6. Buying; can be (Even though *buying* seems like a verb, it's used as a noun in this context and is the subject of the sentence.)

7. Anna; will know

8. Nothing; can compare

9. stories; are

10. We; will leave

Subjects and Verbs Drill 2

1. tissues; are

2. Tamara; is studying

3. Running; can make

4. release; was timed

5. students; have chosen

6. players; leave

7. article; was

8. Going; is

9. girl; is sitting

10. art therapist; does need

Tense Drill

1. am
2. will take
3. have read
4. had taken
5. sent
6. waits
7. had biked
8. will run
9. went
10. have

SUPPLY THE PRONOUN DRILLS ANSWERS

Drill 1

1. I
2. him
3. she
4. me
5. Who
6. her
7. us
8. he
9. They
10. it

Drill 2

1. it
2. them
3. We
4. we
5. she
6. us
7. her
8. whom
9. he
10. him

Drill 3

1. who
2. who
3. Whom
4. Who
5. who
6. whom
7. Whom
8. Who
9. who
10. who

Summary

- When verbs are changing in the answer choices, find the subject and choose a verb that agrees with the subject in terms of being singular or plural. Watch out for phrases that separate the subject and verb.

- When verb tense is changing in the answer choices, look for clues in the sentence or surrounding sentences to determine what tense is needed.

- When pronouns are changing in the answer choices, check that the pronoun agrees with the noun it refers back to, in both number (singular or plural) and case.

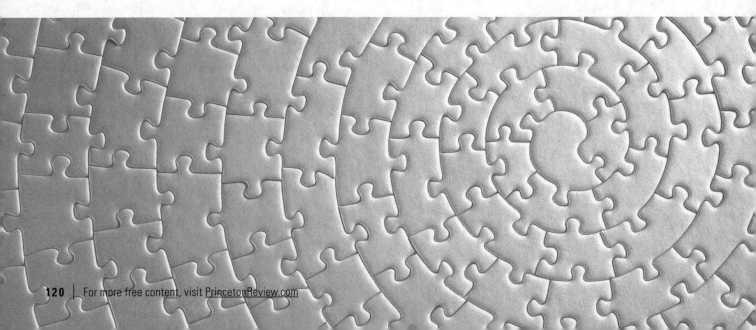

Chapter 9
Sentence Structure

SENTENCE STRUCTURE

In the previous chapter, we discussed the two components that make up the foundation of every sentence: its subject and main verb. Some sentences, like the sentence *I run*, can be complete with just a subject and a verb. Some sentences need an object. For example, *I found* has a subject and a verb, but it isn't a complete sentence because the word *found* needs an object after it. In other words, *I found* leaves us asking, "What have I found?" The answer to that question is the object of the verb *found*. Let's say that I found *the treasure*, and let's add this to the sentence above. *I found the treasure* is complete because it contains a subject, a verb, and an object for the verb *found*.

Though the sentence above is complete, it may quickly become incomplete if we add words. For example, you may recall that transitions can make an idea incomplete. *I found the treasure* is a complete sentence, but *When I found the treasure* and *Because I found the treasure* are not. *When* implies that something happened at the moment that *I found the treasure*, and *Because* implies that something happened because *I found the treasure*. However, neither sentence explains what that something is.

Sometimes you will see questions on the ACT that test this concept. These questions often actually secretly test Stop, Half-Stop, and Go punctuation. However, because the punctuation does not change, this question type is trickier to notice. If you spot this type of question, remember to use the Vertical Line Test and follow the rules from Chapter 4 if the sentence has more than one idea. Let's see a few examples.

<u>Starting to spend time in</u> the park, where a few
₁
locals practiced tai chi.

1. **A.** NO CHANGE
   B. I started to spend time in
   C. In
   D. Spending time in

Here's How to Crack It

First determine what is changing in the answers. Some answer choices have a subject and a verb, while others do not. This is an indication that the question is testing complete sentences. Use the Vertical Line Test where the punctuation appears and the ideas change: between *park* and *where*. The second part of the sentence, *where a few locals practiced tai chi*, is an incomplete idea. A comma is used to connect the two ideas in this sentence. A comma is Go punctuation, which can link anything except two complete ideas. However, remember that the other option for Go punctuation is no punctuation. When a sentence contains two incomplete ideas, there shouldn't be a comma between them. They just make one complete idea. Therefore, since this sentence has a comma, the first part should be complete, in order to form a complete sentence. This means the first part of the sentence should contain both a subject and a verb. Choice (A) does not have a subject indicating who is *starting to spend time*, so eliminate it. Choice (B) has a subject and a verb, so keep it. Choice (C) has neither a subject nor a verb, so eliminate it. Choice (D) lacks a subject, so eliminate it. The correct answer is (B).

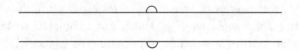

As I drove over to the community center and
₂
signed up for a class.

2. F. NO CHANGE
   G. Driving
   H. While driving
   J. I drove

Here's How to Crack It

Subjects and verbs are changing in the answer choices, so the question is testing complete sentences. In this case, the sentence only has one idea and no punctuation, so there isn't a reason to use the Vertical Line Test. Consider what is needed for a complete sentence: a subject and a verb. The non-underlined portion of the sentence does not contain a subject or a verb. That is, it does not say who went *to the community center and signed up for class*. Use POE. Choice (F) has a subject and a verb, but the word *as* at the beginning makes it an incomplete idea. Eliminate (F). Choices (G) and (H) have verbs but no subject, which makes them incomplete, so eliminate them. Choice (J) has a subject and a verb, so it is the correct answer.

The class, however, was too expensive,

it would cost more than I had left in my budget.
₃

3. A. NO CHANGE
   B. costing
   C. it cost
   D. this class might cost

Here's How to Crack It

Notice that subjects and verbs change in the answer choices, and there is punctuation, so do the Vertical Line Test after the word *expensive*. The first part of the sentence, *The class, however, was too expensive*, is a complete idea. Consider a complete idea followed by a comma: a comma is Go punctuation, so it can link anything except two complete ideas. Thus, if the first part is complete, the second part must be incomplete. Choices (A), (C), and (D) all include a subject and a verb, so they make the second part complete. Eliminate them. Only (B) is incomplete because it has just a verb, no subject. The correct answer is (B).

Now, let's add another wrinkle to this idea. When we say, "a subject and a verb," the verb must be in a particular form. The ACT loves to trick you by adding *-ing* and "*to*" forms to the answer choices. Let's talk about these two in detail. While *The company owns several stores* is a complete idea, *The company owning several stores* is an incomplete idea. This is because the verb *owning* is not the kind of verb that can be "the verb" in a sentence. *-ing* verbs are generally part of incomplete ideas and cannot be the main verb in the sentence. Another type of verb that cannot be "the verb" in a sentence is a verb in the "*to*" form. For example, *to purchase a bike* is an incomplete idea. Adding a subject isn't enough: *The lady to purchase a bike* isn't a complete idea either. Any verb with *to* cannot be the main verb of a sentence.

Here's an example of how these tricky verb forms are tested on the ACT.

The people in the park—both older and younger

adults—meet to practice self-defense and meditation.
                    ―
                    4

4. **F.** NO CHANGE
   G. meeting
   H. to meet
   J. DELETE the underlined portion.

Here's How to Crack It

The answer choices have different verb forms. First, locate the subject of the sentence: *people*. *In the park* is a phrase that describes the people, and *both older and younger adults* is another describing phrase, set off with dashes. Keep going and notice that the verb is *meet*: it explains what the *people* do. To make things a little clearer, cross out all of the describing phrases and read the sentence. This will let you focus on how the main verb, *meet*, relates to the subject. The sentence is saying *The people...meet to practice self-defense and meditation*. This seems fine, so keep it. Choice (G) says *The people...meeting*. This is not a complete sentence because an *-ing* verb cannot be the main verb in a sentence. Eliminate (G). Choice (H) says *The people...to meet*. This also isn't a complete sentence because a *to* verb can't be the main verb in a sentence. Eliminate (H). For (J), the sentence reads *The people...to practice*. Like (H), this doesn't contain a main verb, so eliminate it. The correct answer is (F).

PHRASES

Paying attention to describing phrases in a sentence is key. Generally, in a sentence, the verb follows the subject. However, there may be describing or other phrases in between the subject and verb. In the drills following this section, you'll get some practice with identifying subjects and verbs and dealing with tricky describing phrases. Here are some ways the subject and verb can be separated.

1. Prepositional phrases. You saw these in the previous chapter. Any phrase involving a preposition is a prepositional phrase: *in Georgia, at the beach, with my friend, over the bridge*, and so on.

2. Participial phrases. Whoa! Don't be thrown off by the scary grammar word. You're familiar with these already. As we just saw, *-ing* verbs (also known as present participles) are often used in describing phrases. Here are some examples: *speaking softly, going along with things, walking away*. Another verb form that can create a describing phrase is the past participle, which you saw in Chapter 8. Here are some examples: *stuck in the middle, woken by the loud noise, gone in a flash, eaten in a hurry*. These phrases are often separated from the rest of the sentence with pairs of commas, dashes, or parentheses.

3. Describing phrases using *which, that, who,* etc. Here are some examples: *which is why I'm leaving, that he likes, when you decide to try it.* These are sometimes separated from the rest of the sentence with pairs of commas, dashes, or parentheses.

Punctuation is often a good clue that a phrase is a describing phrase. Remember that if an unnecessary phrase comes in the middle of the sentence, it must have commas, dashes, or parentheses both before and after it. There will not be any punctuation between a sentence's subject and main verb unless there is an unnecessary phrase between them. In this case, you will see not one but two punctuation marks, both before and after the phrase. See the following example:

The people who invented tai chi and other Chinese martial arts, lived a long time ago.

The subject of the sentence is *people.* What did the people do? *Lived,* so that is the verb. Should there be a comma in between the subject and the verb? No, unless there is an unnecessary phrase with two commas. The phrase *who invented tai chi and other Chinese martial arts* is a necessary phrase that clarifies which *people* lived, so it should not have commas around it. Here is the correct version of this sentence:

The people who invented tai chi and other Chinese martial arts lived a long time ago.

That might seem like a lot of words without punctuation, but it follows the rules. A comma is not used when you simply want to take a breath or pause in speech. There must be a grammatical reason. Remember, do not use a comma if there isn't a good reason for it.

Let's see how this concept may be tested on the ACT.

The classes taught by a professor at the
<u>   </u>
          5
community college.

5. **A.** NO CHANGE
   B. classes being
   C. classes are
   D. classes, which are

Here's How to Crack It

Subjects and verbs change in the answers, so identify the subject and verb. The subject is *classes.* There must be a verb to go with *classes.* The original sentence might seem like it has a verb: *taught.* However, the way this sentence is written, that verb is actually part of a describing (participial) phrase: *taught by a professor at the community college.* The *classes* are not the ones that *taught*—the classes are being taught by someone. Therefore, *taught* cannot be the verb to go along with the subject *class.* Eliminate (A). Choice (B) also creates a participial phrase: *being taught by a professor at the community college.* This leaves the rest of the sentence as just *The classes,* so there is no verb. Eliminate (B). Choice (C) creates a subject and verb: *The classes are taught.* This is correct, so keep (C). Choice (D) uses a comma to separate the second part of the sentence, *which are taught by a professor at the community college.* Just like the transitions example earlier, adding a transition word, *which,* to the complete sentence makes the sentence incomplete. Doing so makes *which are taught by a professor at the community college* into a phrase that describes *The classes.* This leaves *The classes* without a verb, so the sentence is incomplete. Eliminate (D). The correct answer is (C).

Some of the tai chi <u>students, primarily hoping</u>
₆
to reduce their stress, using the martial art for its

meditative benefits.

6. **F.** NO CHANGE
   G. students who primarily want
   H. students, by primarily wanting
   J. students primarily hope

Here's How to Crack It

Subjects and verbs change in the answer choices, so identify the parts of the sentence. The second part of the sentence is an incomplete idea following a comma: *using the martial art for its meditative benefits*. This means the first part must be complete. Choice (F) sets *primarily hoping to reduce their stress* off with commas, suggesting that the phrase is an unnecessary describing phrase. This leaves the rest of the sentence as *Some of the tai chi students...using the martial art for its meditative benefits*. Remember that an *-ing* verb cannot be the main verb of a sentence. Therefore, this sentence contains only a subject, no main verb, so it's incomplete. Eliminate (F). Choice (G) includes a describing phrase *who primarily want to reduce their stress*. Remember that describing phrases do not always include commas: here the word *who* indicates that this phrase isn't part of the subject or verb. As with (F), this leaves the first part without a verb, so eliminate (G). Choice (H), similarly, creates a describing phrase *by primarily wanting to reduce their stress* and makes the sentence incomplete, so eliminate (H). Choice (J) provides a verb for the subject: *hope*. This makes the first part of the sentence *Some of the tai chi students primarily hope to reduce their stress*. This is a complete idea, so (J) is the correct answer.

When you first read the sentence above, you might have wanted it to say *Some of the tai chi students, primarily hoping to reduce their stress, use the martial art for its meditative benefits*. That would be completely fine because the verb *use* would go with the subject *students*. However, the verb *using* in the second part of the sentence isn't underlined, so it can't be changed. That means you have to find an answer that adds a main verb to the sentence.

SENTENCE STRUCTURE DRILL

Directions: For the following sentences and fragments, put a check mark next to each complete sentence. If the sentence is not complete, make it complete by adding or removing punctuation, removing a transition word, or changing the main verb.

1. In 2018, writer and professor Carol Anderson, published her fourth book.

2. Starting in childhood, the siblings, born in the city of Toronto, who studied the art of origami.

3. Not knowing which aisle contained beans, Cade wandered around the store.

4. Since the books are due on the tenth, two weeks from today.

5. With a bang, the bright fireworks, launched from the pier, and exploded colorfully in the dark sky.

6. My ankle starting to hurt after I twisted it during volleyball practice.

7. According to the guidebook, grizzly bears, when they are seen in the wild, are best left alone.

8. As Jaylee's phone beeped over and over, so she had to set it to silent.

9. Learning a foreign language requires practice in that language: immersion in a group speaking the language, when possible, is the best method.

10. Singing for a large audience, scared Jackson.

SENTENCE STRUCTURE DRILL ANSWERS AND EXPLANATIONS

1. A single comma cannot go between a subject and a verb, so remove the comma after *Anderson*.

2. The sentence does not have a concrete verb to go with the subject *siblings*. Remove the word *who* to make the sentence complete.

3. Complete

4. Remove the word *since* to make the sentence complete.

5. There is no verb to go with the subject *fireworks*. The sentence should indicate that the fireworks *exploded*, so remove the word *and*. Then the sentence correctly reads *With a bang, the bright fireworks, launched from the pier, exploded colorfully in the dark sky*. The phrase *launched from the pier* describes the *fireworks* and is surrounded by commas.

6. Change the verb to *was starting* or *started* to make the sentence complete.

7. Complete

8. Remove the word *as* to make the first part complete because it has a comma with FANBOYS (*so*), and thus both parts must be complete. Alternatively, remove the word *so* to allow just a comma (Go punctuation) to be used after the incomplete idea.

9. Complete

10. A single comma cannot go between a subject and a verb. The subject here is *singing* and the verb is *scared*. Remove the comma.

Summary

- A complete sentence must contain a subject and a verb. Verbs ending with *-ing* and verbs with *to* do not count.

- If subjects and verbs are changing in the answer choices, consider using the Vertical Line Test to determine whether the parts of the sentence are complete or incomplete.

- A single comma cannot go between a subject and a verb. Watch out for describing phrases that should either have punctuation before and after the phrase or not at all.

Chapter 10
Modifiers

MODIFIERS

Consider the following sentence:

> *Hoping for success, the chef's newest creation would satisfy guests who were looking to eat local, seasonal ingredients.*

Do you spot the error? While you might understand that the chef is hoping for success, the way this sentence is written makes it sound like *the chef's newest creation* is hoping for success. Unless the food has a brain with hopes and dreams, this sentence doesn't make logical sense. This grammar error is called a misplaced modifier. According to this rule, a describing phrase or "modifier" (here *hoping for success*) needs to come as close as possible to the thing it's describing. Here are two ways the sentence above could be rewritten.

> *Hoping for success, the chef had created a dish to satisfy guests who were looking to eat local, seasonal ingredients.*

> *The chef hoped her newest creation would successfully satisfy guests who were looking to eat local, seasonal ingredients.*

As you can see, the sentence can be rewritten so the thing being described comes right before or after the modifying phrase. Another option is to rewrite the sentence entirely to get rid of the modifier.

Having gotten lost and without an idea of where to go, nobody was around to ask for directions.

1. **A.** NO CHANGE
   B. I wanted to find someone to ask for directions.
   C. someone nearby could have given me directions.
   D. directions from someone nearby would have been helpful.

Here's How to Crack It

Check what's changing in the answer choices. The options provide similar meanings, but the order of the words changes. This is a good clue the question is testing modifiers. The beginning of the sentence contains a modifier: *Having gotten lost and without an idea of where to go.* Who was lost? Not *nobody*, so eliminate (A). Not *someone*, so eliminate (C). And *directions* can't be lost, so eliminate (D). *I* was the one who was lost, so the correct answer is (B).

There are two good ways to spot these questions. If you are reading the sentence, you might notice that it contains a misplaced modifier because the word after a modifying phrase isn't the person or thing the modifier describes. Alternatively, by following Step 1 of our basic approach, you may notice that all four answers say something similar, but the words are in a different order or the subject of the answers changes. This is a good clue that the question is testing modifiers.

MODIFIER DRILL

Directions: For each question, choose the sentence that is written correctly.

1. A. Rich in vitamins, nutritionists highly recommend eating kale regularly.
    B. Because kale is rich in vitamins, nutritionists highly recommend eating it regularly.

2. A. Given names like Justify, American Pharaoh, and Seattle Slew, racehorses showed Americans that animals could be a popular form of entertainment.
    B. Given names like Justify, American Pharaoh, and Seattle Slew, horse racing showed Americans that animals could be a popular form of entertainment.

3. A. After dazzling the audience with his rich singing voice, critics praised Astin's performance.
    B. Dazzled by his rich singing voice, critics praised Astin's performance.

4. A. A strong contender for the Olympic gold medal, the swimmer practices for at least four hours every day.
    B. A strong contender for the Olympic gold medal, the swimmer's practices last for at least four hours every day.

5. A. Featuring a fountain, visitors to the garden often take pictures.
    B. Featuring a fountain, the garden is frequently photographed by visitors.

6. A. A talented writer who has had several books published, Ng saw her books on best-seller lists for months.
    B. A talented writer who has had several books published, Ng's books have been on bestseller lists for months.

7. A. After completing a six-month paid internship, successful programmers become full-time employees.
    B. After completing a six-month paid internship, the skills that successful programmers have learned allow them to become full-time employees.

8. A. Since horses are receptive to humans, people have used them throughout history to perform jobs.
    B. Receptive to humans, people have used horses throughout history to perform jobs.

9. A. Moving his audience to tears, the play's viewers shouted, "Bravo!"
    B. Moved to tears, the play's viewers shouted, "Bravo!"

10. A. With titles such as *Lady Bird* and *Little Women*, films directed by Greta Gerwig earned critical acclaim.
    B. With titles such as *Lady Bird* and *Little Women*, Greta Gerwig's film career earned critical acclaim.

MODIFIER DRILL ANSWERS AND EXPLANATIONS

1. **B** Choice (A) mistakenly suggests that *nutritionists* are *rich in vitamins*.

2. **A** The *racehorses* are *given names*, not *horse racing* as a whole.

3. **B** The *critics* were *dazzled* by the singing. Choice (A) suggests that the critics are *dazzling the audience with his rich singing voice*, which doesn't make sense.

4. **A** The *swimmer* is *a strong contender*, not *the swimmer's practices*.

5. **B** The *garden* features a fountain, not the *visitors*.

6. **A** *Ng*, a name of a person, could be *a talented writer*, but *Ng's books* could not be.

7. **A** The *successful programmers* are the ones who are *completing a six-month paid internship*, not *the skills*.

8. **A** Choice (B) suggests that *people* are *receptive to humans*, which doesn't make sense because people are humans. Choice (A) correctly indicates that *horses* are *receptive to humans*. Remember that more words are sometimes needed to make the meaning clear.

9. **B** *The play's viewers* were *moved to tears*. In (A), the modifier is *moving his audience to tears*, which presumably describes a performer, not *viewers*.

10. **A** The *films* have those *titles*, not her *film career*.

Summary

o   The order of words changing in the answer choices is a good clue that modifiers are being tested.

o   Determine the subject of the modifying phrase. The subject should come as close as possible to the modifier.

o   Sometimes the correct answer will rewrite the sentence entirely or add a subject to the modifier so that it is no longer a modifier at all.

Chapter 11
Precision

TESTING PRECISION

Although you (luckily) will not see questions on the ACT that test your knowledge of difficult vocabulary words, you will see some questions on the English test that require you to choose among different individual words, most of which you will likely know. Here's an example.

A loud, shrieking noise <u>dispensed</u> from the device, startling me.
₁

1. **A.** NO CHANGE
   B. emerged
   C. originated
   D. accumulated

Here's How to Crack It

Vocabulary changes in the answer choices, so read the sentence and consider what meaning is necessary for the underlined portion. The underlined portion should mean something like "came out." Use POE. Choice (A), *dispensed*, means something close to "came out," but not exactly. *Dispensed* means "distributed," and it wouldn't be correct to say that a noise "distributed from the device," so eliminate (A). Choice (B), *emerged*, means "came out," so keep it. Choice (C), *originated*, means "began," and it implies that the subject began in a certain location but is no longer there, which isn't the case in this sentence, so eliminate (C). Choice (D), *accumulated*, means "gathered together," which does not match with "came out," so eliminate (D). The correct answer is (B).

As you can see, these questions require you to differentiate between words, sometimes relying on subtle differences in what the words suggest. The best strategy for dealing with these questions is to determine your own word or phrase based on the meaning of the sentence. Then consider how well each answer choice matches with that word or phrase. Unfortunately, these questions do not rely on simple rules that you can apply every time. It's impossible to know which words will be tested and in what contexts, but rest assured that you likely will be familiar with the options provided. Use POE and take your best guess if needed.

Vocabulary questions like the examples above, in which one word changes in the answer choices, are testing you on precision. This means you need to choose the answer that provides the most precise meaning in that sentence. Another, less common type of precision question involves choosing a more specific answer over one with more vague phrasing. Take a look at the following example.

I suspected that the sounding alarm was an

indication that <u>things were not good.</u>

2

2. F. NO CHANGE
   G. it was pretty bad.
   H. something was wrong.
   J. the device was malfunctioning.

Here's How to Crack It

First, identify what's changing in the answers. The answer choices indicate something similar, but some are more specific and others are more vague. Some choices are also more informal than others. Choices (F), (G), and (H) are all vague. Choice (J) is the most specific. Instead of saying *something* or *things* or *it*, (J) says *the device*. Instead of using the words *not good*, *pretty bad*, or *wrong*, (J) uses a more precise word: *malfunctioning*. Because (J) is the clearest phrase, the correct answer is (J).

When dealing with this type of question, there are particular types of words you can watch out for. General words such as *stuff* and *things* can often be replaced with more specific nouns. Like the vocabulary-only precision questions, you may also be asked to choose a word that is more specific and precise, such as *demanded* instead of *said*. These more precise words can make the meaning of the sentence clearer. You may also need to change a pronoun (such as *this, it, they,* and so on) into an actual noun if it is not clear who or what the pronoun refers to. Finally, you may also need to consider tone. As in the example above, you may see overly-casual, slang-y words such as *pretty* (as in *pretty good*), *kind of, cool, awesome, super, totally, wicked,* or *nifty*. ACT English passages generally use an academic tone, so these very informal words tend to be incorrect—they're not consistent with the passage's tone. Remember the 4 Cs!

PRECISION DRILL

Directions: Identify which option is more precise.

1. A. The new evidence presented by the prosecutor **forced** the members of the jury to reconsider their opinions.

   B. The new evidence presented by the prosecutor **restricted** the members of the jury to reconsider their opinions.

2. A. The principal decided to **institute** a new system for addressing students' behavior problems.

   B. The principal decided to **install** a new system for addressing students' behavior problems.

3. A. **When** they have been specially trained, software engineers may not be able to fix computers.

   B. **Unless** they have been specially trained, software engineers may not be able to fix computers.

4. A. At the Olympics, **they** can meet others from all over the world.

   B. At the Olympics, **participants** can meet others from all over the world.

5. A. During a heat wave, lettuce crops may **wither** and eventually die.

   B. During a heat wave, lettuce crops may **deflate** and eventually die.

6. A. Researchers **accused** that the mice's decline in health was related to vitamin deficiency.

    B. Researchers **suspected** that the mice's decline in health was related to vitamin deficiency.

7. A. **In light of this achievement**, we will now be able to offer tax preparation services to our clients.

    B. **Considering this action**, we will now be able to offer tax preparation services to our clients.

8. A. The Hubble Space Telescope has **provided** some of the best images of the galaxy that we have.

    B. The Hubble Space Telescope has **administered** some of the best images of the galaxy that we have.

9. A. Archaeologists have found jewelry, tools, and pottery from **there**.

    B. Archaeologists have found jewelry, tools, and pottery from **locations where Ancient Egyptians lived.**

10. A. Andrew Carnegie was a **rich guy** who eventually helped build hundreds of libraries.

    B. Andrew Carnegie was a **tycoon** who eventually helped build hundreds of libraries.

PRECISION DRILL ANSWERS AND EXPLANATIONS

1. **A** *Restricted* means "confined," and the sentence isn't indicating that the jurors were "confined" to something.

2. **A** While the two words have similar meanings, *install* is used when something is put into a particular place. In this case, the sentence isn't describing something being put into a spot but rather being "implemented," which is similar in meaning to *institute*.

3. **B** The word *when* should be used only when there is a reference to time. There isn't one in this sentence. Furthermore, it does not make logical sense to say that *when* people are trained, they are *not* able to do something.

4. **B** The word *they* is not clear. *Participants* clarifies the subject of the sentence, so it is more precise.

5. **A** While the two words have somewhat similar meanings, *deflate* means "to lose air." A plant isn't filled with air, so *deflate* doesn't work in this context. *Wither* means "shrivel," and that is an appropriate word to describe something that could happen to a plant.

6. **B** The word *suspected* in this context means "guessed," which works in a scientific context. *Accuse* means "blame," and it is only used in the context of some sort of fault or crime, which isn't mentioned in this sentence.

7. **A** Choice (A) is more precise because *achievement* specifies the type of *act*: a positive one. *In light of* is also more specific than *considering*, as it draws a clearer causal relationship.

8. **A** *Administer* means "supervise" or "provide as help." A *telescope* cannot *administer* something, as the word *administer* involves an action taken by a human.

9. **B** Choice (A) is not precise. Although (B) is longer, it specifies what location is being discussed, so it is the clearer option.

10. **B** Choice (A) is overly casual. Both *rich* and *guy* are not formal enough for the academic tone that ACT passages typically take. Choice (B) has a more appropriate tone and also uses a more precise word.

Summary

o   When the answer choices have individual words with similar meanings, read the sentence and understand what type of word should be used first. Then use POE.

o   Watch out for slight differences in definitions and how words should be used.

o   When given the option, choose a precise, specific word over a vague word.

o   When given the option, choose an actual noun over a pronoun, as it is clearer.

o   Watch out for answer choices that are overly casual and thus inconsistent with the passage's tone.

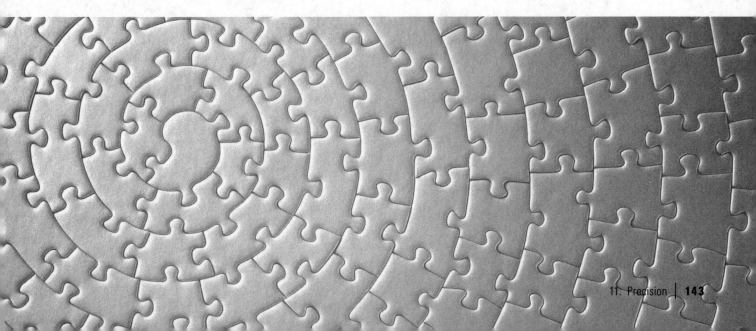

Chapter 12
Idioms and
Frequently
Confused Words

IDIOMS

Like the vocabulary questions we discussed in the previous chapter, idiom questions require you to be familiar with the words or phrases given. An idiom is a common phrase that does not follow a consistent rule. Why do we say *according to* and not *according with*? Why do we say *listening to* and not *listening of*? No real reason—it's just a rule for each particular word. You probably use idiomatic phrases, like the ones above, every day without thinking about why one word is used and not another. That's actually good news: you are probably already familiar with the majority of idioms you can expect to see on the ACT. The bad news is that ACT rarely repeats the same idioms, so unfortunately there is no real way to prepare for them, as there are countless words that could be used.

Here are some examples of idioms that have appeared on recent ACT tests. The word that would be tested in the underlined portion is shown in bold. (You may notice that these questions typically test you on prepositions, the small directional words we discussed in previous chapters.) This list should give you an idea of the types of phrases that could be tested. However, we do not recommend that you sit down and memorize these because, again, it's not necessarily likely that the same idioms will be tested a second time. Luckily, you can expect to see only about 2–3 idiom questions on the test.

According **to**

> *According **to** a recent study, this product may be harmful for children.*

Appetite **for**

> *The list of bestsellers reveals our appetite **for** self-help books.*

Arrive **at**

> *When they arrive **at** the airport, they will give us a call.*

As...**as**

> *There are as many points of view **as** there are members of our class.*

As evidenced **by**

> *He was a minimalist, as evidenced **by** the sparse nature of his apartment.*

At a...pace

> *The lesson was hard to follow because it moved **at** such a rapid pace.*

Based **on** or Based **upon** (both equally acceptable)

> *The movie was based **upon** a book written by a famous chef.*

Characteristic **of**

> *Intrigue is a defining characteristic **of** mystery novels.*

Compared…**to**

> *The artist compared building the sculpture **to** assembling a large puzzle.*

Drew **up**

> *She drew **up** a diagram to explain how the machine worked.*

Famous **for**

> *The dentist became famous throughout the state **for** straightening teeth at low cost.*

Focus **on**

> *The teacher decided to focus the day's lesson **on** grammar after the poor test results.*

Freed **from**

> *The warm weather freed me **from** having to shovel the snow.*

Illumination **of**

> *The illumination **of** the statue was a sight to behold.*

Improved **on** or Improved **upon** (both equally acceptable)

> *The new window design improved **upon** previous, less-insulated models.*

In accordance **with**

> *In accordance **with** the new law, we added reflectors to our bikes.*

In itself

> *I love seeing a new movie, but the popcorn is a treat **in** itself.*

Just South/North/East/West

> *The library is located **just** north of the town square.*

Lag **behind**

> *Try to keep up with the homework so you don't lag **behind** your peers.*

More…**than**…

*More a rough sketch **than** a detailed drawing, the map was difficult to follow.*

Piled high **with**

*The roof, piled high **with** snow, seemed in danger of collapsing.*

Raise…**to**

*Her work raises carpentry **to** the level of art.*

Refer to…**as**

*My teacher refers to it **as** the Awful, Crappy Test.*

Testament **to**

*It was a testament **to** her adaptability that she continued unfazed after the rule change.*

Typical **of**

*Their reaction was typical **of** people who had never seen the show before.*

Well/Better/Best Suited **for** or **to** (both equally acceptable)

*His outfit was better suited **for** the circus than for the prom.*

Here's an example of an ACT-style idiom question.

The MARC train travels between Baltimore with
¯¯¯¯
                                      1
Washington, D.C., primarily to aid commuters on

weekdays.

1. **A.** NO CHANGE
   B. to
   C. and
   D. going to

Here's How to Crack It

Prepositions are changing in the answer choices, so this question is testing idioms. Identify the idiom in the sentence. The sentence says *between Baltimore…Washington, D.C.* The correct idiom is *between…and*. Eliminate (A), (B), and (D) because they don't contain the word *and*. The correct answer is (C).

FREQUENTLY CONFUSED WORDS

A related topic is frequently confused words. Sometimes you will notice that the answer choices have different words, but the words look similar: *then* versus *than* or *rode* versus *road*. While you will never see a word on the ACT that is misspelled, you will occasionally need to choose between two different words that are frequently confused because they have similar spellings. Like with idioms, there is no way to predict which frequently confused words will be tested. However, the following list shows some of the ones that have appeared on the ACT before, along with definitions and examples. Those marked with a ♦ appear the most frequently—we recommend that you learn those. Keep in mind that this topic is tested less frequently than idioms are—once or twice per test.

♦Affect vs. Effect

Affect—(verb) to cause to happen or change

*The rain did not **affect** my weekend plans.*

Effect—(noun) the result of something

*The rain did not have any **effect** on my weekend plans.*

♦Allusion/Illusion/Elusion

Allusion—a reference to something

*The mention of Mount Olympus was an **allusion** to Greek mythology.*

Illusion—a visual trick

*The painting's use of perspective gives it the **illusion** of depth.*

Elusion—escaping or avoiding

*After fifteen minutes of trying to catch my cat, I grew tired of his **elusion**.*

Amount vs. Number

Amount—used for something that cannot be counted

amount of money, amount of love, amount of health, amount of knowledge

Number—used for something that can be counted

number of dollars, number of books, number of resources, number of trees

**Hint: Ask yourself whether you can have 5 of that thing. You can't have 5 money, so it's not countable and needs *amount*. You can have 5 dollars, so it is countable and needs *number*.

**Bonus: *Less* and *fewer* work the same way—*less* if it's not countable, *fewer* if it is. The same goes for *little* (not countable) and *few* (countable).

A Part vs. Apart

A part—being included in something

> *I was lucky to be **a part** of something so influential.*

Apart—separate from

> *We decided to spend the evening **apart** from each other.*

**Hint: If the word *of* comes after, you want *a part*. Only use *apart* if there is some sort of separation or distinction.

♦Cite vs. Site vs. Sight

Cite—to point to or show as a source

> *Opponents of the bill **cite** an increase in pollution as a potential downside.*

Site—the location of something

> *This lot is the future **site** of a new school.*

Sight—related to seeing

> *At the **sight** of the bus approaching, I began to run.*

♦Could/would/might/should of vs. Could/would/might/should have

The correct phrases are *could have, would have, might have,* and *should have. Could of* and any of the others with *of* are never correct, so eliminate them right away.

Dual vs. Duel

Dual—composed of two parts

> *Moving served a **dual** purpose: they would save money and be closer to work.*

Duel—fighting between two people

> *Once the students began to verbally **duel**, the teacher gave them detention.*

♦Lay vs. Lie vs. Laid

Lay—to place or put down

> *Please **lay** the papers on the table.*

Laid—past tense of *lay*

> *I **laid** the papers on the table as you asked me to.*

Lie—to recline

> *I like to **lie** on the couch while I watch TV.*

Lay—past tense of *lie*

> *Yesterday I **lay** on the couch while watching TV.*

**Hint: In present tense, if you can replace it with "put," you want *lay*. If not, it's *lie*. A couple of other idioms to know are *lay the foundation for*, *lay the groundwork for*, and *lay claim to*.

♦Lead vs. led

Lead—(rhymes with deed) to guide or be in charge of something

> *Our choir teacher will **lead** us in the next song.*

Led—past tense of *lead*

> *Our choir teacher **led** us in the last song.*

**Hint: People get this one confused because of the word *lead*, which sounds like *led* but refers to a type of metal. When referring to leadership, *lead* is pronounced with a long -e sound. The past tense is *led*.

♦Passed vs. Past

Passed—went by

> *The deadline for submissions to the contest has already **passed**.*

Past—previous, already happened

> *Your **past** actions will be considered in your evaluation.*

**Hint: *Passed* is a past-tense verb, while *past* is an adjective or noun. The meanings are somewhat similar, but you must choose the correct part of speech for the sentence. For *passed*, ask yourself: Did something pass? If so, *passed* is correct.

Peak vs. Peek

Peak—the highest point

*Climbing to the **peak** of the mountain will take two days.*

Peek—a quick look

*Take a **peek** at the plans for our vacation.*

Principal vs. Principle

Principal—a person with the highest rank, or the most important thing

*The **principal** reason for her promotion was her stellar leadership on a recent project.*

Principle—a basic truth or value

*Their teamwork on the project embodied the **principle** of collaboration.*

Sat vs. Set

Sat—past tense of *sit*

*People **sat** on the floor once the chairs were all taken.*

Set—to put something in a certain spot

*Not pleased with his first attempt at a poem, he **set** it aside and tried again.*

**Bonus: Two more idioms are *set out* (*She set out from Colorado.*) and *set about* (*He set about writing his letter.*) Only use *sat* to describe sitting.

♦Than vs. Then

Than—used to make a comparison

*I have seen more episodes **than** you have.*

Then—used to refer to time

*It was **then** that I decided to major in English.*

**Bonus: "Rather then" is never correct. It's *rather than.*

To vs. Too

To—used for directions

*Please give the scissors **to** me.*

Too—also, or to an overly high degree

*I walked **too** close to the edge and fell off.*

Here's an example of a frequently confused words question.

———————○———————

On the weekends, the train has <u>less passengers</u>
$\overline{2}$
then on weekdays, so it runs less frequently.
$\overline{2}$

2. **F.** NO CHANGE
   G. lesser passengers than
   H. fewer passengers then
   J. fewer passengers than

Here's How to Crack It

The words *less* and *fewer* along with *then* and *than* change in the answer choices, so the question is testing frequently-confused words. Start with *then* and *than*. The sentence draws a comparison between weekend passengers and weekday passengers, so *than* should be used. Eliminate (F) and (H). Next consider the difference between *lesser* and *fewer*. The word *lesser* means "of a worse quality." The sentence is not indicating that the weekend passengers are somehow worse but rather that there are *fewer* of them, so eliminate (G). *Fewer passengers* is correct because *passengers* are countable, so the word *fewer* should be used. Although it's no longer an option here, the word *less* is used only for non-countable words. The correct answer is (J).

———————○———————

IDIOMS AND FREQUENTLY CONFUSED WORDS DRILLS

Drill 1
Directions: Fill in the blank with the correct preposition.

1. I am indebted _____ you.

2. I am resentful _____ you.

3. I am jealous _____ you.

4. I am different _____ you.

5. The women had a dispute _____ you.

6. In our secret clubhouse, a majority is defined _____ two-thirds or more.

7. You have a responsibility _____ take care of your pet.

8. You are responsible _____ your pet.

9. He was horrified to read his sister's diary and find himself depicted _____ a jerk.

10. I am planning _____ get my driver's license soon.

11. Lindsay will try _____ attend Morgan's party.

12. Ana intends _____ major in mathematics.

Drill 2

Directions: Circle the correct word for each sentence.

1. Because I played ice hockey for several years, I found field hockey easier to learn (then/than) football.

2. She found a credit card (lying/laying) on the ground and brought it to the police station.

3. Other aspects, such as the temperature and humidity level of the room, (affect/effect) how long a piano stays in tune.

4. His (passed/past) accomplishments made him a worthy candidate for a promotion.

5. After a brief stop for a snack, the tour guide (lead/led) the way to the next destination.

6. Malia felt that she (should of/should have) taken the day off from work because she was not feeling well.

7. The reference to "hardships" in the speech was an (allusion/illusion) to the city's high unemployment and poverty rates.

8. Scientists hope to determine the (affect/effect) of prolonged exposure to light from electronics.

9. Although they are more expensive, name-brand colored pencils are used by artists more often (then/than) generic ones are because the quality is superior.

10. The principal (cited/sighted) an increase in graffiti as the reason behind the ban on permanent markers.

IDIOMS AND FREQUENTLY CONFUSED WORDS ANSWERS

Drill 1
1. to
2. of
3. of
4. from
5. with
6. as
7. to
8. for
9. as
10. to
11. to
12. to

Drill 2
1. than
2. lying
3. affect
4. past
5. led
6. should have
7. allusion
8. effect
9. than
10. cited

Summary

- o Idiom questions test rules that are different for each word. You probably know enough to at least take a good guess on these questions.

- o Use POE based on what sounds right if you're not sure.

- o Know the most common frequently confused words.

- o Rest assured that frequently confused words appear only a couple times per test, if at all.

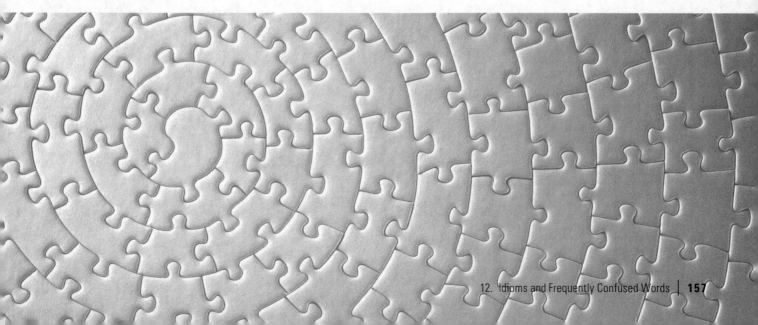

Part V
Practice English Tests

Chapter 13
English
Practice Test 1

ACT ENGLISH TEST

45 Minutes—75 Questions

DIRECTIONS: In the five passages that follow, certain words and phrases are underlined and numbered. In the right-hand column, you will find alternatives for each underlined part. In most cases, you are to choose the one that best expresses the idea, makes the statement appropriate for standard written English, or is worded most consistently with the style and tone of the passage as a whole. If you think the original version is best, choose "NO CHANGE." In some cases, you will find in the right-hand column a question about the underlined part. You are to choose the best answer to the question.

You will also find questions about a section of the passage or the passage as a whole. These questions do not refer to an underlined portion of the passage but rather are identified by a number or numbers in a box.

For each question, choose the alternative you consider best and blacken the corresponding oval on your answer document. Read each passage through once before you begin to answer the questions that accompany it. For many of the questions, you must read several sentences beyond the question to determine the answer. Be sure that you have read far enough ahead each time you choose an alternative.

PASSAGE I

The Man Behind Lassie

Many people are not familiar with the canine star Pal, an American collie, but they have probably heard of the dog he portrayed. Lassie, a beloved character who first appeared in a short story by Eric Knight, was Pal's role for 11 years. While Pal's talent landed him many projects—six movies, two TV pilots, and a national tour, among others—the significant care and instruction provided by the dog's trainer, Rudd Weatherwax; warrant
___
1

recognition. 2

1. **A.** NO CHANGE
   B. Weatherwax, warrant
   C. Weatherwax; who warrants
   D. Weatherwax, who warrants

2. At this point, the writer is considering adding the following true statement:

   > Another important figure was Fred Wilcox, the director who cast Pal in the first Lassie movie.

   Should the writer make this addition here?

   F. Yes, because it clarifies who cast Pal in the "movies" in the preceding sentence.
   G. Yes, because it ends the paragraph in a way that sets up the next paragraph.
   H. No, because it distracts from the paragraph's goal of setting up the main idea of the essay.
   J. No, because it distracts from the paragraph's focus on dogs that have starred in movies.

GO ON TO THE NEXT PAGE.

In 1940, Weatherwax was working as an animal trainer when a friend brought him a young collie for training. Weatherwax trained the dog regularly, guiding him through basic obedience, a training program often used for dogs. [A]

A dog's basic obedience skills include sitting on cue, staying until called, and walk next to its trainer. [B] When Pal had mastered the basics, Weatherwax began training him for the entertainment business. He wanted to ensure that Pal would behave calmly on a bustling movie set. ⑤

[C] While playing the role of Lassie on set, Pal performed complicated stunts with ease. [D] Weatherwax's unfailing compassion and professional attitude ensured a safe working environment.

Before the stunts, Weatherwax was at Pal's side, speaking to him calmly. For instance, at each set, Weatherwax was

constantly off camera, observantly any indications of danger or risk. Additionally, the Society for the Prevention of Cruelty to Animals (SPCA) observed Pal perform stunts, watching for any

3. **A.** NO CHANGE
   B. regularly; guiding
   C. regularly. Guiding
   D. regularly, he guided

4. **F.** NO CHANGE
   G. to walk
   H. walking
   J. they walk

5. At this point, the writer is considering adding the following accurate information:

   > that included many people talking and walking, frequent interaction with child actors, and unusual elements, such as fire.

   Should the writer make this addition here?

   A. Yes, because it gives details about Weatherwax's training program for Pal.
   B. Yes, because it specifies some of the challenges Pal could face on the movie set.
   C. No, because it shows that Pal was a particularly unpleasant dog.
   D. No, because it demonstrates that Weatherwax's training had a minimal effect on Pal's behavior.

6. **F.** NO CHANGE
   G. unfailing, compassion
   H. unfailing compassion,
   J. unfailing, compassion,

7. **A.** NO CHANGE
   B. Thus, at
   C. At
   D. On the other hand, at

8. **F.** NO CHANGE
   G. observant of
   H. observantly of
   J. observation of

GO ON TO THE NEXT PAGE.

dangers <u>that were visible to them.</u>
₉

People <u>of which</u> saw Weatherwax work with Pal were
₁₀

impressed by the clear love he had for the dog. ☐11

    Pal and Weatherwax helped secure Lassie's extraordinary

legacy. <u>Lassie, for example,</u> is one of only three animals with a
₁₂

star on the Hollywood Walk of Fame. After Weatherwax retired,

his animal training work was carried on by not only his

family members <u>but his employee, Carol Riggins</u> too. Pal
₁₃

passed away in 1958 at the age of 18. A picture taken shortly

before his death, showing Pal with his paw resting

on Weatherwax's arm, his eyes <u>gazed</u> at Weatherwax's face,
₁₄

<u>captures the loving relationship that can develop between dog</u>
₁₅
<u>and man.</u>
₁₅

9. **A.** NO CHANGE
    B. visible to it while the dog was performing.
    C. that became evident while observing him perform.
    D. DELETE the underlined portion and end the sentence with a period.

10. **F.** NO CHANGE
    G. of whom
    H. who
    J. whom

11. The writer wants to divide this paragraph into two in order to separate the general information about Pal's training from the information about Pal and Weatherwax on set. The best place to begin the new paragraph would be at:

    A. Point A.
    B. Point B.
    C. Point C.
    D. Point D.

12. Which of the following alternatives to the underlined portion would NOT be acceptable?

    F. For example, Lassie
    G. Therefore, Lassie
    H. To give an example, Lassie
    J. Lassie, for instance,

13. **A.** NO CHANGE
    B. but, his employee Carol Riggins,
    C. but, his employee, Carol Riggins
    D. but his employee, Carol Riggins,

14. **F.** NO CHANGE
    G. gazing
    H. would gaze
    J. gaze

15. Given that all the choices are accurate, which one most effectively concludes the sentence and the essay by reinforcing the essay's main point?

    A. NO CHANGE
    B. is in black and white and accessible through the Los Angeles Public Library.
    C. is a commemoration of one of the most famous canine actors in history.
    D. reveals the deep connection between Pal and Rudd Weatherwax.

GO ON TO THE NEXT PAGE.

PASSAGE II

British Fossils
[1]

In the early 1810s, Mary Anning began collecting fossils with her brother in her hometown of Lyme Regis on the southern coast of Great Britain. Anning's samples, some of the world's earliest recorded fossils, number into the hundreds and represent <u>many interesting species.</u> During the Triassic
₁₆

and Jurassic periods, the area near Lyme Regis was <u>obscured</u>
₁₇
by a shallow sea. Cliffs began to form as shale and limestone

<u>fragments had sunk</u> in the water, settled in layers on the
₁₈
seafloor. [A] Today, the cliffs still contain numerous samples of aquatic prehistoric life. Anning's discoveries

<u>that us see today</u> represent unique species; however, when she
₁₉
first collected them, many thought that they were hoaxes or existing species.

16. The writer is considering revising the underlined portion to the following:

    at least three previously undiscovered species.

    Should the writer make this revision?

    F. Yes, because it provides a specific detail that reveals the significance of Anning's discoveries.
    G. Yes, because it explains why there are so many fossils in Lyme Regis.
    H. No, because it reiterates a detail stated earlier in the paragraph.
    J. No, because it does not indicate the names of the species preserved by Anning's fossils.

17. A. NO CHANGE
    B. covered
    C. buried
    D. shrouded

18. F. NO CHANGE
    G. fragments sank
    H. fragments, have been sinking
    J. fragments, sinking

19. A. NO CHANGE
    B. as we see them
    C. as they are seen by we
    D. as we see it

GO ON TO THE NEXT PAGE.

[2]

Fossils are remains of ancient life and can contain organic remains or records of organisms' activities. Examples include fossilized bones, teeth, footprints, feces, and eggshells. [B] During the creation of a fossil, calcite, a slowly hardening, stable compound that creates fossils, forms around remains to preserve their shape and structure.

Not tolerating rough handling due to their fragility, paleontologists must use extreme care and precise tools when working with the remains. Today's paleontologists and geobiologists has used advanced tools to get a close look at the ancient remains. One of these tools provide scientists with a glimpse into the life of a fossilized organism through electron microscopy. All of this information does a really good job when it comes to determining whether a fossil is from an extinct or existing species.

20. **F.** NO CHANGE
    G. life, and
    H. life; and
    J. life. And

21. **A.** NO CHANGE
    B. stable compound that slowly hardens over a long time,
    C. stable, slowly hardening compound that forms over a long time,
    D. stable compound that slowly hardens,

22. **F.** NO CHANGE
    G. Since they don't tolerate
    H. Because fossils are not tolerant of
    J. Intolerant of

23. **A.** NO CHANGE
    B. uses
    C. use
    D. is using

24. **F.** NO CHANGE
    G. provides
    H. have provided
    J. are providing

25. **A.** NO CHANGE
    B. works pretty well with
    C. is really good for
    D. is especially helpful for

GO ON TO THE NEXT PAGE.

[3]

Age analysis of Lyme Regis's cliffs, combined with information gained from early fossil analysis done on samples taken from them, suggested that some were actually from
<u>26</u>
extinct species. [C] Although many people thought that Anning's fossils were created by modern engineering, scientific analysis of the samples proved that they contained fossils of organisms that lived <u>only a few years ago.</u> [D] Her discoveries
<u>27</u>
helped build a strong case for evolution and extinction.

26. **F.** NO CHANGE
    G. fossils
    H. Anning's fossils
    J. they

27. Which choice draws the most specific contrast between the assumed age of Anning's fossils and the actual age of the fossils she uncovered?

    A. NO CHANGE
    B. not that many
    C. millions of
    D. DELETE the underlined portion.

When <u>anatomist Georges Cuvier</u> learned of Anning's claims, he
<u>28</u>
stated, "Why has not anyone seen that fossils alone gave birth to a theory about the formation of the earth?"

28. **F.** NO CHANGE
    G. anatomist, Georges Cuvier,
    H. anatomist, Georges Cuvier
    J. anatomist Georges Cuvier,

Questions 29 and 30 ask about the preceding passage as a whole.

29. The writer is considering adding the following sentence to the essay:

    > Fossils are made from a wide variety of natural processes involving mineral crystallization.

    If the writer were to add this sentence, it would most logically be placed at:

    A. Point A in Paragraph 1.
    B. Point B in Paragraph 2.
    C. Point C in Paragraph 3.
    D. Point D in Paragraph 3.

30. Suppose the writer's primary purpose had been to provide a short account of the life of an important paleontologist. Would this essay accomplish this purpose?

    F. Yes, because it states that Anning was the one to prove that organisms can go extinct.
    G. Yes, because it outlines one paleontologist's contribution to the theories of evolution and extinction.
    H. No, because it provides details about other paleontologists in addition to Anning.
    J. No, because it centers on how a few fossil discoveries altered a long-established scientific viewpoint.

GO ON TO THE NEXT PAGE.

PASSAGE III

The First Trains in Manhattan

On April 20, 1871, Manhattan's first successful mass transit train, the *Ninth Avenue Elevated*, began operation between Dey Street and 29th Street
<u>　　　　　　　　　　　　　　</u>
31

in Manhattan. The steam-powered locomotive,
<u>　　　　　　　　　　　</u>
32

ironically, ran on a raised platform above the street. New
<u>　</u>
33
Yorkers had long relied on horse-drawn carriages, cable cars, or walking to commute. The *Ninth Avenue* train was faster than any of these methods by a considerable amount, so it quickly gained popularity.

<u>Underground subway trains are now considered to be a</u>
34
<u>staple of New York City transit.</u> The Gilbert Elevated Railway's
34
Sixth Avenue Elevated train began operating in 1878, followed by the *Second Avenue Elevated* train later that year.

Transit lines in Manhattan extended through many of the <u>downtown, but some of the</u> uptown neighborhoods.
<u>　</u>
35

---

31. **A.** NO CHANGE
    B. on the trip to
    C. and also
    D. to

32. **F.** NO CHANGE
    G. signifying the initial ride of a train used for mass transit.
    H. in the 1870s.
    J. DELETE the underlined portion and end the sentence with a period.

33. Which choice most strongly reinforces the information in the rest of the sentence?

    A. NO CHANGE
    B. known as an "elevated train" or "el,"
    C. as reported by journalists,
    D. during that time,

34. Given that all of the choices are true, which one best introduces the topic of the paragraph?

    F. NO CHANGE
    G. It is now possible to travel among four out of the five boroughs in New York City via train.
    H. By the end of the decade, elevated trains ran throughout Manhattan.
    J. Upper Manhattan contained mostly rural land until the late 19th century.

35. **A.** NO CHANGE
    B. downtown and
    C. downtown and,
    D. downtown, and

GO ON TO THE NEXT PAGE.

The train system thus offered a mobility unparalleled in public
transportation in New York City at the time.
                                          36

36. F. NO CHANGE
    G. unparalleled on
    H. unparalleled with
    J. that unparalleled

    Reduced travel time made it feasible for more people
to travel from suburban communities, to workplaces, in
                                37
Manhattan. For instance, the trip from Yonkers, just north of
Manhattan, to the New York Stock Exchange took most of

37. A. NO CHANGE
    B. communities to workplaces,
    C. communities, to workplaces
    D. communities to workplaces

the day: by horse-drawn carriage elevated trains reduced the
         38

38. F. NO CHANGE
    G. day by horse-drawn carriage;
    H. day, by horse-drawn carriage,
    J. day by horse-drawn carriage,

length of the trip noticeably. Real estate development
                     39
skyrocketed, as people decided to settle in more rural areas
surrounding Manhattan and commute to work by way of an
elevated train.

39. Given that all the choices are accurate, which one best completes the contrast set up in the first part of the sentence?
    A. NO CHANGE
    B. with regard to time.
    C. in Manhattan.
    D. to an hour or less.

    During its golden age, the elevated train system carried
         40
millions of people. However, it was not without its flaws.
Though the system allowed people to travel quickly through
Manhattan—an island with an area of approximately 23 square
miles the trains were loud and deposited debris on the streets,
41
buildings, and passersby beneath the tracks.

40. F. NO CHANGE
    G. it's
    H. their
    J. its'

41. A. NO CHANGE
    B. miles;
    C. miles—
    D. miles,

Difficult to operate in the snow and ice, the elevated train was
                                          42
hazardous and unreliable during New York City's cold winters.

42. F. NO CHANGE
    G. riding an elevated train
    H. elevated train transit as a whole
    J. an elevated train ride

GO ON TO THE NEXT PAGE.

By the turn of the twentieth century, an electric underground subway system had risen in popularity, and it was overtaken by the elevated train as the city's most convenient form of transit.

As the subway did not construct debris and was not affected by weather, it gradually replaced many of the elevated trains in Manhattan. However, elevated trains continue their legacy today in Brooklyn, Queens, and the Bronx.

43. **A.** NO CHANGE
    B. overtaken by
    C. overtaken for use by
    D. overtaking

44. **F.** NO CHANGE
    G. manufacture
    H. build
    J. produce

Question 45 asks about the preceding passage as a whole.

---

45. Suppose the writer's primary purpose had been to provide an in-depth comparison of steam-powered elevated trains and electric subway cars that ran in Manhattan in the 1800s. Would this essay accomplish this purpose?

    A. Yes, because the essay discusses the utility, design, and price of both types of trains in Manhattan.
    B. Yes, because the essay shows how electric subway cars were cleaner and less affected by winter weather than elevated trains were.
    C. No, because although the essay provides information about electric subway cars, it centers on the development and operation of steam-powered elevated trains in Manhattan.
    D. No, because the essay centers on the ways in which electric subway cars caused elevated trains to decline in popularity in Manhattan.

GO ON TO THE NEXT PAGE.

PASSAGE IV

Communicating with Chimps

[1] It enables us to watch movies, follow breaking news on television, and learn new concepts remotely. [2] In academia, actions recorded on video can be used as data to inform the work of animal behaviorists. [3] Video recording technology is often used to capture and preserve important actions. ☐46

One of the main forms of communication used by chimpanzees, according to animal behaviorists is visual ──
                                                47
communication. This type of communication is difficult to study.

Technology-averse scientists essentially process data from
                   ─────────────────────────────
                             48
direct observation, causing them to rely only on their memories to form conclusions.

Video technology enables scientists to take a detour around
                                      ──────────────────────
                                              49
sole reliance on memory, allowing them to re-watch videos containing visual gestures as many times as necessary.

Regardless, video technology is useful to the study of visual
──────────
    50
communication.

46. Which sequence of sentences makes this paragraph most logical?
   F. NO CHANGE
   G. 3, 2, 1
   H. 3, 1, 2
   J. 1, 3, 2

47. A. NO CHANGE
   B. chimpanzees according to animal behaviorists, is
   C. chimpanzees, according to animal behaviorists is,
   D. chimpanzees, according to animal behaviorists, is

48. F. NO CHANGE
   G. scientists, essentially processing
   H. scientists who are essentially processing
   J. scientists, who essentially process

49. A. NO CHANGE
   B. bypass
   C. work their way around
   D. cut

50. F. NO CHANGE
   G. Likewise,
   H. Therefore,
   J. However,

GO ON TO THE NEXT PAGE.

Raphaela Heesen and a team of animal behaviorists recently analyzed videos of chimpanzees and made a groundbreaking discovery about chimpanzee communication. Heesen's team traveled to the Budongo Forest Reserve in Uganda to study chimpanzees in their natural habitat. They recorded thousands of instances of gestures being used by wild chimpanzees. Video technology enabled the team to watch the gestures repeatedly, scrutinizing them in the greatest detail possible. As a result, the scientists were able to begin sketching out connections among a number of instances.

Analyzing the results, only 58 unique gestures stood out to the team, meaning many gestures were repeated.

The team then turned to a surprising discipline modern linguistics.

Two rules from this field was used to explain the patterns in chimpanzee gestures: Zipf's law of abbreviation and Menzerath's law.

In fact, Zipf's law states that frequently used words are relatively short. Menzerath's law says that long linguistic

51. A. NO CHANGE
  B. revolutionary, groundbreaking discovery about
  C. discovery that, incredibly, broke new ground about
  D. groundbreaking discovery that revolutionized the study of

52. F. NO CHANGE
  G. drawing
  H. doodling
  J. making representations of

53. A. NO CHANGE
  B. the number of gestures identified by the team is only 58,
  C. the 58 unique gestures were identified by the team,
  D. the team identified only 58 unique gestures,

54. F. NO CHANGE
  G. discipline;
  H. discipline; which is
  J. discipline:

55. A. NO CHANGE
  B. is
  C. were
  D. has been

56. F. NO CHANGE
  G. For instance,
  H. For one thing,
  J. DELETE the underlined portion.

GO ON TO THE NEXT PAGE.

structures are typically broken. 57

The trends of recorded gestures told scientists that these laws may be reliably applied to chimpanzee communication. This

finding is important to animal behaviorists it suggests that chimpanzees use a pattern-based system to communicate. Heesen and her team now hope to expand their work. Since the

study of animal behavior often depends on visual gestures, video recording technology may help to deliver insight into communication across the animal kingdom.

57. At this point, the writer is considering adding the following accurate information:

> into smaller units during speech

Should the writer make this addition here?

- **A.** Yes, because it clarifies how the linguistic structures are being broken.
- **B.** Yes, because it reinforces the writer's statement that Menzerath's law is a language rule.
- **C.** No, because it implies that Menzerath's law is more complex than Zipf's law is.
- **D.** No, because it provides specific information that is not consistent with the rest of the essay.

58. **F.** NO CHANGE
  G. with
  H. by
  J. in

59. **A.** NO CHANGE
  B. behaviorists;
  C. behaviorists; for
  D. behaviorists,

60. **F.** NO CHANGE
  G. gestures as
  H. gestures, with
  J. gestures that

GO ON TO THE NEXT PAGE.

PASSAGE V

A Trailblazing Author

[1] When science fiction literature, entering the mainstream
in the 1950s, readers were captivated by space operas and tales
of technological wonders.

[2] Wanting entertainment but tiring of predictability, readers
looked for science fiction stories that explored new territory.
[3] Their imaginations were no longer captured by formulaic
stories of rocket ships and aliens.

[4] By the 1960s, though, readers' interest was

waning. [64]

An aspiring writer, Octavia Butler, was ready to give
readers something new. A lifelong reader of science fiction,
Butler attended multiple writing programs if she wanted more

literary experience. Thrilled with her strong writing and
impressive world-building, author Harlan Ellison became her
writing mentor and supported her journey. In less than two
years, she sold her first story.

61. A. NO CHANGE
   B. literature entered
   C. literature that entered
   D. literature, which entered

62. F. NO CHANGE
   G. Despite wanting entertainment, readers tired
   H. Though readers wanted entertainment, they tired
   J. Wanting entertainment, but they tired

63. A. NO CHANGE
   B. reader's interest was
   C. reader's interests were
   D. readers' interests were

64. Which sequence of sentences makes this paragraph most
logical?

   F. NO CHANGE
   G. 1, 4, 2, 3
   H. 1, 2, 4, 3
   J. 1, 4, 3, 2

65. A. NO CHANGE
   B. because
   C. provided that
   D. assuming

66. F. NO CHANGE
   G. A thrilling writer
   H. Thrilling him
   J. After thrilling him

GO ON TO THE NEXT PAGE.

Butler broadened the scope of science fiction. She wrote not only about aliens, but also included political and social structures, marginalized groups, and radical transformations. She created stories to more accurately

67. **A.** NO CHANGE
B. also about
C. was also inclusive of
D. DELETE the underlined portion.

consider the world as she experienced it. Her imaginative

68. **F.** NO CHANGE
G. enhance
H. redirect
J. reflect

worlds took readers on fantastical journeys that after them, the real world would never seem the same. Other science fiction authors were impressed by her extensive world-building.

69. **A.** NO CHANGE
B. journeys, which after,
C. journeys, which, after them,
D. journeys, after which

Fellow writers nominated her work for prestigious awards, like

70. **F.** NO CHANGE
G. awards; like
H. awards; like,
J. awards, like,

the Nebula and Hugo awards. 71

71. If the writer were to delete the preceding sentence, this paragraph would primarily lose:

A. a detail about the impressive accomplishments of Butler.
B. an indication of readers' impressions of Butler's work.
C. a suggestion that Butler's work belonged in a different genre.
D. an explanation of how Butler's success made the Nebula and Hugo awards more popular.

Beyond the achievements of her writing, Butler created space for a greater diversity of writers to enter the realm of science fiction. For decades, science fiction consisted of a white, and male group of

72. **F.** NO CHANGE
G. white—and male
H. white (and male),
J. white—and male—

GO ON TO THE NEXT PAGE.

writers. 73 Butler, an African American woman, provided an example for generations of emerging writers, showing them that a career in science fiction was possible. Recognition of her impact goes beyond the writing community. In 1995,

for instance, Butler received a MacArthur Fellowship, 74 colloquially known as a "genius grant." To date, she is the only science fiction writer to receive one. In regards to her work, Butler said, "I wrote myself in, since I'm me and I'm here and I'm writing. I can write my own stories and I can write myself in."

73. Given that all the following statements are true, which one provides the most effective transition between the preceding sentence and the rest of the paragraph?

   A. Many of these writers were responsible for the popularity of science fiction.
   B. Before Butler, science fiction stories were about white, male characters.
   C. Women writers, especially women of color, were vastly underrepresented in the field.
   D. Butler's first novel, *Patternmaster*, features a group of humans with telepathic powers.

74. F. NO CHANGE
     G. likewise,
     H. furthermore,
     J. however,

> Question 75 asks about the preceding passage as a whole.

75. Suppose the writer's main purpose had been to explain the significance of a science fiction author's career. Would this essay accomplish that purpose?

   A. Yes, because it examines how Butler's innovative subjects and expansive world-building affected science fiction literature.
   B. Yes, because it details how the commitment to become a writer changed Butler's personal character and career goals.
   C. No, because it states that, after a few years of success, novels like Butler's no longer interested readers.
   D. No, because it discusses how Butler stopped writing short stories to focus on more literary science fiction novels.

END OF TEST 1
STOP! DO NOT TURN THE PAGE UNTIL TOLD TO DO SO.

Chapter 14
English Practice
Test 1:
Answers and
Explanations

ENGLISH PRACTICE TEST 1 ANSWERS

1.	B		39.	D
2.	H		40.	F
3.	A		41.	C
4.	H		42.	F
5.	B		43.	D
6.	F		44.	J
7.	C		45.	C
8.	G		46.	H
9.	D		47.	D
10.	H		48.	F
11.	C		49.	B
12.	G		50.	H
13.	D		51.	A
14.	G		52.	G
15.	D		53.	D
16.	F		54.	J
17.	B		55.	C
18.	J		56.	J
19.	B		57.	A
20.	F		58.	J
21.	D		59.	B
22.	H		60.	F
23.	C		61.	B
24.	G		62.	F
25.	D		63.	D
26.	H		64.	J
27.	C		65.	B
28.	F		66.	F
29.	B		67.	B
30.	J		68.	J
31.	A		69.	D
32.	J		70.	F
33.	B		71.	A
34.	H		72.	J
35.	B		73.	C
36.	F		74.	F
37.	D		75.	A
38.	G			

SCORE YOUR PRACTICE TEST

Step A

Count the number of correct answers: _____. This is your *raw score*.

Step B

Use the score conversion table below to look up your raw score. The number to the left is your *scale score*: _____.

English Scale Conversion Table

Scale Score	Raw Score	Scale Score	Raw Score	Scale Score	Raw Score
36	72-75	24	53-55	12	23-24
35	70-71	23	51-52	11	19-22
34	68-69	22	48-50	10	16-18
33	67	21	45-47	9	13-15
32	66	20	42-44	8	11-12
31	65	19	40-41	7	9-10
30	64	18	38-39	6	7-8
29	62-63	17	36-37	5	6
28	61	16	33-35	4	4-5
27	60	15	30-32	3	3
26	58-59	14	27-29	2	2
25	56-57	13	25-26	1	0-1

ENGLISH PRACTICE TEST 1 EXPLANATIONS

Passage I

1. **B**   Punctuation is changing in the answer choices, but some of these punctuation marks are commas that change around a phrase, so the question is testing comma rules. The phrase *Rudd Weatherwax* is unnecessary information, since *the dog's trainer* refers only to *Weatherwax*, so it needs a comma before and after. Eliminate (A) and (C) because each uses a semicolon, not a comma, after *Weatherwax*. Both (B) and (D) feature a comma in the correct place, so consider the meaning of the words in each choice. Keep (B) because it makes the sentence complete: *While Pal's talent landed him many projects... the significant care and instruction provided by the dog's trainer, Rudd Weatherwax, warrant recognition.* Eliminate (D) because the addition of *who* makes the sentence incomplete. The answer correct is (B).

2. **H**   Note the question! The question asks whether the sentence should be added, so it's testing consistency. If the content of the new sentence is consistent with the ideas surrounding it, then it should be added. The paragraph introduces *Pal* and his trainer, *Rudd Weatherwax*, and the passage is about their relationship. The new sentence discusses *Fred Wilcox,* who is a secondary figure. This statement is not consistent with the ideas in the text; the sentence should not be added. Eliminate (F) and (G). Keep (H) because it states that the new sentence *distracts from the paragraph's goal*. Eliminate (J) because the text only discusses one dog that has *starred in movies*. The correct answer is (H).

3. **A**   Punctuation is changing in the answer choices, so the question is testing Stop and Go punctuation. Use the Vertical Line Test, and identify the ideas as complete or incomplete. Draw the vertical line between the words *regularly* and *guiding*. The phrase *Weatherwax trained the dog regularly* is a complete idea, and the phrase *guiding him through basic obedience, a training program often used for dogs* is an incomplete idea. To connect a complete idea to an incomplete idea, Half-Stop or Go punctuation is needed. The comma is Go punctuation, so keep (A). The semicolon is Stop punctuation, so eliminate (B). The period is Stop punctuation, so eliminate (C). The comma is Go punctuation, but adding the word *he* before *guided* makes the second part of the sentence complete. A comma cannot connect two complete ideas, so eliminate (D). The correct answer is (A).

4. **H**   Verbs are changing in the answer choices, so the question is testing consistency of verbs. The answer choices are in different forms, so look for a clue in the sentence to identify the appropriate verb form. The underlined verb is part of a list, in which the other two items have verbs that end in *-ing*: *sitting* and *staying*. All verbs in a list must be in the same form to be consistent, so the underlined verb must also have the suffix *-ing*. Eliminate (F), (G), and (J) because they are not consistent with the other verbs. Keep (H) because *walking* correctly includes the suffix *-ing*. The correct answer is (H).

5. **B**   Note the question! The question asks whether the phrase should be added, so it's testing consistency. If the content of the new phrase is consistent with the ideas surrounding it, then it should be added. The sentence that would contain the new phrase says that Weatherwax *wanted to ensure that Pal would behave calmly on a bustling movie set*. The new phrase discusses things that might be found on a *bustling movie set*, so is consistent with the ideas in the text; the sentence should be added. Eliminate (C) and (D). Eliminate (A) because the new phrase does not discuss *Weatherwax's training program for Pal*. Keep (B) because the new phrase does specify *challenges Pal could face on the movie set*. The correct answer is (B).

6. **F** Commas are changing in the answer choices, so the question is testing comma rules. Commas are changing around the word *compassion*, so check to see whether the word is necessary. *Weatherwax's unfailing compassion* is the subject of the sentence, so *compassion* is necessary. Therefore, it should not be surrounded by commas. Eliminate (J) because it surrounds *compassion* with commas. Keep (F) because it does not use commas around *compassion*. There is no reason to use a comma after *unfailing*, so eliminate (G). Likewise, there is no reason to use a comma after *compassion*, so eliminate (H). The correct answer is (F).

7. **C** Transitions are changing in the answer choices, so the question is testing consistency with transitions. Look at the previous sentence to determine how the two ideas are related. The previous sentence describes one action that Weatherwax would take to give Pal a safe working environment, and this sentence explains another such action. These two ideas agree, so eliminate (D), which uses an opposite-direction transition. Eliminate (A) because it suggests that the second sentence states an example of an idea in the first sentence. Eliminate (B) because it implies that the second sentence states a conclusion that follows from an idea in the first sentence. Keep (C) because it preserves the idea that the two sentences are both examples of actions taken by Weatherwax. No transition is needed. The correct answer is (C).

8. **G** Vocabulary is changing in the answer choices, so the question is testing word choice. Determine what meaning of the underlined portion would be consistent with the sentence and would make the sentence complete. The underlined portion must describe *Weatherwax* while he was *off camera*. Eliminate (F) and (H) because *observantly* is an adverb. An adverb describes a verb, not a noun. Since there is no verb for the adverb to describe, both choices make the sentence incomplete. Keep (G) because *observant of* describes Weatherwax's state while he was *off camera*. Eliminate (J) because *observation* does not describe a person. The correct answer is (G).

9. **D** The phrase after *dangers* is changing in the answer choices, so the question could be testing concision. There is also the option to DELETE; consider this choice carefully as it's often the correct answer. First determine whether the underlined phrase is necessary. The sentence already states that the SPCA *observed Pal perform stunts* and *watched for any dangers*. There is no need to repeat the idea that the organization was looking out for *visible* indications of danger, so eliminate (A) and (B). Likewise, there is no need to repeat the idea that the organization was *observing him perform*, so eliminate (C). The correct answer is (D).

10. **H** Pronouns are changing in the answer choices, so the question is testing clarity with pronouns. First determine who or what the pronoun refers to. The subject of the sentence is *People*, and the pronoun refers to this subject. The phrase *of which* does not work because *which* cannot be used to refer to people, so eliminate (F). Since the underlined pronoun must provide a subject for the verb *saw*, a subject pronoun is needed. Eliminate (G) and (J) because each uses the object pronoun *whom*. Keep (H) because it uses the subject pronoun *who*. The correct answer is (H).

11. **C** Note the question! The question asks for *the best place to begin the new paragraph*, so it's testing consistency. Paragraphs should contain information related to one main idea, so look for the main ideas in the existing paragraph. The first part of the paragraph discusses Weatherwax's training program before Pal worked on set, and the second part of the paragraph discusses Pal's work on set. Therefore, the new paragraph should be started with the first sentence that discusses Pal's work on set. Eliminate (A) because it would start the new paragraph too early (while the text still discusses Weatherwax's training program). Choice (B) is tricky because the sentence that follows point B says

that Weatherwax *wanted to ensure that Pal would behave calmly on a bustling movie set*. This sentence only discusses Weatherwax's ambitions, not Pal's actions on set. It is still discussing Pal's *training*. Therefore, it should not be part of the new paragraph. Eliminate (B). Keep (C) because the sentence that follows point C is the first that discusses Pal's actions on set. Eliminate (D) because it would begin the new paragraph too late. The correct answer is (C).

12. **G**   Note the question! The question asks which alternative *to the underlined portion would NOT be acceptable*. Cross off the word *NOT* and label each answer with a checkmark or an X. Notice that each choice contains a transition, so the question is testing consistency with transitions. Look at the previous sentence to determine how the two ideas are related. The previous sentence states a fact, and this sentence gives an example supporting that fact. Therefore, an acceptable transition must indicate that this sentence is an example. Give a checkmark to (F), (H), and (J) because each of these indicates that the information that follows is an example. Give (G) an X because it is the only transition that does not indicate an example (*therefore* implies a conclusion), so it is not an acceptable alternative. The correct answer is (G).

13. **D**   Commas are changing in the answer choices, so the question is testing comma rules. The phrase *Carol Riggins* is unnecessary information. *Carol Riggins* is the only indicated *employee* who carried on Weatherwax's *animal training work*, and the sentence would still make sense without her name, so the name is unnecessary information. *Carol Riggins* needs a comma before and after. Eliminate (A) because it lacks a comma after the phrase. Eliminate (B) because it lacks a comma before the phrase and uses an unnecessary comma after *but*. When dealing with two phrases with the same meaning, the second should be set off in commas, not the first. Eliminate (C) because it surrounds *his employee*, not *Carol Riggins* with commas. Keep (D) because it surrounds *Carol Riggins* with commas. The answer correct is (D).

14. **G**   Verbs are changing in the answer choices, so the question is testing consistency of verbs. The answer choices are in different tenses, so look for a clue in the sentence or surrounding sentences to identify the appropriate tense. The underlined verb is part of a list of two items that describes Pal's expression in a picture. Both or all items in a list must be consistent. The first item is *his paw resting*, so the underlined portion must also use a present tense verb with the suffix *-ing*. Eliminate (F) because *gazed* is past tense. Keep (G) because *gazing* is present tense and has the suffix *-ing*. Eliminate (H) because *would gaze* is not consistent with *resting*. Eliminate (J) because *gaze*, though present tense, doesn't include the suffix *-ing*. The correct answer is (G).

15. **D**   Note the question! The question asks which option reinforces *the essay's main point*. The essay discusses the strong bond between *Pal* and *Weatherwax*. Check each answer choice to see whether it has to do with this strong bond. Eliminate (A) because, though it mentions *a loving relationship between dog and man*, it does not mention Pal or Weatherwax by name and is therefore too vague. Eliminate (B) because it does not mention the bond between Pal and Weatherwax. Eliminate (C) because it refers to Pal but does not mention his bond with Weatherwax. Keep (D) because it mentions *the deep connection between Pal and Rudd Weatherwax*. The correct answer is (D).

Passage II

16. **F**   Note the question! The question asks whether a portion of the sentence should be revised, so it's testing consistency. If the content of the revision is consistent with the ideas surrounding it and more precise than the underlined information, then it should be added. The sentence says that *Anning's samples... represent many interesting species*. The proposed revision indicates that Anning's samples represent *at least three previously undiscovered species*. Since the revision is consistent with the sentence but more clear and specific than the underlined phrase (it mentions a specific fact), it should replace the underlined phrase. Eliminate choices (H) and (J). Keep (F) because it states that the proposed revision provides a *specific detail* about *Anning's discoveries*. Eliminate (G) because the proposed revision does not explain *why there are so many fossils in Lyme Regis*. The correct answer is (F).

17. **B**   Vocabulary is changing in the answers, so the question is testing word choice. Determine what meaning of the underlined portion would be consistent with the sentence. The underlined portion should mean something like "submerged." *Obscured* means "hidden," which doesn't match "submerged" in context. The sentence implies that the area was underwater but not necessarily that it was hidden. Eliminate (A). Keep (B) because *covered* by water means "submerged." Eliminate (C) because *buried* means "underground," not underwater. Eliminate (D) because *shrouded* means "hidden," which does not match "submerged." The correct answer is (B).

18. **J**   Verb forms are changing in the answer choices, so the question is testing sentence structure. Identify the subject and verb of the part of the sentence after the word *as*, which needs to be a complete idea. The subject of that part of the sentence is *shale and limestone fragments*, and the verb is *settled*. There is a comma before the verb, so if there is a comma separating a subject and verb, there must be a second comma around the unnecessary phrase in between. Therefore, the answer must include a comma to go before the phrase. Eliminate (F) and (G) because they do not include a comma. Choice (H) has a verb in a form that could make it the main verb. Since *settled* is the main verb, (H) does not work. Eliminate (H). Choice (J) uses an *-ing* verb, which cannot be the main verb but can start an unnecessary phrase, which is exactly what appears in this sentence. The correct answer is (J).

19. **B**   The wording of the phrase and pronouns change in the answer choices, so the question is testing pronoun case and number. A pronoun must be consistent in number with the noun it is replacing. The underlined portion refers to the noun *cliffs*, which is plural. To be consistent, the pronoun referring to the cliffs must also be plural. Eliminate (D) because *it* is singular. To choose between the remaining choices, consider pronoun case. *We* is a subject pronoun, and *us* is an object pronoun. Eliminate (A) because *us see* incorrectly uses the object pronoun *us* as the subject of the verb. Keep (B) because *we see them* is correct. Eliminate (C) because *seen by we* incorrectly uses the subject pronoun *we* as an object of the preposition *by*. The correct answer is (B).

20. **F**   Punctuation is changing in the answer choices, so the question is testing Stop and Go punctuation. Use the Vertical Line Test, and identify the ideas as complete or incomplete. Because the sentence contains the FANBOYS word *and*, draw two lines around the word *and* and consider the parts of the sentence before and after it. The phrase *Fossils are remains of ancient life* is a complete idea, and the phrase *can contain organic remains or records of organisms' activities* is an incomplete idea. To connect a complete idea to an incomplete idea, Half-Stop or Go punctuation is needed. No punctuation is Go, so keep (F). A comma with FANBOYS is Stop punctuation, so eliminate (G). A semicolon is Stop punctuation, so eliminate (H). A period is Stop punctuation, so eliminate (J). The correct answer is (F).

21. **D**   The length of the phrase is changing in the answer choices, so the question could be testing concision. First determine what parts of the phrase are necessary. The sentence already states that *calcite* does something *during the creation of a fossil* so there is no need to repeat that idea. Eliminate (A) because *that creates fossils* is redundant. There is no need to say *slowly* and *over a long time*, since both indicate that calcite hardens slowly. Eliminate (B) and (C) because both are redundant. Choice (D) is the most concise. The correct answer is (D).

22. **H**   The order of the words is changing in the answer choices, so the question is testing consistency with a modifier. The non-underlined portion says *rough handling due to their fragility, paleontologists must use extreme care and precise tools when working with the remains.* The phrase before the comma modifies the subject of the phrase that comes after the comma. So, the modifying phrase must relate to *paleontologists.* The *paleontologists* are *not tolerating rough handling,* the fossils are. Eliminate (F), (G), and (H) because none of these mentions fossils, and each suggests that the *paleontologists* are tolerant of *rough handling.* Choice (H) correctly states that *fossils* are not tolerant of *rough handling.* The correct answer is (H).

23. **C**   Verbs are changing in the answer choices, so the question is testing consistency of verbs. A verb must be consistent in number with its subject. The subject of the sentence is *paleontologists and geobiologists,* which is plural. The verb must be plural to be consistent. Eliminate (A) because *has used* is singular. Eliminate (B) because *uses* is singular. Keep (C) because *use* is plural. Eliminate (D) because *is using* is singular. The correct answer is (C).

24. **G**   Verbs are changing in the answer choices, so the question is testing consistency of verbs. A verb must be consistent in number with its subject. The subject of the sentence is *one*; *of these tools* is a prepositional phrase and cannot contain the subject. Because *one* is singular, the verb must also be singular. Eliminate (F) because *provide* is plural. Keep (G) because *provides* is singular. Eliminate (H) because *have provided* is plural. Eliminate (J) because *are providing* is plural. The correct answer is (G).

25. **D**   The wording of the phrase is changing in the answers, so the question is testing word choice. Determine which choice would be consistent in meaning and tone with the sentence. The sentence says that *information* helps to determine *whether a fossil is from an extinct or existing species.* All of the choices have the same meaning in context, so consider the tone. The passage is academic and formal in tone. Both *really good* and *works pretty well* are too informal to match the tone of the passage. Eliminate (A), (B), and (C). The phrase *especially helpful* is consistent with the academic tone of the passage, so keep (D). The correct answer is (D).

26. **H**   Pronouns and nouns are changing in the answer choices, so the question is testing clarity with pronouns. Determine who or what the pronoun refers to, and choose an answer that makes the meaning 100% clear. The subject of *were actually from extinct species* pertains to the fossils collected by Anning, so the underlined pronoun should make this meaning clear. The pronoun *some* does not make this meaning clear; eliminate (F). *Fossils* provides a specific noun, rather than a pronoun, but the sentence discusses Anning's fossils, specifically, not all fossils. Eliminate (G). Keep (H) because the sentence discusses *Anning's fossils.* The pronoun *they* does not clearly refer back to one noun; eliminate (J). The correct answer is (H).

27. **C** Note the question! The question asks which option *draws the most specific contrast between the assumed age of Anning's fossils and the actual age of the fossils she uncovered.* Check each answer choice to see what each indicates about the age of fossils. The sentence says that *many people thought that Anning's fossils were created by modern engineering,* so look for the choice that will provide the greatest contrast in age to the present. There is also the option to DELETE; consider this choice carefully as it's often the correct answer. Eliminating the phrase indicates that the organisms lived *years ago.* This could provide a contrast with *modern,* so keep (D) but check the other options. Eliminate (A) and (B) because *only a few years ago* and *not that many years ago* do not strongly contrast *modern.* Keep (C) because *millions of years ago* strongly contrasts with *modern.* The question asks for the *most specific contrast,* so eliminate (D) because *years ago* is not as specific as *millions of years ago.* The correct answer is (C).

28. **F** Commas are changing in the answer choices, so the question is testing comma rules. The phrase *Georges Cuvier* is necessary information (without this phrase, we would not know which *anatomist* is being discussed), so there should be no punctuation around the phrase. Keep (F) because it does not surround the phrase with punctuation. Eliminate (G) because it surrounds the phrase with commas. Eliminate (H) and (J) because there is no reason to use a comma after *anatomist* or *Cuvier.* The correct answer is (F).

29. **B** Note the question! The question asks where the new sentence should be placed, so it's testing consistency. Look for a clue in the sentence to determine what idea it needs to come before or after. The new sentence discusses how *fossils are made.* Only Paragraph 2 discusses the creation of fossils, and the sentence after point B discusses the *creation of a fossil.* Therefore, the new sentence should be placed at point B in Paragraph 2. The correct answer is (B).

30. **J** Note the question! The question asks whether the essay provides *a short account of the life of an important paleontologist.* Consider the main idea of the passage and use Process of Elimination. The passage is about the contribution of one scientist to the field of paleontology; it is not about the life of a paleontologist. Eliminate (F) and (G). Eliminate (H) because the purpose of the passage is not to discuss *other paleontologists.* Keep (J) because it is true that the passage *centers on how a few fossil discoveries altered a long-established scientific viewpoint.* The correct answer is (J).

Passage III

31. **A** Connecting words are changing in the answer choices, so the question is testing consistency. The part before the underlined portion contains the word *between.* The correct idiom is *between…and.* Eliminate (B) and (D) because they do not contain the word *and.* Choice (C) adds the word *also,* which is not necessary because the sentence already uses the word *and.* Eliminate (C). The correct answer is (A).

32. **J** Vocabulary is changing in the answer choices, so the question is testing word choice. There is also the option to DELETE; consider this choice carefully as it's often the correct answer. Choice (F) is redundant because the sentence already used the word *Manhattan's* to describe the train. Eliminate (F). Choice (G) is redundant because the train was already described as the *first successful mass transit train,* so eliminate (G). Choice (H) is redundant because the sentence previously stated that the events occurred in *1871,* so eliminate (H). The correct answer is (J).

33. **B**   Note the question! The question asks which option *most strongly reinforces the information in the rest of the sentence*. First identify the information in the rest of the sentence: it states that the train *ran on a raised platform above the street*. The correct answer must reinforce this idea. Check each answer choice. Eliminate (A) because nothing from the second part of the sentence implies *irony*. Keep (B) because *elevated train* matches with *raised platform above the street*. Eliminate (C) because *journalists* are not consistent with the content of the rest of the sentence. Eliminate (D) because *during that time* doesn't reinforce the fact that the train was *raised*. The correct answer is (B).

34. **H**   Note the question! The question asks which option *best introduces the topic of the paragraph*. First read the paragraph to determine its topic: the paragraph mentions two train lines and then states that *Transit lines in Manhattan extended through* many neighborhoods and provided a great amount of *mobility*. Check each answer choice to see whether it introduces the idea of the trains becoming common throughout the city. Eliminate (F) and (G) because the availability of trains *now* is not relevant to the paragraph's focus on trains in the 1870s. Keep (H) because *by the end of the decade* is consistent with *1878*, and *elevated trains ran throughout Manhattan* is consistent with the paragraph's main idea. Eliminate (J) because it doesn't mention the trains. The correct answer is (H).

35. **B**   Commas are changing in the answer choices, so the question is testing comma rules. Some options have a comma + FANBOYS, so use the Vertical Line Test. Draw lines before and after the FANBOYS word *but*. The phrase *Transit lines in Manhattan extended through many of the downtown* is an incomplete idea (because there must be a plural noun that *many* refers to), and *some of the uptown neighborhoods* is also an incomplete idea. Therefore, a comma + FANBOYS cannot be used because it is Stop punctuation, which only links two complete ideas. Eliminate (A) and (D). Choice (C) places a comma after *and*, but there is no reason to put a comma there, so eliminate (C). The correct answer is (B).

36. **F**   Connecting words are changing in the answer choices, so the question is testing consistency. The word that goes along with *unparalleled* is changing in the answers. The correct idiom is *unparalleled in*. Eliminate (G), (H), and (J) because they do not contain the word *in*. The correct answer is (F).

37. **D**   Commas are changing in the answer choices, so the question is testing comma rules. Consider whether there is a reason to use a comma. The sentence uses the word *to* to connect *suburban communities* to *workplaces in Manhattan*. The *communities* are not *in Manhattan* because they are *suburban*, so the phrase *in Manhattan* applies only to the *workplaces*. This means that *workplaces in Manhattan* is a phrase that should not have a comma in it. Eliminate (A) and (B) because they each put a comma within that phrase. Choice (C) places a comma before *to*. There is no reason to put a comma in that spot, so eliminate (C). The correct answer is (D).

38. **G**   Punctuation is changing in the answer choices, so the question is testing Stop, Half-Stop, and Go punctuation. Use the Vertical Line Test, and identify the ideas as complete or incomplete. Draw the vertical line between the words *day* and *by*. The phrase *For instance, the trip from Yonkers, just north of Manhattan, to the New York Stock Exchange took most of the day* is a complete idea, and the phrase *by horse-drawn carriage elevated trains reduced the length of the trip* could be a complete idea. However, while these are grammatically complete, the second part of the sentence does not make logical sense. *Elevated trains* did not run *by horse-drawn carriage*. This means that the sentence should not be separated into two parts between *day* and *by*. Eliminate (F) and (H) because they put punctuation between those ideas. Next consider (G), which has Stop punctuation between *carriage* and *elevated*. Draw a vertical line there: the first part of the sentence is complete, and so is the second part. This means that the semicolon is correct, so keep (G). Choice (J) puts a comma alone between two complete ideas, which isn't allowed, so eliminate (J). The correct answer is (G).

39. **D** Note the question! The question asks which option *best completes the contrast set up in the first part of the sentence*. First look at the beginning of the sentence to find the contrast. The first part of the sentence states that *the trip from Yonkers…to the New York Stock Exchange took most of the day by horse-drawn carriage*. The second part of the sentence states that *elevated trains reduced the length of the trip*. Check each answer choice to see whether it correctly contrasts with the fact that *the trip…took most of the day by horse-drawn carriage*. Choice (A) indicates a *noticeably* shorter trip by elevated train, so keep it. Choice (B) also indicates a shorter trip *with regard to time*, so keep (B). Choice (C) does not mention the length of the trip, so eliminate it. Choice (D) specifies that the trip was shortened *to an hour or less*. While (A) and (B) have some support, (D) provides the best contrast with the first part of the sentence by comparing the specific amount of time to the duration mentioned previously. Eliminate (A) and (B). The correct answer is (D).

40. **F** Pronouns are changing in the answer choices, so the question is testing consistency of pronouns. A pronoun must be consistent in number with the noun it is replacing. The pronoun refers to the noun *the elevated train system*, which is singular. To be consistent, the pronoun in the answer choice must also be singular. Eliminate (H) because *their* is plural. Next, apostrophes are changing in the answer choices, so the question is also testing apostrophe usage. When used with a pronoun, the apostrophe indicates a contraction, in this case "it is." In this sentence, *it* refers to *the elevated train system* and is possessing the *golden age*. Therefore, the apostrophe is not needed. Eliminate (G) and (J) because they both contain apostrophes. The correct answer is (F).

41. **C** Punctuation is changing in the answer choices, so the question seems to be testing Stop, Half-Stop, and Go punctuation. However, notice that the sentence contains a dash after the word *Manhattan*. The phrase that follows (*an island with an area of approximately 23 square miles*) is unnecessary information that must be set off with commas, dashes, or parentheses. Since the phrase has a dash before it, it must have another dash after it. Eliminate (A), (B), and (D) because they lack the dash after the unnecessary phrase. The correct answer is (C).

42. **F** The precise subject of the sentence is changing in the answer choices, and the subject follows a modifying phrase, so the question is testing consistency with a modifier. The phrase before the underlined portion is *Difficult to operate in the snow and ice*. Consider who or what this phrase describes, and check the answer choices. *The elevated train* could be *difficult to operate*, so keep (F). *Riding an elevated train* can't be *difficult to operate*, so eliminate (G). *Elevated train transit as a whole* can't be *difficult to operate in the snow and ice*—it's the trains specifically that were *difficult to operate*. Eliminate (H). *An elevated train ride* can't be *difficult to operate*, so eliminate (J). The correct answer is (F).

43. **D** Verbs change in the answer choices, so the question is testing consistency with verbs. Consider the difference between *overtaken* and *overtaking*. To overtake means to surpass or move ahead of. The sentence indicates that the *electric underground subway system had risen in popularity*, so the logical conclusion is that the underground subway system "overtook" the elevated train as *the city's most convenient form of transit*. This is confirmed in the next sentence, which states that the subway *replaced many of the elevated trains*. Answer choices (A), (B), and (C) all suggest the reverse: if the subway was *overtaken by* the elevated trains, then the elevated trains would be the most popular, but this contradicts the meaning of the sentence. Eliminate (A), (B), and (C). Choice (D) correctly states that the subway overtook the elevated trains. The correct answer is (D).

44. **J** Vocabulary is changing in the answer choices, so the question is testing word choice. Determine what meaning of the underlined portion would be consistent with the rest of the sentence. The underlined portion should mean something like "give off" because earlier in the paragraph it states that the elevated train *deposited debris on the streets*. Eliminate (F), (G), and (H) because *construct*, *manufacture*, and *build* all mean "assemble," and *debris* is not assembled. While *produce* can mean something like "assemble," it can also mean "give off," so it is consistent with the meaning of the rest of the sentence. The correct answer is (J).

45. **C** Note the question! The question asks whether the essay provides *an in-depth comparison of steam-powered elevated trains and electric subway cars that ran in Manhattan in the 1800s*. Consider the main idea of the passage and use Process of Elimination. The passage is about the rise of elevated trains and how they revolutionized transportation in Manhattan. Near the end, the author mentions the drawbacks of elevated trains and how they were eventually largely *replaced* by the subway in Manhattan. Eliminate (A) and (B) because the author only briefly mentions *electric subway cars* at the end of the passage, and its focus is on the *elevated trains*. Keep (C) because it is true that the essay *provides information about electric subway cars* but *centers on* the *steam-powered elevated trains*. Eliminate (D) because the *decline* of *elevated trains* is not the main focus of the passage. The correct answer is (C).

Passage IV

46. **H** Note the question! The question asks which sequence of sentences makes the paragraph logical. Look for a clue in one sentence to determine what idea that sentence needs to come before or after. Sentence 1 begins with the pronoun *It*, so the pronoun must have a clear reference noun in another sentence. The reference noun must *enable us to* do the things in the rest of the sentence. *Video recording technology* enables us to do the things in the list from Sentence 1. Therefore, Sentence 1 must follow Sentence 3. Eliminate (F), (G), and (J) because none of these has Sentence 3 followed by Sentence 1. The correct answer is (H).

47. **D** Commas are changing in the answer choices, so the question is testing comma rules. The phrase *according to animal behaviorists* is unnecessary information, so it needs a comma before and after. Eliminate (A) because it lacks a comma after the phrase, and eliminate (B) because it lacks a comma before the phrase. There is no need for a comma after *is*; eliminate (C). The correct answer is (D).

48. **F** The wording of a phrase is changing in the answer choices, and some of the choices contain a comma, so the question is testing sentence structure. Locate the subject and verb of the sentence. The part after the comma is incomplete, so the first part must be complete. The subject is *scientists*, and there is no verb, so the underlined portion must contain the verb. Keep (F) because it contains a verb: *process*. Eliminate (G) because an *-ing* verb like *processing* cannot be the main verb in a sentence. Eliminate (H) and (J) because each choice also turns the underlined portion into a phrase that modifies the subject, leading to an incomplete sentence without a verb in each case. The correct answer is (F).

49. **B** Vocabulary is changing in the answers, so the question is testing word choice. Determine what meaning of the underlined portion would be consistent with the sentence. The underlined portion should mean something like "avoid" and should convey that *scientists* avoid *sole reliance on memory*. Eliminate (D) because *cut* does not match "avoid" in context. The remaining choices can match "avoid," so pick the one that is most concise. *Bypass* is the most concise option, and it preserves the meaning of the sentence. Keep (B) and eliminate (A) and (C) because they are overly wordy. The correct answer is (B).

50. **H** Transitions are changing in the answer choices, so the question is testing consistency with transitions. Look at the previous sentence to determine how the two ideas are related. The previous sentence describes a benefit of *video recording technology*, and this sentence states that the technology is *useful*, which is a conclusion based on the previous information. The two ideas agree, so a same-direction transition is needed. Eliminate (F) and (J) because *Regardless* and *However* are opposite-direction transitions. Eliminate (G) because *Likewise* indicates two distinct things that have something in common; it does not suggest that the second idea is a conclusion drawn from the first. Keep (H) because *Therefore* indicates that the second idea is a conclusion that follows from the first. The correct answer is (H).

51. **A** The number of words is changing in the answer choices, so the question could be testing concision. First determine what parts of the phrase are necessary. *Revolutionary* and *groundbreaking* mean the same thing in context, so there is no need to use both. Eliminate (B) and (D) because each suggests that the discovery was both revolutionary and groundbreaking. Choice (C) is also redundant compared to (A) because the word *incredibly* does not need to be applied to something that *broke new ground*, as the two ideas are similar. Choice (A) is the most concise. The correct answer is (A).

52. **G** Vocabulary is changing in the answers, so the question is testing word choice. Determine what meaning of the underlined portion would be consistent with the sentence. The underlined portion should mean something like "making" and should convey that *scientists* made *connections*. Eliminate (F) because *sketching out* does not match "making" in context. Keep (G) because *drawing* matches "making" in context: scientists drew connections. Eliminate (H) because *doodling* is an alternative meaning of drawing and does not match "making" in context. Eliminate (J) because the scientists were not *making representations of* connections—they were making the actual connections. The correct answer is (G).

53. **D** The order of the words is changing in the answer choices, so the question is testing consistency with a modifier. The non-underlined portion contains the modifier *Analyzing the results*. The word after the modifying phrase should indicate who was *analyzing the results*. The results are analyzed by the scientists, so the word or phrase that directly follows the modifying phrase should refer to the scientists. Eliminate (A) and (C) because *58 unique gestures* are not the ones *analyzing the results*. Eliminate (B) because *the number of gestures* is not *analyzing the results*. Keep (D) because *the team* is *analyzing the results*. The correct answer is (D).

54. **J** Punctuation is changing in the answer choices, so the question is testing Stop and Go punctuation. Use the Vertical Line Test, and identify the ideas as complete or incomplete. Draw the vertical line between the words *discipline* and *modern*. The phrase *The team then turned to a surprising discipline* is a complete idea, and the phrase *modern linguistics* is an incomplete idea. To connect a complete idea to an incomplete idea, Half-Stop or Go punctuation is needed. A lack of punctuation is Go punctuation, so keep (F). The semicolon is Stop punctuation, so eliminate (G). Choice (H) adds the phrase *which is* to the sentence. Adding this phrase still makes the second idea incomplete, so a semicolon still cannot be used to connect the two ideas. Eliminate (H). A colon is Half-Stop punctuation, so keep (J). The idea in the second part of the sentence explains a general statement in the first part of the sentence (it explains what discipline the team turned to), so there must be a punctuation mark separating the two ideas. Eliminate (F). Keep (J) because a colon is used to introduce an idea that explains or clarifies the idea before it. The correct answer is (J).

55. **C**   Verbs are changing in the answer choices, so the question is testing consistency of verbs. A verb must be consistent in number with the subject of the sentence. The subject of the sentence is *two rules* from the field of modern linguistics, which is plural. In order to be consistent, the underlined portion must also be plural. Eliminate (A) because *was* is singular. Eliminate (B) because *is* is singular. Keep (C) because *were* is plural. Eliminate (D) because *has been* is singular. The correct answer is (C).

56. **J**   Transitions are changing in the answer choices, so this question is testing consistency with transitions. There is also the option to DELETE; consider this choice carefully as it's often the correct answer. Look at the previous sentence to determine how the two ideas are related. The previous sentence says that *two rules* were *used to explain the patterns in chimpanzee gestures*, and this sentence describes one of those rules in detail. *In fact* is generally used to emphasize how true an earlier idea is, not to provide more detail about an earlier idea. Eliminate (F). *For instance* introduces an example. The second idea is not an example of the first, so eliminate (G). *For one thing* introduces the first of two reasons that support an earlier idea. The second idea is a definition of, not a reason for, part of the first idea. Eliminate (H). Since there is no acceptable transition among the answer choices, the phrase should be deleted to make the sentence more concise. The correct answer is (J).

57. **A**   Note the question! The question asks whether the phrase should be added, so it's testing consistency. If the content of the new phrase is consistent with the ideas surrounding it, then it should be added. The sentence to which the phrase may be added says, *Menzerath's law says that long linguistic structures are typically broken.* This suggests that the *structures* have something wrong with them. With the new phrase, the sentence says, *Menzerath's law says that long linguistic structures are typically broken into smaller units during speech.* Therefore, the phrase clarifies the sentence's meaning: the sentences are not flawed, but they are segmented in speech. The new phrase clarifies the meaning of the sentence, so it is consistent with the ideas in the text; the phrase should be added. Eliminate choices (C) and (D). Keep choice (A) because it correctly states that the phrase *clarifies how the linguistic structures are being broken.* Eliminate (B) because the new phrase does not discuss the idea that *Menzerath's law is a language rule.* The correct answer is (A).

58. **J**   Prepositions are changing in the answer choices, so this question is testing consistency with prepositions and idioms. The preposition must connect *trends* and *recorded gestures*. *Trends of* describes an attribute of something, rather than patterns in data, so it does not work in context. Eliminate (F). *Trends with* and *trends by* are not correct phrases. Eliminate (G) and (H). *Trends in* is the correct idiom to describe patterns in data, so keep (J). The correct answer is (J).

59. **B**   Punctuation is changing in the answer choices, so the question is testing Stop and Go punctuation. Use the Vertical Line Test, and identify the ideas as complete or incomplete. Draw the vertical line between the words *behaviorists* and *it*. The phrase *This finding is important to animal behaviorists* is a complete idea, and the phrase *it suggests that chimpanzees use a pattern-based system to communicate* is a complete idea. To connect a complete idea to a complete idea, Stop or Half-Stop punctuation is needed. A lack of punctuation is Go punctuation, so eliminate (A). The semicolon is Stop punctuation, so keep (B). Choice (C) adds a word, *for*, to the sentence. Adding this word makes the second idea incomplete. A semicolon (Stop punctuation) cannot be used to connect a complete idea to an incomplete idea, so eliminate (C). A comma is Go punctuation, so eliminate (D). The correct answer is (B).

60. **F**   The word after *gestures* changes, or is removed, in the answer choices, so the question is testing complete sentences. Identify the sentence construction. The first part of the sentence is an incomplete idea: *Since the study of animal behavior often depends on visual gestures.* An incomplete phrase beginning with *since* must be followed by a comma. Eliminate (G) and (J) because they do not contain a comma.

The second part of the sentence is a conclusion that follows from the information in the first part and must be a complete idea because the first part is incomplete and followed by a comma. Keep (F) because the second part of the sentence has a subject, *video recording technology* and a verb, *may help*. Eliminate (H) because adding *with* makes the second part of the sentence incomplete. The correct answer is (F).

Passage V

61. **B**   Verb forms and connecting words change in the answer choices, so the question is testing complete sentences. Notice that all of the choices include a verb, but not every choice includes a pronoun. Consider whether a pronoun is necessary. The part of the sentence before the comma must include a subject and a verb for the whole sentence to be complete. Adding the pronoun *that* or *which* puts the verb into a describing phrase, which means the idea lacks a verb outside of the describing phrase. Eliminate (C) and (D). To choose between (A) and (B), consider verbs. An *-ing* verb cannot be main verb in an idea. Alternatively, the sentence discusses an event that happened *in the 1950s*, so a past tense verb is needed. Eliminate (A) because *entering* is present tense and also cannot be the main verb. Keep (B) because *entered* is past tense and in the correct verb form. The correct answer is (B).

62. **F**   Sentence structure changes in the answer choices, so the question is testing complete sentences. The non-underlined portion contains the subject and verb: *readers looked for science fiction stories that explored new territory*. The underlined portion must supply a phrase that modifies or describes the subject. Modifiers can be tricky, so use the Vertical Line Test to determine which choice makes the sentence is complete. Though the Vertical Line Test is typically used when punctuation changes and the answer choices require a decision about punctuation marks, it can be useful for sentence structure questions as well. Draw the vertical line between the words *predictability* and *readers*. Notice that there is a comma between these two words, and the comma can't change. A comma is Go punctuation, and Go punctuation can connect anything except two complete ideas. Look for an answer choice that matches this idea. In (F) the comma connects an incomplete idea, *Wanting entertainment but tiring of predictability*, to a complete idea: *readers looked for science fiction stories that explored new territory*. Keep (F), since the comma does not connect two complete ideas. In (G), the comma connects two complete ideas: *Despite wanting entertainment, readers tired of predictability* and *readers looked for science fiction stories that explored new territory*. Eliminate (G). Likewise, eliminate (H) because it also uses a comma to connect two complete ideas. Choice (J) uses a comma with a FANBOYS word (*but*), which is Stop punctuation. *Wanting entertainment* is an incomplete idea, so Stop punctuation cannot be used. The correct answer is (F).

63. **D**   Apostrophes and verbs are changing in the answer choices, so the question is testing apostrophe usage and consistency of verbs. There is no indication that only one reader is being discussed, so there are multiple readers. When used with a noun, on the ACT, the apostrophe indicates possession. In this sentence, the interests belong to the readers. Therefore, the apostrophe is needed, and because *readers* is plural, the apostrophe should be placed after the *s*. Eliminate (B) and (C) because *reader's* is singular, placing the apostrophe before the *s*. Since *readers* is plural, *interests* must also be plural. Eliminate (A) because *interest* is singular, and it needs to agree with the noun *readers* since multiple readers have multiple interests. Keep (D) because *interests* is plural. The correct answer is (D).

64. **J**   Note the question! The question asks which sequence of sentences makes the paragraph most logical, so it's testing consistency. Look for a clue in the paragraph to determine what idea a particular sentence needs to come before or after. Sentence 4 begins with the phrase *By the 1960s, though*. Since the word *though* implies a contrast between two time periods, it must come after some mention of a prior time period. Sentence 1 discusses an event that happened in the 1950s, so Sentence 4 should follow Sentence 1. Eliminate (F) and (H) because neither has Sentence 1 followed by Sentence 4. Sentence 3 begins with the word *Their*, which refers to readers, so Sentence 3 must come after some mention of readers. Sentence 2 mentions *readers*, so Sentence 3 must follow Sentence 2. Eliminate (G). The correct answer is (J).

65. **B**   Vocabulary is changing in the answers, so the question is testing word choice. Determine what meaning of the underlined portion would be consistent with the sentence. The underlined portion precedes a reason why *Butler attended multiple writing programs*, so it should mean something like "since." Eliminate (A) because *if* does not match "since." *Because* matches "since," and it is appropriate for introducing a reason, so keep (B). *Provided that* means "on the condition that." Butler did not attend writing programs on a condition, so eliminate (C). There is no evidence that Butler *assumed* that *she wanted more literary experience*, so eliminate (D). The correct answer is (B).

66. **F**   The order of the words is changing in the answer choices, so the question is testing consistency with a modifier. The non-underlined portion after the comma contains the subject and verb of the sentence: *author Harlan Ellison became her writing mentor and supported her journey*. The portion of the sentence before the comma must be an action taken by *Harlan Ellison*. Look for a choice that is consistent with this idea. Keep (F) because *Ellison* could have been *Thrilled with her strong writing and impressive world-building*. Choice (G) implies that Ellison was *A thrilling writer*. Since this part of the sentence refers to Butler, not Ellison, this is not the correct meaning of the sentence. Eliminate (G). Likewise, (H) and (J) both imply that Ellison was *thrilling him*. Ellison was not doing the *thrilling*, and *him* doesn't refer to anyone specific, so eliminate (H) and (J). The correct answer is (F).

67. **B**   Vocabulary is changing in the answer choices, so this question is testing word choice. There is also the option to DELETE; consider this choice carefully as it's often the correct answer. Without the underlined phrase, the sentence would be incomplete. The phrase *not only* must be followed by "but also," and without the phrase there is no "also." Eliminate (D) because a phrase is necessary. Consider which of the remaining choices is most concise and precise. *Was also inclusive of* is a longer version of *also included*, so eliminate (C) because (A) is more concise and has the same meaning. To choose between (A) and (B), consider the meaning of the word after *also* in each choice. The beginning of the sentence says that *She wrote not only about aliens, but*. The phrase *not only about* implies a parallelism between two things: *aliens* and the list of items after the underlined portion. When two things are parallel, they should be consistent with one another. Keep (B) because *also about* matches *not only about*. Eliminate (A) because *included* is not parallel with the first part of the sentence. The correct answer is (B).

68. **J**   Vocabulary is changing in the answers, so the question is testing word choice. Determine what meaning of the underlined portion would be consistent with the sentence. The underlined portion should mean something like "show." Eliminate (F) because *consider* means "contemplate." Eliminate (G) because *enhance* means "improve upon." Eliminate (H) because *redirect* means "change the direction of." Keep (J) because *reflect* means "represent," which matches "show." The correct answer is (J).

69. **D** Pronouns and nouns are changing in the answer choices, so the question is testing clarity with pronouns. Determine who or what the pronoun refers to, and choose an answer that makes the meaning 100% clear. The sentence says that *Her imaginative worlds took readers on fantastical journeys* and that after these journeys *the real world would never seem the same* to readers. Look for a choice that makes this meaning of the sentence clear. Eliminate (A) and (C) because it is unclear whether *them* refers to *readers* or *journeys*. *Which after* is not a correct phrase—the correct wording is "after which," so eliminate (B). Keep (D) because it preserves the meaning of the sentence by using the phrase *after which* to indicate that something happened after the *journeys*. The correct answer is (D).

70. **F** Punctuation is changing in the answer choices, so the question is testing Stop and Go punctuation. Use the Vertical Line Test, and identify the ideas as complete or incomplete. Draw the vertical line between the words *awards* and *like*. The phrase *Fellow writers nominated her work for prestigious awards* is a complete idea, and the phrase *like the Nebula and Hugo awards* is an incomplete idea. To connect a complete idea to an incomplete idea, Half-Stop or Go punctuation is needed. The comma without FANBOYS is Go punctuation, so keep (F) and (J). The semicolon is Stop punctuation, eliminate (G) and (H). Notice that commas are changing after the word *like*. Consider the four ways to use a comma. There is no reason to use a comma after *like*, so eliminate (J). The correct answer is (F).

71. **A** Note the question! The question asks what the paragraph would lose if the sentence were deleted. Consider the purpose of the sentence. The sentence explains that other *writers nominated* Butler's *work* for *prestigious awards*, so it reveals Butler's accomplishments. Check the answers and eliminate any choice that is not consistent with this purpose. Keep (A) because it mentions Butler's *accomplishments*. Eliminate (B) because the sentence does not discuss *reader's impressions of Butler's work*. Eliminate (C) because the sentence does not suggest *that Butler's work belonged in a different genre*. Eliminate (D) because the sentence does not mention *how Butler's success made the Nebula and Hugo awards more popular*. The correct answer is (A).

72. **J** Commas, long dashes, and parentheses are changing in the answer choices, so the question is testing punctuation around unnecessary information. The phrase *and male* is unnecessary information, so it needs matching punctuation marks before and after. Eliminate (F) because it lacks a comma after the phrase. Eliminate (G) because it lacks a long dash after the phrase. Eliminate (H) because, though the unnecessary phrase is surrounded by matching parentheses, there is no reason to use a comma after the ending parenthesis. Keep (J) because it surrounds the phrase with long dashes. The correct answer is (J).

73. **C** Note the question! The question asks which option provides the most effective transition between the preceding sentence and the rest of the paragraph, so it's testing consistency. The preceding sentence says that, *For decades, science fiction consisted of a white—and male—group of writers* and the paragraph discusses the accomplishments of *Butler, an African American woman*, in the field. Therefore, the transition must indicate that Butler's work helped to promote diversity in a field that was not previously diverse. Eliminate (A) because it does not mention the previous lack of diversity of the field. Eliminate (B) because it essentially restates information from the previous sentence and does not *transition* into the next point. Keep (C) because it discusses a lack of diversity in the field and transitions from the idea that earlier writers were white and male to the idea that Butler *provided an example* for people who hadn't been included. Eliminate (D) because *Butler's first novel* does not relate to a lack of diversity in the field. The correct answer is (C).

74. **F**   Transitions are changing in the answer choices, so the question is testing consistency with transitions. Look at the previous sentence to determine how the two ideas are related. The previous sentence describes a fact about Butler, and this sentence provides an example to support that fact. Keep (F) because *for instance* implies that the sentence with the transition contains an example of a previous idea. *Likewise* and *furthermore* indicate agreement between two ideas, but neither suggests that the sentence with the transition gives an example of the previous idea. Eliminate (G) and (H). Eliminate (J) because *however* implies that the two sentences contrast. The correct answer is (F).

75. **A**   Note the question! The question asks whether the essay explains *the significance of a science fiction author's career.* Consider the main idea of the passage and use Process of Elimination. The passage is about an author's career contribution to the field of *science fiction* literature. Therefore, this passage does fulfill such a goal. Eliminate (C) and (D) because they say that the essay doesn't fulfill the purpose. Keep (A) because it says that *Butler's innovative subjects and expansive world-building affected science fiction literature.* Eliminate (B) because the passage does not discuss *how the commitment to become a writer changed Butler's personal character and career goals.* The passage focuses on Butler's importance in her field, rather than her personal attributes. The correct answer is (A).

Chapter 15
English Practice
Test 2

ACT ENGLISH TEST

45 Minutes — 75 Questions

DIRECTIONS: In the five passages that follow, certain words and phrases are underlined and numbered. In the right-hand column, you will find alternatives for each underlined part. In most cases, you are to choose the one that best expresses the idea, makes the statement appropriate for standard written English, or is worded most consistently with the style and tone of the passage as a whole. If you think the original version is best, choose "NO CHANGE." In some cases, you will find in the right-hand column a question about the underlined part. You are to choose the best answer to the question.

You will also find questions about a section of the passage or the passage as a whole. These questions do not refer to an underlined portion of the passage but rather are identified by a number or numbers in a box.

For each question, choose the alternative you consider best and blacken the corresponding oval on your answer document. Read each passage through once before you begin to answer the questions that accompany it. For many of the questions, you must read several sentences beyond the question to determine the answer. Be sure that you have read far enough ahead each time you choose an alternative.

PASSAGE I

What You See Isn't What You Get

[1]

Two first-year students stand, looking uncertainly at what appears to be a pleasant seating area just ahead. There are two tables: one is occupied by a young woman, but the other is empty. Nevertheless, no one else seems to be considering walking in.
₁

1. Which of the following alternatives to the underlined portion would NOT be acceptable?

  A. However,
  B. Therefore,
  C. Still,
  D. And yet,

That's because the seating area is actually a life-size painting
₂
on the wall of one of the campus buildings.
₂

2. **F.** NO CHANGE
  G. painting, on the wall,
  H. painting, on the wall
  J. painting; on the wall

[2]

A life-size seating area that's only a painting? [A] That's John Pugh's specialty: large-scale public art that is available
₃
for anyone to see. He employs the trompe l'oeil, or
₃
"trick of the eye," style. His paintings are strikingly realistic, having carefully included shadows and reflections, making his
₄
paintings appear to be three-dimensional, as well as numerous details. [B] The café scene includes not only the young woman and also a statue, a framed piece of art, and a small cat,
₅

3. **A.** NO CHANGE
  B. large-scale public art
  C. public art for everyone
  D. art that is public and freely available

4. **F.** NO CHANGE
  G. always including a variety of
  H. due to Pugh's inclusion of
  J. being careful to include

5. **A.** NO CHANGE
  B. nor
  C. or
  D. but

GO ON TO THE NEXT PAGE.

peering around a corner. [6]

[3]

In another of his paintings, a wave looms across the entire front of a building. [C] The painting is immense, the wave looks like it's about to crash, and three children appears
7

to stand directly in its path. Being life-size and incredibly life-like, a group of firefighters ran over to save the "children"
8
8
shortly before the piece was completed. When the men got close enough to realize it was only a painting, they had a good laugh. [D] Most people, like the firefighters, are just impressed by Pugh's skill.

[4]

Pugh believes that by creating public art, he can
9
communicate with a larger audience than if his art were in a
9
gallery. Many of his pieces, including the café scene described
9
above, use the existing architecture. One of his other pieces

created the illusion that part of a building's wall has collapsed,
10
revealing an ancient Egyptian storeroom in the middle of Los Gatos, California. Like the café scene, the Egyptian scene includes a human figure. In this case, however, the woman is not part of the scene. Instead, she appears to be a passer-by,

6. If the writer were to delete the question "A life-size seating area that's only a painting?" from this paragraph, the essay would primarily lose:

   F. an acknowledgement that Pugh's work might seem unusual to some.

   G. a statement of the writer's central thesis for the remainder of the essay.

   H. an argumentative and persuasive tone.

   J. nothing, because the question simply confuses the main idea.

7. **A.** NO CHANGE
   B. appeared
   C. appear   .
   D. was appearing

8. **F.** NO CHANGE
   G. Stopping their truck in the middle of traffic,
   H. Appearing young enough to be swept away,
   J. Like so many of Pugh's other works,

9. Given that all the choices are true, which one best conveys the theory behind Pugh's method as discussed in the remainder of the paragraph?

   A. NO CHANGE

   B. Pugh prefers incorporating his work into the pre-existing environment to simply adding his art without regard for its surroundings.

   C. Drawing his inspiration from many different cultures, Pugh enjoys startling the viewer by placing objects in an unexpected context.

   D. The firefighters may not have been upset at Pugh's trick but they were certainly startled, just like so many other people who see Pugh's work.

10. **F.** NO CHANGE
   G. is creating
   H. creates
   J. creating

GO ON TO THE NEXT PAGE.

peering into the revealed room. Cities around the world have
commissioned works from Pugh. It is Pugh's ability to create
an apparent mystery in the middle of everyday life that makes
his work speak to so much people. After all, who doesn't
appreciate being tricked once in a while?

11. **A.** NO CHANGE
    B. (Do NOT begin new paragraph) Surprisingly, cities
    C. (Begin new paragraph) Cities
    D. (Begin new paragraph) Surprisingly, cities

12. **F.** NO CHANGE
    G. more
    H. most
    J. many

> Questions 13 and 14 ask about the preceding passage as a whole.

13. The writer is considering adding the following sentence to the essay:

    > No one seems to mind being fooled by Pugh's paintings.

    If the writer were to add this sentence, it would most logically be placed at:

    A. Point A in Paragraph 2.
    B. Point B in Paragraph 2.
    C. Point C in Paragraph 3.
    D. Point D in Paragraph 3.

14. Suppose the writer's goal had been to write a passage exploring some of the current trends in the art community. Would this essay accomplish that goal?

    F. Yes, because it looks at a variety of styles popular among muralists throughout the Los Angeles area.
    G. Yes, because is considers some of the reasons for Pugh's preference for large-scale public art.
    H. No, because it only explores Pugh's artistic vision without considering the broader context of the art world.
    J. No, because it details a number of incidents in which people have been confused by Pugh's artwork.

PASSAGE II

Leaving the Nest

My mother flew out with me and stayed for a few days,
to make the transition easier for me. We went shopping and
bought odds and ends for my dorm room—pillows, small
decorative items, even a few pots and pans—to make it feel
more like home. It felt more like a vacation than anything else.

15. **A.** NO CHANGE
    B. pans; to
    C. pans: to
    D. pans. To

GO ON TO THE NEXT PAGE.

Then suddenly her brief stay was over. Her plane was leaving for San Juan, and I realized I wasn't going with her. She was going home, but I already was home. This strange new city was my home now. Sitting on my bed in the dorm room that remained half-empty, it hit me. I had just turned eighteen. I was about to start college in a new place, with a new language, a new culture. I had just said my first real farewell to a mother whom I had never before been away from for more than a weekend. I had to learn how to live on my own, with *mi*

familia so many miles away and me all by myself.

During high school, I had fantasized about moving to the United States someday. I was born in a sleepy, rural village in southern Puerto Rico. My high school class had fifty people in it, and the small town where I grow up was a very close-knit community. I had spent hours imagining what it would be like to be surrounded not by a few dozen people but by a few million.

Living in such a small town, I was used to knowing everyone and having everyone know me. The very first

16. **F.** NO CHANGE
    G. As I sat on the bed in my half-empty dorm room,
    H. Nervously looking around the half-empty dorm room,
    J. Looking around the half-empty dorm room from my bed,

17. Which of the following choices is most logically supported by the first part of the sentence?

    A. NO CHANGE
    B. who had always done my laundry, prepared my meals, and kissed me goodnight.
    C. whom I hoped was having a pleasant flight back to San Juan and then on to our village.
    D. who had herself spent some years living in the United States in her twenties, before I was born.

18. **F.** NO CHANGE
    G. and no one with me.
    H. not with me any more.
    J. DELETE the underlined portion and end the sentence with a period.

19. **A.** NO CHANGE
    B. grew
    C. grown
    D. growth

20. Given that all the choices are true, which provides the best transition to the topic discussed in the rest of the paragraph?

    F. NO CHANGE
    G. The idea of being surrounded by so many people, and being able to meet and talk with any of them seemed like a dream come true.
    H. When the time came to apply to colleges, I picked several, all in major metropolitan areas in the continental United States.
    J. I had considered applying to colleges in San Juan but decided that it was still too close to home, too familiar, too easy.

GO ON TO THE NEXT PAGE.

acceptance received by me was from this school, located in the
<u>_____</u>
₂₁
middle of a city with millions of inhabitants. My parents

were so proud that I get this opportunity to see the world
₂₂
outside of our village. They had spent enough time outside

of Puerto Rico in the United States to know that the English
<u>_____</u>
₂₃
language was not the only thing that was different. We

celebrated the weekend before I left, inviting all the neighbors

over to my parents home. We played music and ate and danced
<u>_____</u>
₂₄

past midnight. [25]

21. A. NO CHANGE
    B. acceptance I received
    C. acceptance, I received,
    D. acceptance, receiving by me

22. F. NO CHANGE
    G. will get
    H. was getting
    J. had to get

23. The best placement for the underlined portion would be:
    A. where it is now.
    B. after the word time.
    C. after the word language.
    D. after the word different (and before the period).

24. F. NO CHANGE
    G. parents's
    H. parent's
    J. parents'

25. At this point, the writer is considering adding the following true statement:

    My favorite dance has always been la bomba.

    Should the writer make this addition here?

    A. Yes, because it adds a detail that helps explain the personality of the narrator.
    B. Yes, because it provides a smooth transition to the following paragraph.
    C. No, because it gives the false impression that the narrator will study dance in college.
    D. No, because it would be an unnecessary digression from the main point of the paragraph.

As the memory faded; I looked around my new room
<u>_____</u>
₂₆
again. Sure, it was small and a little bit dingy. True, I didn't

know anyone yet. None of that mattered, though. I had finally

made it. My new roommate would be arriving the next day.

Hopefully she would be a new friend and even if she wasn't,

my classes were starting in a few days. I had literally millions

of people to meet; surely a few of them would become my new

friends. I smiled, suddenly feeling nervous but excited, not
<u>_____</u>
₂₇

26. F. NO CHANGE
    G. faded, and
    H. faded,
    J. faded.

27. Which of the following alternatives to the underlined portion would NOT be acceptable?

    A. excitement nervous
    B. nervously excited
    C. nervous excitement
    D. excitedly nervous

GO ON TO THE NEXT PAGE.

lonely any more. I was eighteen, in the city, and <u>had to face</u>
                                                         28

the world. [29]

28. Which choice most effectively expresses the narrator's confidence about her new life?

    F. NO CHANGE
    G. ready to take on
    H. all alone in
    J. about to enter

29. The writer is considering adding a concluding sentence here. Which of the following would be most logical and best express one of the main ideas of the essay?

    A. Still, I knew I would miss Puerto Rico and my friends I had left behind.
    B. Little did I know that my new roommate would become a lifelong friend.
    C. My dreams of living in the big city were finally going to become a reality.
    D. I hoped that my classes would be as exciting as my move had been.

PASSAGE III

Dual Personalities

[1]

When Lois Lane finds herself in serious danger, she looks to Superman for help. When <u>she needed</u> help with an article,
                30
on the other hand, she calls on Clark Kent. Of course, as the reader knows, the two men are actually the same person. [A]

30. **F.** NO CHANGE
    G. in need of
    H. she was needing
    J. needed

[2]

The tradition of giving superheroes alternate names and characters, or "alter-egos," goes back as far as superhero stories do. [B] Today, <u>when</u> it's a commonplace writing technique.
         31
Batman fights crime by night, but he poses as millionaire Bruce

31. **A.** NO CHANGE
    B. where
    C. because
    D. DELETE the underlined portion.

GO ON TO THE NEXT PAGE.

Wayne at day. Spider-Man protects the streets of New York—
₃₂

when he's not busy going to school as Peter Parker. [33]

[3]

Each of the superheroes have something in his (or her)
₃₄
back-story to explain the dual character. [C] They all have a

few things in common too, though. Superheroes have a certain

image—the costume and the name, for example; that helps
₃₅

them maintain their authority. If Batman didn't fight crime, he

would probably do something else to deal with his past. Peter
₃₆

32. **F.** NO CHANGE
    G. for
    H. by
    J. DELETE the underlined portion.

33. At this point, the writer is thinking about adding the following true statement:

    > Wonder Woman, on the other hand, is always herself, since she comes from a tribe of warrior women.

    Should the writer make this addition here?

    A. Yes, because it provides a balance for the previous examples of Batman and Spider-Man.
    B. Yes, because it emphasizes the author's earlier claim that the alter-ego is commonplace.
    C. No, because it strays from the primary focus of the passage by providing irrelevant information.
    D. No, because it poses the unnecessary hypothetical that no superhero really needs an alternate identity.

34. **F.** NO CHANGE
    G. has
    H. is having
    J. are having

35. **A.** NO CHANGE
    B. example,
    C. example.
    D. example—

36. Given that all the choices are true, which one provides the best support for the statement in the preceding sentence?

    F. NO CHANGE
    G. Batman, who lost his parents when he was young, were younger, he might have a harder time.
    H. Batman were just a regular-looking man, it would be harder for him to strike fear into the heart of criminals.
    J. Batman needed to, he could probably fight criminals without his gadgets since he knows several martial arts.

GO ON TO THE NEXT PAGE.

Parker isn't a very awe-inspiring name, but Spider-Man is. At
the same time, the hero often has friends and family members

who are somehow completely unaware of their loved ones'
                                                        38

other identity. Providing the superheroes with everyday names
                     39

and jobs helps in their attempts to fit in with the people around
                 40
them.

[4]

Stan Lee, creator of Spider-Man, and dozens of other
                   41
superheroes, often commented on what he believed makes a

true hero. His opinion was that in order for the reader to care

about the hero, the hero has to be flawed. Do you agree with
                                              42
him? According to Lee, without some kind of flaw, the hero
42

wouldn't really seem human. [D] Lee built tension, in his
                                              43
stories, by putting those human flaws and the hero's quest into
43
conflict. It is that tension, perhaps, that makes his storylines so

gripping. Even Superman, the least "normal" of all the heroes,

has to deal with the tension between his love for Lois Lane and

her love for Superman, not Clark Kent. 44

37. Which of the following alternatives to the underlined portion
would NOT be acceptable?

   A. name; on the other hand,
   B. name, because
   C. name, although
   D. name; however,

38. **F.** NO CHANGE
   G. one's
   H. individuals
   J. individuals'

39. **A.** NO CHANGE
   B. Assuming
   C. Offering
   D. Allowing for

40. **F.** NO CHANGE
   G. it's
   H. his
   J. one's

41. **A.** NO CHANGE
   B. Lee creator of Spider-Man,
   C. Lee creator of Spider-Man
   D. Lee, creator of Spider-Man

42. Which choice provides the most logical and effective transition
to the rest of this paragraph?

   F. NO CHANGE
   G. Why would anyone want a hero to be less than perfect?
   H. Are you familiar with Lee's various characters?
   J. What kind of flaw could a superhero have?

43. **A.** NO CHANGE
   B. tension in his stories
   C. tension in his stories,
   D. tension, in his stories

44. The writer is considering deleting the preceding sentence.
Should this sentence be kept or deleted?

   F. Kept, because it provides a specific example of the theory
   being discussed throughout the paragraph.
   G. Kept, because it demonstrates that the ultimate superhero
   will not seem human under any circumstances.
   H. Deleted, because it takes away from the persuasiveness
   of the point made in the previous sentences.
   J. Deleted, because it switches the focus from the more
   "human" superheroes to the "least" human of them.

GO ON TO THE NEXT PAGE.

Question 45 asks about the preceding passage as a whole.

45. The writer is considering adding the following sentence to the essay:

> Even though many readers feel that Lane's ignorance is hard to believe, the Clark Kent persona provides a valuable, and time-honored, element to the Superhero story: the alter-ego.

If the writer were to add this sentence, it would most logically be placed at:

A. Point A in Paragraph 1.
B. Point B in Paragraph 2.
C. Point C in Paragraph 3.
D. Point D in Paragraph 4.

PASSAGE IV

Curly Hair: The Circular Trend

Is curly hair a blessing or a curse? Passing trends, which can last a day or a decade, typically influence hairstyles, which can vary dramatically; every bit as much as clothing. Some segment of the population will therefore always be fighting the natural tendency of their hair, unless the fashion becomes natural hair.

[47] In the 1950s, curls were in, and the average American woman spent countless hours pinning, rolling, and curling her hair every week. Without blowdryers or curling irons, women were left with few options, maintaining properly stylish

46. F. NO CHANGE
G. dramatically, being every
H. dramatically, every
J. dramatically. Every

47. Given that all of the following statements are true, which one, if added here, would most clearly and effectively introduce the main subject of this paragraph?

A. Some people don't care for curly hair because it is considered more difficult to style than straight hair is.
B. As far back as the Renaissance, people have faked having curly hair by wearing wigs and using curlers.
C. Curly hair has bounced in and out of the American fashion scene for at least the last fifty years.
D. Clothing styles also change frequently, and sometimes influence hairstyles in a direct, easily visible way.

GO ON TO THE NEXT PAGE.

hair-dos to work hard and a great deal of time. By the mid-
1960s, a lot of women started to wonder whether all that work
was really necessary. Suddenly, natural hair was all the rage.
Women began to grow they're hair out and allow it to remain in
its natural state, whether curly or straight. For a brief moment,
it looked like women would be able to embrace their natural
hair, whether straight or curly, light or dark, or having length or
being short.

The change was short-lived, however, and didn't last for
long, perhaps unsurprisingly. The desire to have long, natural
hair somehow turned into the desire to have long, straight hair.
During the 1970s, the movie and television star Farrah Fawcett
popularized a look that involved long hair that seemed naturally
straight and feathered—cut into layers designed to frame the
face—yet slightly messy. [53] Women who had

naturally curly hair were suddenly the ones to suffer now, as
they painstakingly ironed their hair to achieve that "natural"
look. The fashions of the 1980s, however, turned everything
around yet again. Big was in, and that went for hair as well as
clothes. Curly hair became incredibly popular, and the main
fashion goal was to make one's hair as curly and as big as
possible. Women who didn't have natural curls got "permanent

---

48. F. NO CHANGE
   G. was hardly work
   H. with hard work
   J. by working hard

49. A. NO CHANGE
   B. their
   C. there
   D. her

50. F. NO CHANGE
   G. and regardless of length.
   H. which can be long or short.
   J. long or short.

51. A. NO CHANGE
   B. wasn't fated to continue, though, so it
   C. predictably enough failed to stick and
   D. DELETE the underlined portion.

52. F. NO CHANGE
   G. star, Farrah Fawcett
   H. star, Farrah Fawcett,
   J. star Farrah Fawcett,

53. The writer is considering deleting the phrase "cut into layers designed to frame the face" from the preceding sentence (adjusting the punctuation as needed). Should this sentence be kept or deleted?

   A. Kept, because it contrasts the style popularized by Fawcett with earlier styles.
   B. Kept, because it defines the word used immediately before the phrase.
   C. Deleted, because it fails to adequately explain the term it is intended to modify.
   D. Deleted, because it digresses from the main point of the paragraph.

54. F. NO CHANGE
   G. suddenly we're
   H. sudden were
   J. sudden we're

55. A. NO CHANGE
   B. the curlier, the better.
   C. it.
   D. it didn't seem possible to have hair that was too curly, or too big to be fashionable.

GO ON TO THE NEXT PAGE.

waves," or "perms," to create the rampant curls <u>modeled</u> by
their pop icons, such as Cyndi Lauper and Gloria Estefan.

[1] By the middle of the 1990s, however, the perm had
lost its appeal, and straight hair was back in fashion where it
remains today. [2] Some <u>commentator's</u> have recently claimed
that curly hair is making a comeback, but only time will
tell. [3] Instead of using an iron, women can have their hair
chemically straightened in a sort of "reverse perm." [4] While
it's hard to know what the trend of tomorrow will be, one thing
seems certain: no style lasts forever. [58]

56. Which of the following alternatives to the underlined portion would NOT be acceptable?

    F. worn
    G. displayed
    H. imitated
    J. popularized

57. A. NO CHANGE
    B. commentators
    C. commentators'
    D. commentators's

58. For the sake of the logic and coherence of this paragraph, Sentence 3 should be placed:

    F. where it is now.
    G. before Sentence 1.
    H. after Sentence 1.
    J. after Sentence 4.

Question 59 asks about the preceding passage as a whole.

---

59. Suppose the writer had been instructed to write an essay discussing modern attitudes toward curly hair. Would this essay meet that requirement?

    A. Yes, because it explains why some women prefer to wear their hair straight, regardless of current fashions.
    B. Yes, because it analyzes the reasons behind changes in fashion that affect the popularity of curly hair.
    C. No, because it focuses more on the changeability of fashions than the attitudes toward them.
    D. No, because it focuses primarily on the popularity of straight hair and the effort of style maintenance.

GO ON TO THE NEXT PAGE.

PASSAGE V

Marie Curie: Physicist, Chemist, and Woman

Marie Curie is famous today for two main reasons: her
scientific discoveries and her defiance of gender stereotypes.
She, along with her husband, identified two new elements,
polonium and radium. She then coined the term "radioactive"
<u>polonium and radium</u>. She then coined the term "radioactive"
60

60. The writer is considering deleting the underlined phrase
and adjusting the punctuation accordingly. If the phrase
were removed, the paragraph would primarily lose:

   F. a specific detail that provides information about the result
of some of Curie's research.

   G. an explanation of how Curie was able to make such a
variety of important scientific discoveries.

   H. information that identifies the reason Curie was awarded
two Nobel prizes.

   J. a definition of radioactivity included by the writer and
necessary to the paragraph as a whole.

and developed a theory to explain the phenomenon. <u>Curie first</u>
<u>began to research radioactivity after noticing that the amount</u>
61
<u>of radiation produced by a sample depended wholly on the</u>
61
<u>quantity of uranium in the sample.</u>
61

61. Given that all of the choices are true, which provides the
most effective transition from this paragraph into the rest
of the essay?

   A. NO CHANGE

   B. Due to her discoveries, she was both the first woman to
receive a Nobel Prize and the first person to receive two
Nobel Prizes, though her road to success was paved with
difficulties.

   C. Although physics and chemistry are treated as separate
fields, like so many other branches of science, the two
are so interconnected in some areas that it can be difficult
to tell them apart.

   D. Curie's husband, Pierre, was also a noted scientist who
wrote several famous pieces on magnetism, including
one that detailed the relationship between temperature
and paramagnetism.

Curie was proficient in the fields of physics and chemistry,
though her education was somewhat <u>unusual, which prevented</u>
62
<u>her</u> from attending university due to a lack of money, Curie
62
initially studied in a laboratory run by her cousin. Determined
to pursue her love of science, Curie eventually enrolled at the
University of Paris, <u>where</u> she later became the first female
63
professor.

62. **F.** NO CHANGE
   G. unusual, prevented
   H. unusual. Prevented
   J. unusual prevented her

63. **A.** NO CHANGE
   B. like
   C. when
   D. DELETE the underlined portion.

GO ON TO THE NEXT PAGE.

While Curie is widely given recognition and credit for discovering radioactivity, this is not entirely accurate. Henri Becquerel, a French scientist, has that honor. When Curie

made her discovery, Becquerel had already saw that rays, functioning much like X-rays but produced by uranium salt, existed; however, he did not identify the underlying process.

Becquerel of radioactivity was performing

experimental involving photographic paper, and the discovery was accidental. He realized that something was exposing the photographic paper to rays even before he placed the paper in the sunlight. Nevertheless, further experiments revealed that the substance emitting rays was the fluorescent substance, potassium uranyl sulfate.

However, Becquerel didn't identify the underlying scientific principal, namely, that the rays were produced not by a molecular interaction but by the atom itself. Curie was

the first to make this discovery; it was she who isolated, and identified radium and polonium. The earliest scientist to realize that there was an element in the fluorescent substance more

reactive than uranium, Curie dedicated the next twelve years to developing a method for isolating that substance,

64. F. NO CHANGE
G. credited and acknowledged as the person responsible for
H. generally credited with
J. appreciated often as deserving credit and recognition for

65. A. NO CHANGE
B. has already seen
C. had already seen
D. has already saw

66. The most logical placement of the underlined portion would be:

F. where it is now.
G. after the word *performing*.
H. after the word *paper*.
J. after the word *discovery*.

67. A. NO CHANGE
B. an experimental
C. experimentally
D. an experiment

68. F. NO CHANGE
G. Subsequently, further
H. Further
J. In contrast, further

69. A. NO CHANGE
B. principle
C. principal
D. principle:

70. F. NO CHANGE
G. isolated
H. isolated it
J. isolated—

71. A. NO CHANGE
B. uranium;
C. uranium
D. uranium:

GO ON TO THE NEXT PAGE.

which <u>was not yet known but later came to be identified and is</u>
<u>now called "radium."</u>
72

72

Curie was progressive for a <u>chemist; much less for a</u>
73

woman. Women in science <u>would of</u> often had a difficult
74

time, and Curie was no exception. She was refused a position
at Krakow University due to her gender, and was ultimately
denied membership in the French Academy of Sciences.
However, the general consensus is that Curie was not bitter
about these rejections. Instead, she <u>worked as hard as she</u>
75

<u>could even when she wondered whether she would ever be</u>
75

<u>recognized.</u> She was a woman who knew her own worth, even
75

when others did not: a trait as valuable today as during the
eighteenth century.

72. **F.** NO CHANGE
    G. we now know as radium.
    H. scientists and laypeople alike are familiar with today under the name "radium."
    J. people in the present day refer to under the name of "radium."

73. **A.** NO CHANGE
    B. chemist,
    C. chemist; moreover,
    D. chemist so

74. **F.** NO CHANGE
    G. might of
    H. have
    J. has

75. Given that all the choices are true, which one provides the most consistent description of Curie's personality as described in this paragraph?

    A. NO CHANGE
    B. became somewhat reclusive in her later years, preferring her work to society.
    C. spent many years in her eventually successful attempt to identify the source of Becquerel's mysterious rays.
    D. was generally described by those who knew her as persistent, friendly, and humble.

END OF TEST 2
STOP! DO NOT TURN THE PAGE UNTIL TOLD TO DO SO.

Chapter 16
English Practice
Test 2:
Answers and
Explanations

ENGLISH PRACTICE TEST 2 ANSWERS

1.	B		39.	A
2.	F		40.	F
3.	B		41.	D
4.	H		42.	G
5.	D		43.	B
6.	F		44.	F
7.	C		45.	A
8.	G		46.	H
9.	B		47.	C
10.	H		48.	H
11.	C		49.	B
12.	J		50.	J
13.	D		51.	D
14.	H		52.	F
15.	A		53.	B
16.	G		54.	F
17.	A		55.	B
18.	J		56.	H
19.	B		57.	B
20.	H		58.	H
21.	B		59.	C
22.	H		60.	F
23.	D		61.	B
24.	J		62.	H
25.	D		63.	A
26.	H		64.	H
27.	A		65.	C
28.	G		66.	J
29.	C		67.	D
30.	G		68.	H
31.	D		69.	D
32.	H		70.	G
33.	C		71.	A
34.	G		72.	G
35.	D		73.	B
36.	H		74.	H
37.	B		75.	D
38.	G			

SCORE YOUR PRACTICE TEST

Step A

Count the number of correct answers: _____. This is your *raw score*.

Step B

Use the score conversion table below to look up your raw score. The number to the left is your *scale score*: _____.

English Scale Conversion Table

Scale Score	Raw Score	Scale Score	Raw Score	Scale Score	Raw Score
36	72-75	24	53-55	12	23-24
35	70-71	23	51-52	11	19-22
34	68-69	22	48-50	10	16-18
33	67	21	45-47	9	13-15
32	66	20	42-44	8	11-12
31	65	19	40-41	7	9-10
30	64	18	38-39	6	7-8
29	62-63	17	36-37	5	6
28	61	16	33-35	4	4-5
27	60	15	30-32	3	3
26	58-59	14	27-29	2	2
25	56-57	13	25-26	1	0-1

ENGLISH PRACTICE TEST 2 EXPLANATIONS

Passage I

1. **B**   The question asks you to find the answer choice that is NOT acceptable as a replacement for the underlined portion—remember, that means the passage is correct as written. Look at the answer choices—they are all transition words, so you need to find the one that can't be used to connect the two ideas. The original word, *Nevertheless*, is used to connect two different ideas. Choices (A), (C), and (D) are all used in the same way. Choice (B), *Therefore*, is used to connect two similar ideas, so it can't be used to replace *Nevertheless*.

2. **F**   When you see answer choices "stacked" like this, using all (or mostly all) the same words with Stop and Go punctuation changing in the same spot, check for Complete/Incomplete on either side of that spot. In this case, *That's because the seating area is actually a life-size painting* is a complete idea, and *on the wall of one of the campus buildings* is incomplete. Since Stop punctuation can separate only complete ideas, eliminate (J). There's not a good reason to insert a comma either after *painting* or *wall*, so the best answer is (F).

3. **B**   The answer choices here all say the same thing in slightly different ways, but none contains an obvious grammatical error. Remember your fourth "C," concise! *Public* denotes the same idea as *for anyone/everyone* and *freely available*, so there's no need to say both—eliminate (A), (C), and (D).

4. **H**   Here you have three answer choices with different "-ing" forms of verbs, and one without. We know ACT doesn't like the "-ing" form—it's not concise—and (H) has no grammatical errors; therefore, it's the best answer.

5. **D**   The answer choices are all transition words, but this time ACT is testing idioms—specifically the "*not only, ___ also*" construction. The proper word to use is *but*, (D).

6. **F**   To identify what the essay would lose by deleting the sentence, you must first determine the purpose of that sentence. In this case, the author asks, "A life-size seating area that's only a painting?" rhetorically, anticipating the reader's possible surprise at such a notion. Choice (F) is the only answer choice that expresses that purpose.

7. **C**   You need to find the correct form of the verb here. Eliminate (A) and (D)—they are singular forms and don't agree with the plural subject, *children*. Choice (B) is the correct plural form but the wrong tense—the correct answer choice has to be consistent with the other present-tense verbs in the passage: *looms, is*, and *looks*—that is (C).

8. **G**   Verbs are changing in the answer choices. Choice (J) actually creates an error, because in this question, the answer choices are all modifying phrases, and ACT wants a modifying phrase to be right next to the thing that it describes. That means you need to find the phrase that describes a *group of firefighters*. Choice (F) describes the image of the wave, (H) describes the children, and (J) describes the painting itself, leaving (G) as the only possible choice.

9. **B**   The remainder of the paragraph talks about how Pugh uses his art to transform the appearance of an existing building, which agrees with (B). There is no comparison with gallery displays as in (A), nor is there discussion of multicultural influence on his work, as in (C). Choice (D) refers to the preceding paragraph.

10. **H** The correct form of the verb needs to be consistent with the preceding sentence: *use* is present-tense, so eliminate (F). Remember, ACT doesn't like "-ing" verbs, so you should only choose one if you have eliminated every other answer choice. In this case, even though (G) and (J) are both present-tense, (H) is as well, and it isn't an "-ing" verb, making it the best answer.

11. **C** The answer choices give the option to start a new paragraph or not. Since the focus of the paragraph changes with the underlined portion from descriptions of some of Pugh's works to a more general statement about cities around the world, there should be a new paragraph here. Eliminate (A) and (B). The word *Surprisingly* isn't necessary, so eliminate (D). The correct answer is (C).

12. **J** There is no comparison being made here, so eliminate (G) and (H). The author is trying to express a large number of people, so you have to use *many*—(J).

13. **D** The new sentence says that no one minds being fooled by the paintings. At point [D], the firefighters "had a good laugh" at being fooled and are "impressed" by his skill. This indicates that they don't mind being fooled, so the correct answer is (D).

14. **H** The question asks about "trends" in the plural, and only one artist and one style was discussed in the essay—eliminate (F) and (G). Choice (J) is incorrect because, although the essay does talk about people being confused by Pugh's art, that's not the reason the essay doesn't accomplish the stated goal—it's a problem of scope, as outlined in (H).

Passage II

15. **A** On the ACT, a semicolon is used in exactly the same way as a period, so you can eliminate (B) and (D)—they can't both be correct! Besides, *to make it feel more like home* is an incomplete idea, and Stop punctuation can be used only to separate two complete ideas. The colon in (C) comes after a complete idea, which is correct, but saying *to make it feel more like home* after it is awkward. You'll need a dash to be consistent with the rest of the sentence and set off the unnecessary *pillows, … pots and pans* from the rest of the sentence—(A).

16. **G** The answer choices here all say the same thing in slightly different ways. Choices (H) and (J) contain grammatical errors. If used in the sentence, they would create dangling modifiers. Remember your fourth "C"—concise! Choice (G) is the only answer choice that doesn't use an "-ing" form of the verb (which ACT doesn't like), and has no grammatical errors, so it's the best choice.

17. **A** You need to find an answer choice that agrees with *I had just said my first real farewell to a mother*. The sentence as written accomplishes this by explaining that she had never been away from her mother *for more than a weekend*. Choices (B), (C), and (D) all introduce new and off-topic information.

18. **J** When you see DELETE or OMIT as an answer choice, do that first. If you can take out the underlined portion without creating an error, chances are you've found your answer. In this case, deleting *and me all by myself* doesn't create an error, and leaving it in would be redundant—the narrator has already described herself as *on my own*—so eliminate (F). Choices (G) and (H) are redundant for the same reason.

19. **B** The correct tense of the verb here needs to be consistent with the non-underlined portion of the passage. The narrator is talking about her life before coming to college, so you must use the past tense,

grew, to be consistent with the other verbs in the sentence, *had* and *was*. Choice (A), *grow*, is present tense, and (D), *growth*, isn't a verb, so eliminate them. Choice (C), *grown*, could be past tense, but needs to be paired with a helping verb.

20. **H**   The task here is to transition from a discussion of the narrator's life in high school to her acceptance at a major university in the United States. Choice (H) begins with her in high school—*when the time came to apply to colleges*—and ends with her applying to several in the United States. Choices (F) and (G) don't talk about applying to college at all, and (J) talks about applying to college only in Puerto Rico.

21. **B**   There are a couple of things changing in the answer choices here—commas and pronouns—work with one first and then the other. Remember that unless you have a reason to use a comma, no punctuation is preferable. Here, we have no reason to use a comma after *acceptance*, so eliminate (C) and (D). Now it's a matter of comparing *acceptance received by me* or *acceptance I received*. They both say the same thing, but the latter is more concise—choose (B).

22. **H**   The answer choices are forms of the verb "to get." To choose the correct one, look at the non-underlined portion of the sentence. The narrator says her parents *were* proud, so you need a past-tense verb to agree with that—eliminate (F) and (G). Choice (J) changes the meaning of the sentence, so the only answer choice left is (H), even though it uses the "-ing" form of the verb.

23. **D**   The difference being talked about here is between Puerto Rico and the United States, so *in the United States* needs to be placed in the spot that will make that most clear. Choice (A) makes it sound like Puerto Rico is in the United States—eliminate it. Neither (B) nor (C) makes it clear that the United States is where things are different—only (D) does.

24. **J**   Apostrophes are used to show either possession or contraction. The word after *parents* is *house*, so you want to show possession. The narrator is referring to the house that belongs to both of her parents, and with a plural noun that ends in "s," all you need to do is add an apostrophe—(J).

25. **D**   Remember that on the ACT, less is more, so you should have a really compelling reason to add something. In an essay discussing the narrator's feelings about being away from her home and family for the first time, it's not really important to know what her favorite dance is—eliminate (A) and (B). The reason it's not important isn't because of any false impression created, so (D) is the best answer.

26. **H**   Here you see nicely "stacked" answer choices with Stop and Go punctuation changing in the same spot. Check for Complete/Incomplete on either side: *As the memory faded* is Incomplete, so no matter what, you're not going to be able to use Stop punctuation—that can connect only two complete ideas. Eliminate (F), (G), and (J), and you're done.

27. **A**   You're looking for the answer choice that can NOT be used in place of the underlined portion—remember, that means the sentence is correct as written. Choices (B), (C), and (D) all express either how the narrator was feeling or what she was feeling; (A) is the only choice that makes no sense—you wouldn't feel *excitement nervous*—and is therefore the one to choose.

28. **G**   The assignment here is to *express the narrator's confidence*, so the correct answer choice must do exactly that. Choice (G), *ready to take on*, does that much more effectively than *had to face*, *all alone in*, or *about to enter*.

29. **C** Make sure to read the question carefully—the goal here is to not only pick a logical concluding sentence but also the one that *best expresses one of the main ideas of the essay*. A main idea is one that recurs throughout the essay, so you can eliminate (B) and (D). While Puerto Rico is certainly mentioned throughout the essay, it wouldn't be logical for the narrator to express her regret at leaving home—the preceding sentence has an upbeat and confident tone, which (C) continues while including another main idea—her dream of living in a large city.

Passage III

30. **G** Three of the four answers are in past tense, so start with one that is not in past tense, (G). That makes the sentence read *When in need of help with an article, she calls on Clark Kent*, which is a present-tense sentence that is consistent with the first: *When Lois Lane finds herself in serious danger, she looks to Superman for help*. The verbs in (F), (H), and (J) are all past tense, so (G) is the best answer.

31. **D** DELETE is an answer choice, so do that first—if you don't create an error by taking out the underlined portion, it's probably the correct choice. In this case, taking out the question word *when* leaves *Today it's a commonplace writing technique*—a perfectly good complete sentence. Leaving *when, where,* or *because* in there would make the sentence incomplete, so you shouldn't choose (A), (B), or (C).

32. **H** You've got DELETE as an option, so try it. This time, it creates an error: *...he poses as millionaire Bruce Wayne day* doesn't make sense, so eliminate (J). Now your choices are all prepositions, which means ACT is testing idioms. To express the notion that something occurs during the day, you need to say *by day*—(H).

33. **C** To decide whether to make the addition here, take a look at the main theme of the passage—Dual Personalities—and what's going on in the paragraph. The author is talking about *the tradition of giving superheroes alternate names and characters*, so adding a sentence about a superhero that doesn't need an alter-ego would be a bad idea—eliminate (A) and (B). Choice (D) is incorrect because the sentence poses no hypothetical situation.

34. **G** The correct verb here needs to agree in number with the subject, *Each*. Careful—*of the superheroes* is a prepositional phrase, so it's not the subject, but it can make the wrong verb sound correct. To avoid confusion, you should cross out prepositional phrases you find inserted between a verb and its subject, one of ACT's favorite tricks. Now you know the subject is *Each*, a singular noun, so it needs a singular verb—eliminate (F) and (J). Choices (G) and (H) are both singular and present-tense, but beware the "-ing" form! They both say the same thing, but (G) is more concise, making it the better answer choice.

35. **D** The phrase *the costume and the name, for example* is unnecessary. Unnecessary info can be offset by either a pair of commas or a pair of dashes, but you can't open with one and close with another. The dash used in the non-underlined text means a dash must be used here.

36. **H** You need to provide support for the preceding sentence, which states that impressive costumes and names help superheroes maintain their authority. Only (H) addresses anything to do with this theme by stating that it would be more difficult for Batman to fight crime if he lacked those things.

37. **B** You need to find the answer choice that can NOT be used to replace the underlined portion in the passage. A quick glance at the answer choices might give you the impression that Stop/Go punctuation is being tested here, but look closer; the words changing after the punctuation are all transition words,

and that typically means ACT is testing direction. Remember, when NO CHANGE is not an answer choice, the sentence in the passage is correct as written, and that gives you an important clue: the transition word used is *but*, an opposite-direction transition—that means a suitable replacement will also have to use one. *On the other hand*, *although*, and *however* in (A), (C), and (D) are all opposite-direction transitions, but *because* in (B) is same-direction, and so can NOT be used—making (B) the correct answer.

38. **G** There are two things changing here: apostrophes showing possession and word choice between *one* and *individual*. In the sentence, the *loved one/individual* with the *other identity* refers back to *the hero*, so you know you need to choose a singular noun, and to show possession, you need to add an *'s*. Choice (G), *one's*, is the only one that offers that construction.

39. **A** The superheroes are given these alter-egos by their creators in order to help the characters fit into a societal context. *Providing* best communicates this meaning; there is no assumption being made, as in (B), and (C) and (D) make it seem as if the fictional characters had a choice in the matter.

40. **F** This is a pronoun question, so find the noun that's being replaced. In this case, it's the superheroes who are making the attempts, and *superheroes* is plural. That helps a lot, since, apostrophes or not, you can eliminate (G), (H), and (J)—they're all singular pronouns and can't be used to replace a plural noun.

41. **D** This is a comma question, so keep your comma rules in mind. There is unnecessary information in this sentence: *creator of Spider-Man and dozens of other superheroes*. This needs to be set off with commas—one after *Lee* (eliminate (B) and (C)) and one after *superheroes*. The only answer choice that offers this without adding additional, unnecessary commas is (D).

42. **G** The rest of the paragraph discusses the reasons Stan Lee gave his superheroes human flaws, so if you're going to introduce that sort of discussion with a rhetorical question, the natural choice for that question would be one that asks, "Why?" Choice (G) is the only one that asks that question.

43. **B** This question is testing comma usage, but none of the situational rules seem to apply—there's no introductory idea, list, or unnecessary information. Therefore, the issue is whether there is a definite need to pause at any point in *Lee built tension in his stories by putting those human flaws and the hero's quest into conflict*. If it helps, you can take an exaggerated pause at the spots ACT suggests putting commas. If the pause creates a little tension, you probably need the comma; if the pause just seems irritating or awkward, you don't. This sentence is a little on the long side, but it doesn't need the commas—(B).

44. **F** The sentence should be kept, since it's giving an example of what the entire previous paragraph is talking about—eliminate (H) and (J). Choice (G) is the direct opposite of what's happening in the sentence: the ultimate superhero does in fact have human feelings.

45. **A** This sentence fits best with the discussion in the first paragraph about Lois Lane's misconception that Superman and Clark Kent are two different individuals. It also introduces the concept of the alter-ego, the subject of the second paragraph, so it functions nicely as a transition sentence as well.

Passage IV

46. **H**   Here you have nicely "stacked" answer choices with Stop and Go punctuation changing in the same spot—check for Complete/Incomplete on either side. *Passing trends...vary dramatically* is Complete, and *every bit as much as clothing* is Incomplete. You'll need Go punctuation to connect these two— eliminate (F) and (J). Choice (G) uses the less-concise "-ing" form of the verb, making (H) the best answer.

47. **C**   The assigned task is to introduce the main subject of the paragraph, which begins by talking about curly hair being the fashion in the 1950s and the progression toward "natural" hair by the mid-1960s. Choice (A) is addressed in the paragraph, but it's not a main subject. The Renaissance is never mentioned, so eliminate (B), and (D) introduces a new topic—clothing styles—so the best answer is (C).

48. **H**   The answer choices here are all very similar and don't contain any obvious errors. You'll need to check the non-underlined portion on either side and make sure the answer is consistent with both. To the left you have *maintaining properly stylish hair-dos*, and to the right you have *and a great deal of time*. Choices (F) and (J) aren't consistent with both, and (G) is not only inconsistent, but it also contradicts the preceding sentence—these hairdos took a lot of work.

49. **B**   There are pronouns changing in the answer choices, and an apostrophe in the sentence as written. If you're in doubt about whether you need the contraction or a pronoun, expand out the contraction: in this case, *they're* becomes "they are," which doesn't make sense—eliminate (A). The noun being replaced here is *Women*, which is plural, so you need a plural pronoun—eliminate (D). Choice (B) is the possessive, plural pronoun you're looking for, but watch out for its sound-alike, *there*, in (C).

50. **J**   All the answer choices basically say the same thing, and none creates a grammatical error, so pick the one that says what they all do in the most concise way. That's (J)—*long or short*.

51. **D**   DELETE is an answer choice, so try that first. Taking out the underlined portion leaves *The change didn't last long, perhaps unsurprisingly.* That is a complete sentence, and the meaning hasn't changed, so it's the best answer.

52. **F**   This question is testing comma usage, so keep your comma rules in mind. It might be tempting to think of *Farrah Fawcett* as unnecessary information, but if you remove it from the sentence, it is no longer clear who *the movie and television star* is. Because it's necessary, no commas are needed, which corresponds with (F), NO CHANGE.

53. **B**   Be careful—the question is asking whether the phrase inside the dashes *should* be deleted, not whether it *can* be. In this case, the author is using the phrase inside the dashes to define a term with which the reader may not be familiar, and you know ACT likes things to be clear. Therefore, the phrase should be kept—eliminate (C) and (D). Choice (A) is incorrect because there is no contrast made to an earlier style.

54. **F**   There are two things changing here: apostrophes showing contraction and word choice between *sudden* and *suddenly*. You need the adverb *suddenly*, so eliminate (H) and (J). Choice (G) is incorrect because *we're* is a contraction of "we are," which wouldn't make sense in the sentence.

55. **B**   Three of the answer choices say the same thing in slightly different ways, while one just says *it*. While you may be tempted to read *it* in the slang sense of "something really popular," remember there's no

slang on the ACT—eliminate (C). Now you're left with the three answer choices that don't contain errors, but all say the same thing—pick the one that's most concise, (B).

56. **H**   You need to find the answer choice that can NOT replace the underlined portion in the sentence, and since NO CHANGE isn't an option, you know the sentence in the passage is correct. The option here is to find an alternate word for *modeled*, so this is just a vocabulary question. Choices (F), (G), and (J) all work as replacements in the context of the sentence, so select (H), the one that does NOT. If this question tricked you, you may have picked *imitated*, since the sentence talks about women imitating the pop icons, but the pop icons are the ones doing the modeling.

57. **B**   If you're unsure about whether an apostrophe is showing possession or contraction, expand it out. In this case, "commentator is" wouldn't make sense, so if you need an apostrophe at all, it would be to show possession. However, look at the word after the underlined portion: *have*. Only nouns can be possessed, and *have* is not a noun; therefore, you can't use an apostrophe here at all—eliminate (A), (C), and (D).

58. **H**   Sentence 3 talks about how women can now have their hair chemically straightened. Both sentence 2 and sentence 4 talk about curly hair, so eliminate (F) and (J). Sentence 3 would naturally follow sentence 1, which transitions from the previous paragraph and introduces the idea of straight hair being the fashion now, so (H) is a better answer choice than (G).

59. **C**   The essay mentions the "modern" preference for straight hair, but that's a long way from *discussing modern attitudes toward curly hair*—eliminate (A) and (B). Choice (D) is incorrect for the same reason: the primary focus is not on the popularity of straight hair.

Passage V

60. **F**   The phrase *polonium and radium* names the *two new elements* discovered by the Curies. It doesn't provide an explanation as (G) claims, nor does it offer the reason Marie Curie won the Nobel Prize, as in (H). Choice (J) is incorrect because the phrase does not define radioactivity—it simply lists two radioactive elements—leaving (F) as the best answer.

61. **B**   The assigned task is to *provide the most effective transition* to the rest of the essay. The next paragraph talks about some of the problems Curie encountered in her academic and professional career, so an *effective transition* will need to incorporate that theme, as (B) does. Choice (A) provides a specific detail only about Curie's research, (C) doesn't mention Curie at all, and (D) talks only about Curie's husband, Pierre.

62. **H**   Here you see nicely "stacked" answer choices with Stop and Go punctuation changing in the same spot, but before checking for Complete/Incomplete on either side to see which kind of punctuation you need, notice you have one answer choice with *which* in it, and three without. Start with the one that is different, (F). In (F), the idea after the comma would be *which prevented her from attending university due to a lack of money, Curie initially studied in a laboratory run by her cousin*, which doesn't make sense—eliminate (F). The remaining three answer choices all have *prevented* as the first word in the second idea, but (J) has *prevented her*, which creates another error—eliminate (J). Now it's down to a choice between a period and a comma. The ideas on either side are both complete (make sure to read the entire sentence!), so you need Stop punctuation—(H).

63. **A** You're given the option to DELETE the underlined portion, so try that first. Taking out *where* in this case leaves you with a comma joining two complete ideas, so eliminate (D). *Like* doesn't make sense, so eliminate (B). Both *when* and *where* might seem to work, but keep in mind that the two things happening in the sentence are Curie enrolling at the University of Paris and becoming the first woman professor there. Those two things didn't happen simultaneously, so you can't use *when* to connect them—choose (A).

64. **H** All the answer choices here say basically the same thing, and none creates a grammatical error, so pick the one that says what they all do in the most concise way. That's (H)—*generally credited with*.

65. **C** There are two things changing in the answer choices: *seen* vs. *saw* and *has* vs. *had*. Start with whichever seems easier, and eliminate answer choices that don't agree. The correct form of the verb (regardless of whether you use *has* or *have*) is *has/have seen*, so delete (A) and (D). To figure out which tense you need, check the non-underlined rest of the passage for context. In the same sentence, you have past-tense verbs: *made, existed, did*—(C) is past tense and therefore consistent with the rest of the sentence.

66. **J** Here it's really just a matter of inserting the underlined portion, *of radioactivity*, in each of the places in the answer choices; the only place it makes any sense at all is after *discovery*, (J).

67. **D** This question is basically just testing word choice. From the context of the (now altered) passage, you know that *Becquerel was performing* [something] *involving photographic paper*, not *performing* [in some manner] involving photographic paper. If you need a thing, you need a noun, and the only choice you have is (D).

68. **H** There are transition words changing in the answer choices, which can often be an indication that ACT is testing direction, but notice that one option does not have a transition, which is usually the way to go. If you try the one without, you're left with *Further experiments revealed... potassium uranyl sulfate*, which is a perfectly good sentence, and more concise than the other three. There's no real need for a transition at all here, so (H) is the best answer.

69. **D** This is another word choice question with some punctuation thrown in to confuse the issue—start easy! *Principal* means something that is highest in rank or value; *principle* means a fundamental assumption. In the context of the sentence, you need to use *principle*—eliminate (A) and (C). Using a colon after *principle* might seem obviously preferable to the comma after *namely*, which seems awkward, but remember that ACT mandates that a colon must follow a complete idea, and must itself be followed by a list, definition, expansion, or explanation of that complete idea; make sure to check that. *However, Becquerel...principle* is a complete idea, and the idea after the colon is a definition (as evidenced by the introductory word *namely*)—pick (D).

70. **G** All the answer choices have *isolated* by itself with some kind of punctuation, and one that adds *it*—that's probably a good place to start. Adding the pronoun *it* here, though, creates an error: the pronoun is not replacing any noun—eliminate (H). The action in the idea after the semicolon is *she* (Curie) *isolated and identified* the two elements, so there's no need for any punctuation in between the two verbs—choose (G).

71. **A** The answer choices have Stop and Go punctuation changing in the same spot and all use the same word, so check for Complete/Incomplete on either side: before the punctuation you have *The earliest scientist to realize that there was an element in the fluorescent substance more reactive than uranium*—an incomplete idea, and afterward you have *Curie dedicated the next twelve years to developing a method*

for isolating that substance, which was not yet known but later came to be identified and is now called "radium," which is a complete idea, so you need Go punctuation to separate them—eliminate (B) and (D), which has a colon, which you know has to follow a complete idea. You definitely need to pause after the incomplete idea, so leave the comma where it is—(A).

72. **G**   You know ACT is testing concise when all the answer choices here say basically the same thing, and none creates a grammatical error. That's what's happening here, so pick the one that says what they all do in the most concise way. That's (G)—*we now know as radium*.

73. **B**   Here you see Stop and Go punctuation changing in the same spot and nicely "stacked" answer choices, so check for Complete/Incomplete on either side: before the punctuation you have *Curie was progressive for a chemist*—a complete idea, and afterward you have *much less for a woman*, which is an incomplete idea, so you need Go punctuation to separate them—eliminate (A) and (C). Choice (D) is awkward and doesn't really make sense—choose (B).

74. **H**   There are two things changing in the answer choices here: word choice and helping verbs. It's incorrect to say *would of* or *might of*—it's "would have" and "might have." Eliminate (F) and (G). Helping verbs need to agree with the subject in number, just like regular verbs. In this case, the subject is *Women*, which is plural, so choose (H), *have*.

75. **D**   The correct answer choice will provide *the most consistent description of Curie's personality as described in this paragraph*. There is no mention in the paragraph of her seeking recognition as in (A), and likewise in (B), no proof that she became reclusive. Choice (C) doesn't talk about her personality at all, leaving (D) as the best answer choice.

Chapter 17
English Practice
Test 3

ACT ENGLISH TEST

45 Minutes—75 Questions

DIRECTIONS: In the five passages that follow, certain words and phrases are underlined and numbered. In the right-hand column, you will find alternatives for each underlined part. In most cases, you are to choose the one that best expresses the idea, makes the statement appropriate for standard written English, or is worded most consistently with the style and tone of the passage as a whole. If you think the original version is best, choose "NO CHANGE." In some cases, you will find in the right-hand column a question about the underlined part. You are to choose the best answer to the question.

You will also find questions about a section of the passage or the passage as a whole. These questions do not refer to an underlined portion of the passage but rather are identified by a number or numbers in a box.

For each question, choose the alternative you consider best and blacken the corresponding oval on your answer document. Read each passage through once before you begin to answer the questions that accompany it. For many of the questions, you must read several sentences beyond the question to determine the answer. Be sure that you have read far enough ahead each time you choose an alternative.

PASSAGE I

A Day in the City

When I woke up this morning, I made myself a bowl of cereal and sat, listening to the traffic. Some of my friends ask me how I can stand living somewhere so noisy. It's true that

1. Which of the following alternatives to the underlined portion would NOT be acceptable?
   A. cereal and sat while listening
   B. cereal, sat listening
   C. cereal, sat, and listened
   D. cereal before sitting and listening

there's always some kind of noise in my neighborhood—taxi drivers honking their horns, kids playing their radios so loud that the bass makes my teeth vibrate, or people yelling in the street. I know that some people wouldn't like it, but to me, these are the sounds of life. [3]

2. F. NO CHANGE
   G. neighborhood, taxi
   H. neighborhood; taxi
   J. neighborhood taxi

3. If the writer were to delete the preceding sentence, the essay would primarily lose:
   A. a contrast to the positive tone of the essay.
   B. an explanation for the narrator's trip to the park.
   C. information that shows the author's attitude toward the place she lives.
   D. nothing at all; this information is not relevant to the essay.

It's Saturday, so this morning I decided to go to the park. The train is the fastest way to go but I took the bus instead.

4. F. NO CHANGE
   G. Since today it is finally
   H. Allowing for it being
   J. The day of the week is

When I ride the bus, you get to see so much more of the city. It can be kind of loud on the bus, with some people talking

5. A. NO CHANGE
   B. one is riding
   C. you ride
   D. they are riding

GO ON TO THE NEXT PAGE.

on their phones, others chatting sociable with their friends, and
_____
6

others playing music. Just like the traffic's sounds, though, the

noise on the bus represents people working, relaxing, and living.
_____
7

Once I get to the park, I pick a bench over near the play

area. The city added the bench so they could play while their
____
8

parents sit nearby, obviously I like to sit there because there's a
_____
9

great big oak tree for shade. I can see and hear almost

everything from there. I sit there watching, and listening to the
_____
10

people around me. People-watching is one of my favorite

things to do, I like listening even better. The park is the best
_____
11

place because you get to see and hear everything. The only

problem is that there's so much to see and hear!

That's why people get so tired after a little while. That way,
_____
12

I can pay more attention to the sounds and not get distracted by

what I see. With my eyes closed, I can pick out parts of

two old men's familiar conversation. One of them is telling the
_____
13

other about something his grandson said. I can't hear the rest,

but whatever it was must have been hilarious because his

friends' laugh is so loud, it startles me.
_____
14

Later that night, after I've ridden the bus back home, I think

about those old men. When I'm old, I hope that I too will have

a friend who will sit in the park with me, and who will enjoy

listening to the sounds of the city as much as I do.

6. F. NO CHANGE
   G. sociably, with
   H. sociable with,
   J. sociably with

7. A. NO CHANGE
   B. people, working;
   C. people; working
   D. people, working,

8. F. NO CHANGE
   G. kids
   H. because they
   J. that it

9. A. NO CHANGE
   B. nearby.
   C. nearby,
   D. nearby, because

10. F. NO CHANGE
    G. there, watching, and listening,
    H. there, watching and listening
    J. there watching and listening,

11. A. NO CHANGE
    B. do, nevertheless,
    C. do, but
    D. do, however

12. Which choice most effectively introduces the idea discussed in this rest of the paragraph?

    F. NO CHANGE
    G. I close my eyes
    H. the park is interesting
    J. some people like quiet

13. Which choice would emphasize the narrator's curiosity and interest in the old men's conversation in the most logical and effective way?

    A. NO CHANGE
    B. noisy chatter.
    C. animated discussion.
    D. entertaining stories.

14. F. NO CHANGE
    G. friends's
    H. friends
    J. friend's

GO ON TO THE NEXT PAGE.

Question 15 asks about the preceding passage as a whole.

15. Suppose the writer's assignment was to write an essay analyzing one reason people might choose to live in a large city. Would this essay fit that description?

   A. Yes, because it discusses the convenience of public transportation.

   B. Yes, because it explains the narrator's enjoyment of one of the city's parks.

   C. No, because it focuses on one detail of city living that most people dislike.

   D. No, because it only discusses why the narrator prefers listening to watching.

PASSAGE II

The Bridge They Said Couldn't Be Built

Visible in the fog as well as the sun, the Golden Gate Bridge is a symbol of San Francisco. The bridge was once famous for having the longest suspension span in the world; even today, its suspension span is the second longest in the United States. It is open to cars and pedestrians alike and has only been shut down three times in that seventy-year history. The amount of concrete needed to anchor the bridge was

16. **F.** NO CHANGE
   G. their
   H. its
   J. DELETE the underlined portion.

enough to construct a sidewalk five feet wide, all the way from San Francisco to New York City. Since the Golden Gate opened, almost two billion cars have crossed the bridge and it has been featured in countless movies.

17. **A.** NO CHANGE
   B. sidewalk five feet wide
   C. sidewalk—five feet wide
   D. sidewalk, five feet wide

The fame of the Golden Gate Bridge wasn't always assured. [A] When Joseph Strauss announced his intention of building the bridge, people flocked to support him. A combination of factors made building a bridge in that location difficult: cold, stormy seas below, foggy and damp weather, and winds that regularly reach speeds of 60 miles per hour.

18. Which choice provides the conclusion that relates to the rest of the paragraph in the most logical way?

   F. NO CHANGE
   G. many said it was impossible.
   H. some admired his vision.
   J. he had already built other bridges.

GO ON TO THE NEXT PAGE.

[B] After two years of discussion, the voters approved a

bond: that would raise $35 million, all dedicated to building the
19

bridge. Even then, there were many skeptics whom believed
20

that it couldn't be done.

Strauss, a veteran bridge builder, refused to give up.

Construction began in 1933 and ended in 1937, and lasted a
21

little more than four years. On May 28, 1937. The bridge,
22

arching grandly over the water, opened to pedestrians. More
22

than 200,000 people walked across the bridge that day to

celebrate the grand achievement.
23

[C] By the time it was completed, the bridge had exceeded

everyone's expectations. Not only was it built, it was also

ahead of schedule and under budget. To top it off,

it was beautiful. Nevertheless, the Golden Gate Bridge is
24

considered an artistic masterpiece, recognizable all around the

world. At its highest point, the bridge rises 746 feet into the

air—191 feet taller than the Washington Monument.
25

The name "Golden Gate" refers not to the color of the

bridge, which is actually orange, but to the stretch of water

below, where the San Francisco Bay connects to the Pacific

Ocean. [D] The color, called "International Orange," was

chosen partly because it matched the natural surroundings and
26

19. **A.** NO CHANGE
    B. bond,
    C. bond;
    D. bond

20. **F.** NO CHANGE
    G. that
    H. who
    J. DELETE the underlined portion.

21. **A.** NO CHANGE
    B. being completed by 1937,
    C. ending four years later
    D. DELETE the underlined portion.

22. **F.** NO CHANGE
    G. 1937; the bridge arching grandly
    H. 1937, the bridge, arching grandly
    J. 1937, the bridge, arching grandly,

23. **A.** NO CHANGE
    B. an achievement that was extremely impressive because it symbolized a significant victory over difficult circumstances.
    C. the successful completion of a project that was amazing both because of the obstacles that had been overcome and because of the magnitude of the product that was the result of the project.
    D. DELETE the underlined portion and end the sentence with a period.

24. **F.** NO CHANGE
    G. At the time,
    H. Regardless,
    J. Even today,

25. **A.** NO CHANGE
    B. air;
    C. air
    D. air, rising

26. **F.** NO CHANGE
    G. nature surrounding
    H. nature surrounded
    J. natural surrounds

GO ON TO THE NEXT PAGE.

partly because it would allow the bridge to remain visible on foggy days. [27]

Today, the bridge is divided into six lanes for cars, plus pedestrian lanes for people and bicycles. On sunny days, crowds of people flock to the bridge to enjoy the view. Rising out of the sea like a vision from a dream, the Golden Gate Bridge captures the imagination today, just as it did when

Strauss first envisioned it. [28]

27. The writer is considering deleting the phrase "on foggy days" from the preceding sentence in order to make the paragraph more concise. If the writer were to make this deletion, the sentence would primarily lose information that:

A. explains why the color of the bridge is referred to as "International Orange."

B. demonstrates the ways in which the bridge's color matches the environment.

C. reveals the danger that the bridge can cause for some ships during bad weather, regardless of color.

D. adds a detail that provides a specific situation in which the bridge's visibility is particularly important.

28. The writer is considering adding a sentence that demonstrates the wide variety of the bridge's uses today. Given that all the following statements are true, which one, if added here, would most clearly and effectively accomplish the writer's goal?

F. On weekdays, during the busiest times of day, the direction of certain lanes changes to accommodate rush hour commuters.

G. The weather in San Francisco is often foggy, but when the sky is clear, the bright orange of the bridge stands out against its surroundings.

H. The bridge is 1.7 miles long, so some people walk across in one direction but hire a taxi or take the bus to return.

J. People use it to commute to work, to go on day trips to Marin or San Francisco, and even just to enjoy the beauty of the bridge itself.

Question 29 asks about the preceding passage as a whole.

---

29. Upon reviewing the essay, the writer realizes that some information has been omitted. The writer wants to incorporate that information and composes the following sentence:

> The local community began to consider building a bridge to connect the San Francisco peninsula in 1928.

If the writer were to add this sentence to the essay, the most logical place to insert it would be at:

A. Point A in Paragraph 2.

B. Point B in Paragraph 3.

C. Point C in Paragraph 5.

D. Point D in Paragraph 6.

GO ON TO THE NEXT PAGE.

Father of a Language

The Italian language wasn't always the single, unified,
$\underset{30}{}$
language that it is today. In fact, during the Middle Ages, Italy
wasn't a unified country. Even today, though Italy is politically
unified, each region speaks its own dialect. In some regions,
such as Tuscany, the dialect is virtually identical to the "official"
Italian language. In other regions, such as Venice, however, the
language is still distinct in many ways.

Dante Alighieri, more commonly known simply as Dante,
is sometimes called the "father of the Italian language." He
was born in Florence during the thirteenth century and was
$\underset{31}{}$
a prolific writer. In approximately 1305, he published an
essay entitled "De Vulgari Eloquentia," or "In Defense of the
Vernacular." About three years later, Dante began work on his
masterpiece: *The Divine Comedy*. Today he is considered one

of the greatest writers of the Western world. [32] During his

life, however, his work was more controversial. Some of the
$\underset{33}{}$
main reasons for this was his decision not to write in Latin, but
in "Italian."

30. F. NO CHANGE
    G. single yet unified,
    H. single, and unified,
    J. single, unified

31. The writer is considering removing the underlined phrase.
    The primary effect of the deletion would be the loss of a
    detail that:
    A. provides context that may be helpful in understanding
        the passage.
    B. creates confusion regarding the writer's point in this
        paragraph.
    C. interrupts the flow of the passage without adding any new
        information.
    D. provides a grammatically necessary connection.

32. The writer is considering adding the following phrase to
    the end of the preceding sentence (changing the period
    after "world" to a comma)

    > alongside other recognized greats such as Homer,
    > Shakespeare, and Sophocles.

    Should the writer make this addition?

    F. Yes, because it provides necessary context for the sen-
        tence's previous statement.
    G. Yes, because it explains the important role the creation
        of Italian played in Western literature.
    H. No, because it adds details that distract from the primary
        point of the sentence.
    J. No, the list of important writers does not include all
        important writers in the Western tradition.

33. A. NO CHANGE
    B. One
    C. Few
    D. Each

GO ON TO THE NEXT PAGE.

At that time, high literature was written not in the various local languages and in Latin. Dante believed that literature

should be available not only to the educated elite who had education but also to the common people. In order to make

this dream possible, Dante "created" a new language as he called "Italian." This new language wasn't really new at all; it consisted of bits and pieces from the different languages already spoken throughout Italy, and drew most heavily on Dante's native Tuscan dialect. Dante's creation laid the foundation for the unified language to be spoken in Italy today.

The Divine Comedy is, in some ways, the beginning of national Italian literature. By writing it in the language spoken by the Italian people; Dante made *The Divine Comedy*

available to the people. Dante for his opinion that literature to anyone should be accessible drew criticism. However, the

movement that Dante helped begin led to diminished literacy among the Italian people, which, in turn, eventually led to the Renaissance.

The title of *The Divine Comedy* confusing some people. At one time, the label of "comedy" was attached to any work not written in Latin. *The Divine Comedy* wasn't written in

Latin, but it was considered a comedy; however, today it is widely considered a masterpiece of serious literature. Dante's

---

34. F. NO CHANGE
   G. for
   H. as
   J. but

35. A. NO CHANGE
   B. who had been taught
   C. with a school background
   D. DELETE the underlined portion.

36. F. NO CHANGE
   G. and called
   H. that he called
   J. calling

37. A. NO CHANGE
   B. spoken
   C. if spoken
   D. to speak

38. F. NO CHANGE
   G. people,
   H. people.
   J. people:

39. A. NO CHANGE
   B. Dante should be accessible for his opinion that literature to anyone drew criticism.
   C. Dante drew criticism for his opinion that literature should be accessible to anyone.
   D. Dante drew criticism to anyone for his opinion that literature should be accessible.

40. The writer wants to imply that prior to Dante's development of "Italian," illiteracy was common. Which choice best accomplishes that goal?

   F. NO CHANGE
   G. an increase in
   H. a passion for
   J. compulsory

41. A. NO CHANGE
   B. confusing
   C. confuses some
   D. that confuses

42. F. NO CHANGE
   G. since
   H. because
   J. so

GO ON TO THE NEXT PAGE.

brave decision, while, in defiance of the common beliefs of
his time, demonstrated that it was not necessary for a literary
masterpiece to be written in Latin, paved the way for future
writers and readers alike. Nevertheless, *The Divine Comedy*
remains a symbol of both literature and innovation today.

43. **A.** NO CHANGE
    B. and
    C. which,
    D. so that,

44. **F.** NO CHANGE
    G. In contrast,
    H. However,
    J. DELETE the underlined portion.

PASSAGE IV

Baking Lessons

[1]

Both of my parents worked full-time when I was a little
girl, so my grandmother would stay at our house during the day.
We would sit in the living room on the couch at my family's
house and watch game shows. Our favorite was

The Price is Right. We would call out their answers along with
the contestants. When our answers were right, we would

scream with excitement, and when the contestants were wrong,
we would moan with disappointment. [A]

[2]

[1] When I got older and started going to school, we
couldn't watch our game shows regular. [2] That was okay
with me, though, because the one thing I liked better than
watching game shows with my grandmother was helping her
bake. [49] [3] Watching her in the kitchen was magical: she
never seemed to need the recipes but everything she made
tasted like heaven.

45. **A.** NO CHANGE
    B. on the couch in the living room at my family's house
    C. in the living room at my family's house on the couch
    D. at my family's house on the couch in the living room

46. **F.** NO CHANGE
    G. my
    H. our
    J. her

47. Which of the following alternatives to the underlined portion would NOT be acceptable?

    A. excitement, when
    B. excitement; when
    C. excitement. When
    D. excitement, or when

48. **F.** NO CHANGE
    G. as regular.
    H. but regularly.
    J. as regularly.

49. The writer is considering deleting the preceding sentence. If the sentence were removed, the essay would primarily lose:

    A. a transition from the narrator's discussion of watching game shows to the subject focused on in the remainder of the essay.
    B. unnecessary information that serves only to detract from the primary subject being discussed in the paragraph.
    C. details that are critical to understanding why the narrator took such pleasure in watching game shows with her grandmother.
    D. an insight into why the narrator would choose to spend her afternoons watching television with her grandmother.

GO ON TO THE NEXT PAGE.

[3]

[1] As I got older, she let me help with the easy parts, such
as sifting the flour and measuring the sugar. [2] At first I would

just sit on the kitchen stool and watch, even though I didn't
understand what she was doing. [3] The day she let me separate

the eggs, I felt like I had reached the pinnacle of success. 52

[4]

Eventually, my parents decided that I could take care of myself,
and my grandmother stopped coming over every day because I
didn't need someone to keep an eye on me anymore. [B] The love
of baking that she had inspired, however, stayed with me. I
started baking by myself, and even if the cookies ended

up burned

sometimes, more often they turned out pretty well. I dropped
in new recipes, and whenever I got to a tricky part, I would call
my grandmother for advice. Sometimes I would call her just to
talk, too. I felt like I could talk to her about anything.

50. Which of the following alternatives to the underlined portion would NOT be acceptable?

F. during
G. her with
H. out with
J. along

51. Which of the following would best express the narrator's respect for her grandmother's abilities in the kitchen, and the enjoyment the narrator feels at watching her grandmother bake?

A. NO CHANGE
B. or work on whatever homework I had for the next day.
C. awed by her skills and eager to taste whatever she was creating.
D. confused by all the different steps that went into each dish.

52. Which of the following is the most logical ordering of the sentences in Paragraph 3?

F. NO CHANGE
G. 3, 1, 2
H. 2, 3, 1
J. 2, 1, 3

53. A. NO CHANGE
B. since I was considered old enough to stay home by myself.
C. due to my parents' decision that I didn't need a babysitter.
D. DELETE the underlined portion and end the sentence with a period.

54. Which of the following alternatives to the underlined portion would NOT be acceptable?

F. spoiled
G. burnted
H. ruined
J. burnt

55. A. NO CHANGE
B. auditioned for
C. tried out
D. fell into

GO ON TO THE NEXT PAGE.

[5]

[C] Last week, I found a recipe book she made for me. It included her recipes for brownies, cookies, and my favorite, lemon meringue pie. As I <u>flipped through</u> the pages, I thought
56

for a moment I could hear her <u>voice, although</u> she's gone, I
57
know that in the way that matters most, she'll never really be

gone at all. She was the one <u>which</u> taught me not just about
58

baking, but about life. <u>I imagine that I will enjoy baking for</u>
59
<u>the rest of my life.</u> [D]
59

56. Which of the following alternatives to the underlined portion would NOT be acceptable?

   F. leafed through
   G. looked through
   H. tossed out
   J. read over

57. **A.** NO CHANGE
   B. voice; but
   C. voice. Although
   D. voice although

58. **F.** NO CHANGE
   G. whom
   H. who
   J. whose

59. Given that all the choices are true, which one would provide a concluding sentence that best captures the main idea of the essay?

   A. NO CHANGE
   B. To this day, I love watching game shows and baking delicious food for my family.
   C. Baking is a great way to relax, and it's often less expensive than buying cakes and pastries from a bakery.
   D. Every day, when I enter the kitchen, I remember my grandmother and everything she taught me.

Question 60 asks about the passage as a whole.

---

60. The writer is considering adding the following true statement to the essay:

> My grandmother passed away ten years ago, but I still think of her every day.

If the writer were to add this sentence, it would most logically be placed at:

   F. Point A in Paragraph 1.
   G. Point B in Paragraph 2.
   H. Point C in Paragraph 5.
   J. Point D in Paragraph 5.

GO ON TO THE NEXT PAGE.

PASSAGE V

Global Rat-titudes

[1]

The relationship between humans and animals have always
been complicated. [A] Some cultures have developed entire
belief systems around favored animals. For example, cows
are treated with reverence in Hindu societies, in part because
some followers of the Hindu religion believe that any cow
could carry the spirits of one of their ancestors. Certain Native
American tribes believe that they're favored animal, the buffalo,
had a connection to the divine. The tribes still hunted

the buffalo, but carefully, according to such strict rules that the
hunt seemed more like a religious ritual. Even in cultures

with less formalized belief systems, regular interactions
between people and animals still lead to common opinions.

[2]

These stories usually develop around the animals that
interact with humans most frequently. [B] Therefore, it should
not be surprising that so many stories surround the most
common of animals: rats. Rats live side-by-side with humans

all over the world, regularly interact with people. Human-rat

61. A. NO CHANGE
B. should of
C. had
D. has

62. F. NO CHANGE
G. their
H. theirs
J. there

63. A. NO CHANGE
B. so that
C. as to mean
D. because

64. Given that all of the choices are true, which of the following concludes this paragraph with the clearest allusion to the story of "The Pied Piper of Hamlin," which is discussed later in the essay?

F. NO CHANGE
G. it is well-known that other cultures hold religious beliefs about some animals.
H. people still tend to have beliefs, either individual or cultural, relating to animals.
J. folklore and stories relating to humans' relationship with animals abound.

65. Which of the following alternatives to the underlined portion would NOT be acceptable?

A. tales
B. legends
C. narrators
D. fables

66. F. NO CHANGE
G. world and regularly
H. world, regular
J. world, regularly,

GO ON TO THE NEXT PAGE.

coexistence may be common all around the world, with
<u>67</u>
different cultures respond to that closeness in different ways.

[3]

In the United States and Europe, one typical attitude is that
the rat is a pest. This could be due to the common belief that
<u>68</u>

rats spread disease. They <u>don't, at least not directly; but many</u>
<u>69</u>
people don't know that. [C] "The Pied Piper of Hamlin," a
well-known children's story, is one example of how rats have
been portrayed in a <u>different way</u> in Western literature: in that
<u>70</u>
story, rats cause such a problem that a town has to hire a piper
to call them all away.

[4]

<u>What's really wild is that in</u> many Latin American countries,
<u>71</u>
and some European countries as well, the rat is portrayed in
a very different light. The tooth fairy legend is common all
over the world, but in Latin America, the "fairy" is a rat! Rats
do have <u>very strong teeth,</u> which could explain the association.
<u>72</u>
Clearly, this shows another attitude toward rats that is much
more positive.

[5]

<u>Yet another</u> attitude toward the rat can be seen in the
<u>73</u>

Chinese *Zodiac*. The Rat is <u>one of the animals, of the zodiac</u>
<u>74</u>
along with the Sheep, the Rooster, the Boar, and eight others.
Like the other zodiac animals, the Rat is neither entirely good

67. A. NO CHANGE
   B. world,
   C. world, but with
   D. world, but

68. F. NO CHANGE
   G. pest, which is a common opinion.
   H. pest, a belief many people share.
   J. pest, moreover.

69. A. NO CHANGE
   B. don't, at least not directly,
   C. don't: at least not directly,
   D. don't, at least not directly

70. Given that all the choices are true, which one states a
detail that most clearly relates to the information conveyed
at the end of this sentence?
   F. NO CHANGE
   G. mystical
   H. negative
   J. juvenile

71. A. NO CHANGE
   B. In
   C. Dig this: in the minds of those born and raised in
   D. You'll be shocked to discover that in

72. Given that all the choices are true, which one provides a
physical detail about rats that relates most clearly to the
preceding sentence?
   F. NO CHANGE
   G. particularly curious natures,
   H. a reputation for excessive chewing,
   J. long and somewhat unusual tails,

73. A. NO CHANGE
   B. China's
   C. Chinese mysticism's
   D. Their

74. F. NO CHANGE
   G. one of the animals, of the zodiac,
   H. one of the animals of the zodiac,
   J. one, of the animals of the zodiac

GO ON TO THE NEXT PAGE.

nor entirely bad. It's described as clever and friendly, but also tricky and not entirely honest. That may be the most accurate description of the rat so far. Whether you like rats or not, it's hard to deny their reputation for cleverness. [D] As many people are discovering these days, rats can even make excellent pets, so long as you remember to latch the cage carefully! ☐75

75. The writer is considering adding the following sentence to the essay:

> In fact, many still believe that the bubonic plague is directly caused by rats.

If the writer were to add this sentence, it would most logically be placed at:

A. Point A in Paragraph 1.
B. Point B in Paragraph 2.
C. Point C in Paragraph 3.
D. Point D in Paragraph 5.

END OF TEST 3
STOP! DO NOT TURN THE PAGE UNTIL TOLD TO DO SO.

Chapter 18
English Practice Test 3:
Answers and Explanations

ENGLISH PRACTICE TEST 3 ANSWERS

1.	B		39.	C
2.	F		40.	G
3.	C		41.	C
4.	F		42.	J
5.	C		43.	C
6.	J		44.	J
7.	A		45.	B
8.	G		46.	H
9.	B		47.	A
10.	H		48.	J
11.	C		49.	A
12.	G		50.	J
13.	D		51.	C
14.	J		52.	J
15.	B		53.	D
16.	H		54.	G
17.	B		55.	C
18.	G		56.	H
19.	D		57.	C
20.	H		58.	H
21.	D		59.	D
22.	H		60.	H
23.	A		61.	D
24.	J		62.	G
25.	A		63.	A
26.	F		64.	J
27.	D		65.	C
28.	J		66.	G
29.	A		67.	D
30.	J		68.	F
31.	A		69.	B
32.	H		70.	H
33.	B		71.	B
34.	J		72.	F
35.	D		73.	A
36.	H		74.	H
37.	B		75.	C
38.	G			

SCORE YOUR PRACTICE TEST

Step A
Count the number of correct answers: _____. This is your *raw score*.

Step B
Use the score conversion table below to look up your raw score. The number to the left is your *scale score*: _____.

English Scale Conversion Table

Scale Score	Raw Score	Scale Score	Raw Score	Scale Score	Raw Score
36	72-75	24	53-55	12	23-24
35	70-71	23	51-52	11	19-22
34	68-69	22	48-50	10	16-18
33	67	21	45-47	9	13-15
32	66	20	42-44	8	11-12
31	65	19	40-41	7	9-10
30	64	18	38-39	6	7-8
29	62-63	17	36-37	5	6
28	61	16	33-35	4	4-5
27	60	15	30-32	3	3
26	58-59	14	27-29	2	2
25	56-57	13	25-26	1	0-1

ENGLISH PRACTICE TEST 3 EXPLANATIONS

Passage I

1. **B** The question asks you to find the answer choice that is NOT acceptable as a replacement for the underlined portion—remember, that means the passage is correct as written. Look at the answer choices—some change words, and some change punctuation. In a case like this, you'll need to check each answer choice. Choices (A), (C), and (D) can all be inserted in place of the underlined portion without creating an error, but (B) makes the sentence *When I woke up this morning, I made myself a bowl of cereal, sat listening to the traffic*, which isn't an appropriate way to join the two ideas and therefore can NOT be used.

2. **F** When you see answer choices "stacked" like this, using all the same words with Stop and Go punctuation changing in the same spot, check for Complete/Incomplete on either side of that spot. In this case, *It's true that there's always some kind of noise in my neighborhood* is complete, and *taxi drivers honking their horns, kids playing their radios so loud that the bass makes my teeth vibrate, or people yelling in the street* is incomplete. Since Stop punctuation can separate only two complete ideas, eliminate (H). You definitely need some kind of pause after *neighborhood*, so (J) can be eliminated. Now you must choose between a comma and a dash. Using a comma would make it seem like the sentence is giving a list of things that are true, when the intention is to list the kinds of noises in the neighborhood. Remember a single dash is the same thing as a colon—it must follow a complete idea and must itself be followed by a list, definition, or explanation of the first complete idea. That's what the sentence has as written, so choose (F).

3. **C** The preceding sentence is *I know that some people wouldn't like it, but to me, these are the sounds of life.* This is almost the exact opposite of what (A) says—the narrator is putting a positive spin on what many would find an annoyance. There is no trip to the park mentioned as in (B), and (D) is incorrect because this sentence is very much relevant to the essay—choose (C).

4. **F** The sentence has a comma with the FANBOYS word *so*, which is Stop punctuation, so the sentence must have two complete ideas. This means the first part of the sentence needs to be complete. Eliminate (G) and (H) because they make the first part incomplete. Between (F) and (J), (F) is more concise, so it is the correct answer.

5. **C** Careful—all of these answer choices may seem fit to use, but on the ACT, there is always a reason to choose the best answer choice. In this case the entire sentence reads *When I ride the bus, you get to see so much more of the city.* The underlined portion you select must have a pronoun that is consistent with the non-underlined *you get*, which is (C), *you ride*.

6. **J** Here you need to choose between *sociable* and *sociably*, but there's punctuation changing as well—start easy! You need the adverb *sociably* because it's describing how the people are chatting—eliminate (F) and (H). Choice (G) is incorrect because there's no need for a pause after *sociably*, so no comma is needed.

7. **A** The answer choices have "stacked" words with Stop and Go punctuation changing in one spot, so check for Complete/Incomplete on either side of that spot. *Just like the traffic's sounds, though, the noise on the bus represents people* is complete (but awkward), and *working, relaxing, and living* is incomplete,

so you need Go punctuation—eliminate (B) and (C). Choice (D) is incorrect because you don't need a comma after *people*—you need commas only to separate the items in the list of things the people are doing.

8. **G** Here you have three answer choices using pronouns and one that uses the noun *kids*, so check that one first. *Kids* makes sense in the context of the sentence and is consistent with the non-underlined *their parents*.

9. **B** In the answer choices, you see Stop and Go punctuation changing after the word *nearby*, so check for Complete/Incomplete on either side of the punctuation. *The city added the bench so kids could play while their parents sit nearby* is complete, and, regardless of whether it begins with *obviously*, or not, *I like to sit there because there's a great big oak tree for shade* is also complete. Two complete ideas must be connected with Stop punctuation—eliminate (A) and (C). While adding the word *because* in (D) makes the second idea incomplete and might make you think it's okay to use a comma, it's still incorrect: to use the word *because*, you need a causal relationship between the ideas, and there is none in this case.

10. **H** This question is testing proper comma placement. You don't need a comma after either *watching* or *listening*, since the idea being expressed is *watching and listening to the people around me*—eliminate (F), (G), and (J).

11. **C** In the answer choices, you see Stop and Go punctuation changing after the word *do*, so check for Complete/Incomplete on either side of the punctuation. *People-watching is one of my favorite things to do* is complete, and *I like listening even better* is complete as well. Two complete ideas must be connected with Stop punctuation—eliminate (A). You can also eliminate (B) and (D), because even though they respectively add *nevertheless* and *however* after the punctuation change, both of those are transition words that only indicate direction—they don't make a complete idea incomplete. Choice (C), which uses a comma + FANBOYS (but), is the only choice that gives you the Stop punctuation you're looking for.

12. **G** The following sentence says *That way, I can pay more attention to the sounds and not get distracted by what I see*, so the most logical introduction would be one that has the narrator closing her eyes—(G).

13. **D** You need to emphasize the narrator's curiosity and interest in the old men's conversation, so the correct answer choice needs to incorporate the narrator's point of view. Choices (A), (B), and (C) are all objective descriptions of the conversation itself or the old men. Choice (D) characterizes the stories as entertaining, meaning *entertaining* to the narrator, and so is the best answer.

14. **J** Here apostrophes are being used to show possession. You know there are two old men having the conversation, so the laugh that comes in response to the story one of them is telling must come from his *friend*, not his *friends*. To show possession for a singular noun, all you have to do is add *'s*—(J).

15. **B** This essay is definitely pro-city living, and really explores only one aspect of what the narrator likes about the city, so you can eliminate (C) and (D). Choice (A) is incorrect, because although public transportation is mentioned, it isn't the convenience the narrator enjoys—it's the sounds and sights of the city.

Passage II

16. **H**   When you see DELETE as an answer choice, try that first. In this case, taking out *that* causes a syntax error—you wouldn't say *…three times in seventy-year history*. You need to find the correct pronoun, so the first step is to identify the noun that the pronoun replaces—it's *bridge*. Since *bridge* is a singular noun, eliminate (G); you can't replace a singular noun with a plural pronoun. The pronoun *that* in the sentence as written is incorrect; you can't use it because there is no prior reference to the seventy-year history.

17. **B**   The sentence is saying the amount of concrete was *enough to construct a sidewalk five feet wide all the way from San Francisco to New York City*. There isn't a reason to use commas here, so eliminate (A) and (D). Choice (C) has a dash (which is the same as a colon) after *sidewalk*, which creates an awkward and unclear construction afterward.

18. **G**   The sentence immediately following details the various reasons San Francisco Bay is a bad spot for bridge-building, so a logical introduction will introduce this theme. Neither (F), (H), nor (J) does this as well as (G) does.

19. **D**   Here you see Stop and Go Punctuation changing after the word *bond* in each answer choice, so check for Complete/Incomplete on either side of the punctuation. *After two years of discussion, the voters approved a bond* is complete, and *that would raise $35 million, all dedicated to building the bridge* is incomplete, so eliminate (C). Choice (A) has a colon after a complete idea, but the incomplete idea after it is awkward and unclear. Choice (B) is incorrect because the phrase *that would raise $35 million* is necessary, and thus there is no need for a comma here.

20. **H**   You have the option to DELETE the underlined portion, so try that first. That leaves *Even then, there were many skeptics believed that it couldn't be done*, which is a bad sentence—eliminate (J). Now you have to choose the correct pronoun, so identify the noun that's being replaced—it's *skeptics*. You can't use *that* to replace skeptics: it's singular and *that* can't be used to refer to people, so eliminate (G). If you have trouble deciding between *who* and *whom*, try substituting a different pronoun: there are multiple skeptics, so you can use "they" and "them." You would use the subject-case "they believed it couldn't be done," not the object-case "them believed it couldn't be done." That means you need to use the subject-case *who*—(H).

21. **D**   When DELETE is an option, you should always check that first—you know ACT likes things concise. Taking out the underlined portion leaves *Construction began in 1933 and lasted a little more than four years*. That's a perfectly good sentence, and you're not adding any new information with (A), (B), or (C)—(D) is the best (most concise) answer.

22. **H**   The answer choices have "stacked" words with Stop and Go punctuation changing after *1937*, so check for Complete/Incomplete on either side of that spot. *On May 28, 1937* is an incomplete idea, so you know you can't use Stop punctuation—that's only for connecting two complete ideas—eliminate (F) and (G). Choices (H) and (J) both give you the comma you need after *1937*, but (J) goes a little too far by adding another that you don't need after *grandly*. Choice (H) is correct.

23. **A**   DELETE the underlined portion first, since that's an option. That leaves *More than 200,000 people walked across the bridge that day to celebrate*, which is a complete idea, but is not as clear as it could be (celebrate what?). The better option is (A)—it's a little less concise, but much more clear. Choices (B) and (C) are much too wordy; neither says anything that (A) doesn't.

24. **J** The answer choices are all transition words, which is usually a sign that the question is testing direction. The two sentences on either side are *To top it off, it was beautiful* and *the Golden Gate Bridge is considered an artistic masterpiece*—two similar ideas (although note the shift in tense between the two from past to present.) You can eliminate the two opposite-direction transitions, (F) and (H), and eliminate (G) because it's still past tense; you want a transition that will make the change to present tense, as *Even today* does.

25. **A** The answer choices all have Stop and Go punctuation (and a dash) changing after the word *air*, so check for Complete/Incomplete before and after the punctuation. Before the punctuation is *At its highest point, the bridge rises 746 feet into the air*, which is complete, and afterward is *191 feet taller than the Washington Monument*, an incomplete idea. Eliminate (B)—you can't use Stop punctuation here. We can do without the extra *rising*, so eliminate (D). We do, however, need some kind of pause after *air*, so eliminate (C).

26. **F** The answer choices are all different word combinations—you just have to pick the correct one. The idiomatic expression for "environment" is *natural surroundings*—(F). If you're not sure here, you can try substituting each answer choice into the sentence; you should at least be able to eliminate one or two answer choices. Always keep in mind that NO CHANGE is going to be correct about 25 percent of the time it appears, so don't be afraid to pick it—especially if you can't identify an error in the sentence as it's written.

27. **D** The whole sentence says *The color, called "International Orange," was chosen partly because it matched the natural surroundings and partly because it would allow the bridge to remain visible on foggy days*. Saying *on foggy days* provides a detail about when the bridge might be hard to see, so if you take out that portion, you would lose that detail. That most closely matches (D).

28. **J** You need to emphasize the *wide variety of the bridge's uses* here, so the correct answer choice must do that. Choice (F) talks only about commuter traffic, (G) describes the bridge itself, not how it is used, and (H) talks about how some people cross the bridge—none of which describe *a wide variety of uses*. Choice (J) talks about the bridge's multiple uses for commuters and travelers and as a tourist destination in its own right, so it is the best answer choice.

29. **A** The added sentence talks about the original idea for building the bridge, so it belongs somewhere very early in the discussion of its construction—eliminate (C) and (D). Between (A) and (B), the more logical choice for the placement of the original idea for the bridge would be (A), just before the decision to actually build it.

Passage III

30. **J** Here you have nicely "stacked" answer choices with Stop (comma + FANBOYS) and Go punctuation changing after *single*—check for Complete/Incomplete on either side. *The Italian language wasn't always the single* is incomplete, as is *unified, language that it is today*. You'll need Go punctuation to connect these two—eliminate (H). Remember your comma rules; there's no reason to use a comma after *unified*—eliminate (F) and (G), leaving (J) as the best answer choice.

31. **A** The phrase *during the thirteenth century* introduces the time period the passage will be talking about, so that's what you lose if you take it out—there's no confusion created as in (B), no interruption as in (C), and it's not grammatically necessary as (D) claims; (A) is the best answer.

32. **H** Remember that less is more on the ACT; any time you have the option to add anything, make sure you have a compelling reason to do so. In this case, the sentence (not to mention the passage as a whole) is talking about Dante Alighieri, so adding a list of other writers doesn't add anything necessary to the essay. If you're still unsure, you can check the reasons given in the answer choices and eliminate those that don't agree with the passage: you can eliminate (F) as previously stated, there's no discussion of the creation of Italian as (G) states, and the reason you aren't adding the list isn't because it's not exhaustive, as (J) claims—it's because it's unnecessary.

33. **B** The underlined portion acts as the subject of the singular verb *was* in the non-underlined portion. Choices (A) and (C) are plural. Choice (D) doesn't fit the context of the sentence.

34. **J** The meaning of the sentence is not to say that literature was not written in the local languages and also not in Latin; the idea is that high literature was written in Latin instead of the local languages. To express that, you need to say *literature was written not in the various local languages but in Latin*—(J).

35. **D** DELETE is an answer choice, so try that first. Taking out the underlined portion leaves *Dante believed that literature should be available not only to the educated elite but also to the common people*. That is a complete sentence, and the meaning hasn't changed, so (D) is the best answer.

36. **H** Three of the answer choices use *called* and one uses *calling*, so you should check that one first, but remember that ACT doesn't really like the "-ing" form of verbs, and you should pick it only when all the other answer choices have an actual error. In this case, however, it doesn't make sense in the sentence—Dante was not literally calling out the word "Italian"—you can eliminate (J), and also (F) and (G), which make the sentence read the same way.

37. **B** Three of the answer choices use *spoken* and one uses *speak*, so you should check that one first. However, *to speak* doesn't make sense in the context of the sentence, so eliminate (D). There's no need to include *to be* or *if* as in (A) and (C); (B) makes the most sense—and it's the most concise—so it's the best answer choice.

38. **G** The answer choices all have Stop and Go punctuation (plus a colon) changing after the word *people*, so check for Complete/Incomplete on either side to see which you need. In this case, *By writing it in the language spoken by the Italian people* is incomplete, and since Stop punctuation can connect only two complete ideas, you can now eliminate (F) and (H). You can also eliminate (J), since a colon can follow only a complete idea. That leaves (G) as the only possible choice.

39. **C** All of the answer choices use the exact same words, just in different orders—you'll need to select the one that is most clear. Dante thought literature should be available to everyone, and was criticized for that opinion. The answer choice that expresses that idea in the clearest fashion is (C).

40. **G** Remember when ACT gives you a task to accomplish with an answer choice, you must read very literally—an answer choice that does the thing you want is a better choice than one that "could" do the thing you want. In this case, we need an answer choice that will imply that illiteracy changed from more common to less common. Be careful! If you just look at the words in the answer choices, *diminished* might seem the perfect candidate, but the passage is talking about *literacy*, not illiteracy. Therefore, you want the answer choice that says that literacy became more common, which would *imply* that illiteracy became less common—(G). Although both (H) and (J) might conceivably accompany an increase in literacy, neither states that as clearly as (G) does.

41. **C** A good place to start here is to decide which verb form you need—always keeping in mind ACT's opinion of the "-ing" form. *Confuses* agrees with the subject, *title*, so eliminate (A) and (B). The use of *that* in (D) makes the sentence an incomplete idea, so the best answer is (C).

42. **J** There are transition words changing in the answer choices, but not punctuation, which will typically mean ACT is testing direction. Make sure you read enough to get the proper context! The two ideas we have to connect are *The Divine Comedy wasn't written in Latin* and *it was considered a comedy*. The sentence prior to this says *the label of "comedy" was attached to any work not written in Latin*, so you're going to need a same-direction transition—eliminate (F). Choices (G), (H), and (J) are all same-direction transitions, but (G) and (H) have the relationship wrong—*The Divine Comedy* wasn't written in Latin as a result of being considered a comedy; it was the other way around. Note that in this case, (G) and (H) are "same" answer choices: *since* and *because* mean the exact same thing in this context, which means one cannot be more correct than the other; therefore, you cannot select either one.

43. **C** The answer choices all feature different transition words, but there's some punctuation changing as well. In fact, three of the answer choices use a comma and one doesn't—start there. In this instance, *and* causes an error, so eliminate (B). All the other answer choices end in a comma, which means the phrase *in defiance of the common beliefs of his time* is unnecessary since it's set off by a pair of commas—it may help to cross it out or simply ignore it to help answer the question. Without the unnecessary phrase (and its commas), the sentence now reads *Dante's brave decision, while demonstrated that it was not necessary for a literary masterpiece to be written in Latin, paved the way for future writers and readers alike*. That's not correct, so eliminate (A), and substituting *so that* for *while* doesn't help either—eliminate (D). That leaves (C), *which*, as the correct answer.

44. **J** You have the option to DELETE the underlined portion, so try that first. You're left with a complete sentence, so it's at least possible to take out that word without creating an error. However, notice that the other choices are all transition words, so it may be a good idea to assess whether a transition is needed here. The prior sentence (now) reads *Dante's brave decision, which, in defiance of the common beliefs of his time, demonstrated that it was not necessary for a literary masterpiece to be written in Latin, paved the way for future writers and readers alike*, and then you have *The Divine Comedy remains a symbol of both literature and innovation today*. No transition is really needed here, and even if one were, it wouldn't be an opposite-direction one, as are (F), (G), and (H).

Passage IV

45. **B** The answer choices are all different arrangements of the same three modifying phrases. On the ACT, (and in good writing in general), a modifying phrase must be placed next to the thing it's modifying. In this case, the words right before the underlined portion are *We would sit*, and the phrase that most directly modifies that is *on the couch*, so the correct answer choice must start with that phrase. Only (B) matches that description.

46. **H** You have possessive pronouns changing in the answer choices, so to choose the correct one, you'll need to find the context in the non-underlined part of the passage. The answers being called out belong to the narrator and her grandmother, and since the passage is written in the first person, you need to use *our*, (H). If you're still unsure, notice that using *our* is consistent with the following sentence: *When our answers were right....*

47. **A**   You need to find the answer choice that is NOT a suitable replacement for the correctly written underlined portion in the passage. The answer choices all have Stop and Go punctuation changing after the word *excitement*, so you should check for Complete/Incomplete on either side. Notice the sentence as written uses Stop punctuation (comma + FANBOYS), so you know the two ideas are complete. Choices (B), (C), and (D) all use different forms of Stop punctuation and therefore work to connect the two complete ideas. What can NOT be used as a replacement is (A), which uses a comma to separate two complete ideas.

48. **J**   The first decision to make here is whether you need *regular* or *regularly*. The verb *watch* is being modified, so you need the adverb *regularly*—eliminate (F) and (G). Choice (H) is incorrect because it uses the correct adverb but the wrong conjunction—the narrator and her grandmother don't watch the shows *as regularly* as they did prior to school starting.

49. **A**   The sentence *That was okay with me, though, because the one thing I liked better than watching game shows with my grandmother was helping her bake* introduces the main idea of the essay, and so serves as a transition between the discussion of the two activities the narrator enjoys with her grandmother. That's not unnecessary or detracting information as in (B), and (C) and (D) can be eliminated because they talk only about watching television.

50. **J**   You need to find the answer choice that is NOT a suitable replacement for the correctly written underlined portion in the passage. Choices (F), (G), and (H) all keep the original meaning of the sentence, but *help along* has a different meaning, and *help along the easy parts* doesn't really make sense; therefore (J) is NOT a suitable replacement.

51. **C**   Choice (C) describes the narrator as *awed* and *eager to taste*, which accomplishes both tasks: expressing both respect and enjoyment. Choices (A) and (D) express lack of understanding and confusion, and (B) talks about homework.

52. **J**   The three sentences describe a progression in the amount of help the narrator was allowed to give her grandmother in the kitchen: *At first* she only sat and watched (sentence 2). *As* [she] *got older*, she helped with the easier tasks (sentence 1). Finally, she reaches *the pinnacle of success* when she gets to separate the eggs (sentence 3). Choice (J) is correct.

53. **D**   Whenever DELETE is an option, you should try that first. In this case, taking out *because I didn't need someone to keep an eye on me anymore* does not create an error or change the meaning; in fact, it gets rid of redundancy because the narrator has already said *my parents decided that I could take care of myself*. Choices (B) and (C) are both redundant and wordy as well—pick (D).

54. **G**   You need to find the answer choice that is NOT a suitable replacement for the correctly written underlined portion in the passage. Choices (F), (H), and (J) can all be used in place of *burned* in this context, but (G), *burnted*, far from being a replacement, can NOT be used—it's not even a word.

55. **C**   The answer choices all have different pairs of words; notice the second word in each is a preposition. When you see prepositions changing, that's a good sign that ACT may be testing idioms. In this case, in order to express the idea of "attempted something for the first time," you need to use *tried out*, (C).

56. **H**   You need to find the answer choice that is NOT a suitable replacement for the correctly written underlined portion in the passage. Notice the answer choices all have different pairs of words, and the second word in each is a preposition: that's a good sign that ACT is testing idioms. In the context of

the sentence, *flipped through* means "quickly read the contents of a book." Choices (F), (G), and (J) all convey that same meaning, but *tossed out* in (H) would imply she threw the book away, and so can NOT be used as a replacement.

57. **C** The answer choices all have Stop and Go punctuation changing after the same word: *voice*. Check for Complete/Incomplete on both sides. *As I flipped through the pages, I thought for a moment I could hear her voice* is complete, as is *although she's gone, I know that in the way that matters most, she'll never really be gone at all*. You need to use Stop punctuation to separate two complete ideas—eliminate (A) and (D). Choice (B) is incorrect because the transition word *but* makes the second idea incomplete, so you can't use it with a semicolon.

58. **H** When you see pronouns changing in the answer choice, find the noun that's being replaced: *She* (referring to the narrator's grandmother). Eliminate (F) because you can't use *which* to refer a person. Choice (J) is the possessive pronoun *whose*, so look at the word that follows it; only nouns can be possessed. You can't possess *taught*, so eliminate (J). In this case, the pronoun is the subject of the verb *taught*, so you need *who*—(H).

59. **D** The main focus of the passage isn't baking; it's the relationship between the narrator and her grandmother—eliminate (A). Choices (B) and (C) have the same problem. Choice (D) is the only answer choice that mentions the narrator's grandmother.

60. **H** This sentence doesn't fit in the narrative of either paragraph 1 or 2, so eliminate (F) and (G). It should also come before the narrator says *Although she's gone* so that it's clear to the reader that her grandmother has passed away—(H) is the better answer choice for that reason.

Passage V

61. **D** You have helping verbs changing in the answer choices, and recall the helping verbs need to agree with the subject, just like regular verbs. In this case, the subject of the sentence is *relationship*, which is singular, so eliminate (A), which is plural. Choice (B) is an incorrect construction: it's "should have," not "should of." Choice (C) makes the sentence seem to imply that the relationship was only complicated in the past, and isn't anymore, but there's no support for the latter in the passage. Choice (D) is the best answer choice: the relationship *has always been complicated*.

62. **G** The answer choices are all similar-sounding, so your ear isn't going to help much on this question. Expand out (F)—it means "they are," which doesn't make sense here. You need a word that shows the buffalo was the favored animal of the tribes, and in this context, that's the possessive pronoun *their*, (G).

63. **A** The passage says the hunts were carried out *according to such strict rules…the hunt seemed more like a religious ritual*. When you use the word *such* in this context, you have to pair it with *that*, (A). If you chose (D), you may have misunderstood the relationship; the rules weren't strict as a result of the hunts seeming like a religious ritual—it's the other way around.

64. **J** You need to choose an answer choice that makes a *clear allusion* to a story later in the essay. The only answer choice that even mentions a story is (J): *folklore and stories relating to humans' relationship with animals*.

65. **C**   You need to find the answer choice that is NOT a suitable replacement for the correctly written underlined portion in the passage. Choices (A), (B), and (D) all mean the same thing as the underlined word, *stories*. *Narrator* does NOT mean the same thing—it refers to someone who tells stories—so (C) is the correct choice.

66. **G**   You have three answer choices with *regularly* and one with *regular*, so check that one first. You need an adverb to modify the verb *interact*, so eliminate (H). In both (F) and (J), the verb *interact* has no subject, so eliminate them—(G), which joins the two verbs *live* and *interact* with *and*, giving them both a subject, is correct.

67. **D**   The answer choices all have Stop (comma + FANBOYS) and Go punctuation changing after the same word: *world*, so check for Complete/Incomplete on either side. *Human-rat coexistence may be common all around the world* is complete, and so is the part after the underlined portion: *different cultures respond to that closeness in different ways*. Choice (A) has Go punctuation and adds *with*, which makes the second idea incomplete, but also doesn't make sense. Choice (B) joins two complete ideas with a comma—eliminate it. Choice (C) has the FANBOYS conjunction you're looking for, but like (A), adds *with*, which makes no sense. Choice (D) is the best answer choice—it uses Stop punctuation to separate the two complete ideas.

68. **F**   All four answer choices say the same thing in slightly different ways, and none contains a grammatical error. Therefore, pick the one that is the most concise: (F), NO CHANGE.

69. **B**   The answer choices mostly have commas changing around, but one uses a colon, so start there. The colon follows a complete idea, *They don't*, which is proper, but what follows the colon is not a list, definition, or expansion of that idea (not to mention it's an extremely awkward construction), so eliminate (C). To choose the correct comma placement, remember your comma rules: *at least not directly* is unnecessary information, so you need to set it off with commas—the only answer choice that does that is (B).

70. **H**   In the end of the sentence, you have the statement *rats cause such a problem that a town has to hire a piper to call them all away* and you need to find the word to describe how rats have been portrayed that agrees with that most closely. Choice (H), *negative*, agrees with the notion of the rats being a *problem* better than *different*, *mystical*, or *juvenile*.

71. **B**   Aside from being the most concise, (B) avoids the problems found in the other choices. Remember, there's no slang on the ACT! Choices (A) and (C) are too informal, besides being far too wordy. Choice (D) might be tempting, but it's not concise as well as being a bit too strong; remember the author has already told you different cultures respond to that [human-rat] closeness in different ways, so an example of one of those ways shouldn't really shock you.

72. **F**   The correct answer choice has to provide a physical detail about rats, so (G) and (H) can be eliminated—neither of those is a physical detail. Choice (J) certainly is a physical characteristic, but probably has less to do with the rat's association with teeth than a description of the rat's *very strong* teeth.

73. **A**   The underlined portion introduces a new paragraph and the sentence *attitude toward the rat can be seen in the Chinese zodiac.* Choices (B) and (C) cause redundancy in the sentence: the phrase *Chinese zodiac* already tells you you're talking about mysticism in China. Choice (D) is temptingly concise, but the pronoun *their* has no noun to refer to, so you can't use it. Choice (A) is the best answer since it both makes sense in the sentence and acts as an effective transition to the new paragraph after the discussion of a different example of people's attitude toward rats in the previous paragraph.

74. **H**   Remember your comma rules here: this isn't a list, introductory idea, or unnecessary information, so there's really no reason to use a comma between any of the underlined words—eliminate (F), (G), and (J); the only choice you have is (H).

75. **C**   The new sentence states that some people believe rats cause the plague. Paragraph 3 discusses that people believe that *rats spread disease,* so the new sentence should be placed in that paragraph.

Chapter 19
English
Practice Test 4

ACT ENGLISH TEST

45 Minutes—75 Questions

DIRECTIONS: In the five passages that follow, certain words and phrases are underlined and numbered. In the right-hand column, you will find alternatives for each underlined part. In most cases, you are to choose the one that best expresses the idea, makes the statement appropriate for standard written English, or is worded most consistently with the style and tone of the passage as a whole. If you think the original version is best, choose "NO CHANGE." In some cases, you will find in the right-hand column a question about the underlined part. You are to choose the best answer to the question.

You will also find questions about a section of the passage or the passage as a whole. These questions do not refer to an underlined portion of the passage but rather are identified by a number or numbers in a box.

For each question, choose the alternative you consider best and blacken the corresponding oval on your answer document. Read each passage through once before you begin to answer the questions that accompany it. For many of the questions, you must read several sentences beyond the question to determine the answer. Be sure that you have read far enough ahead each time you choose an alternative.

PASSAGE I

Cheeseburgers and Cats That Can Make You "lol"

Everyone knows that cats love to chase mice, <u>but who knew they also love to eat cheeseburgers?</u> [A] It's a very special kind of cat that does: a *lolcat*. The concept, which originated in 2006, was simple: take a funny

1. If the writer were to delete the underlined portion (changing the comma after *mice* to a period), the sentence would primarily lose:
   A. a description of one of the things that make lolcats unique.
   B. a scientific fact describing a well-known species.
   C. a concise statement of the essay's main idea.
   D. nothing at all, because it strays from the topic unnecessarily.

photograph of a cat and <u>written</u> a humorous caption over it. [B] The name is a compound word combining *cat* and *lol*, the slangy Internet abbreviation for "laughing out loud." [C] In some ways, the phenomenon of the lolcat was nothing new. [D] In the 1870s, Brighton-based <u>photographer, Henry Pointer</u> took a series of images of his pet cats. The images were intended to form the backgrounds for *cartes de visite*, <u>having at times been called</u> "visiting cards." To enhance a photo's appeal, Henry Pointer would often add a humorous caption.

2. F. NO CHANGE
   G. is writing
   H. wrote
   J. write

3. A. NO CHANGE
   B. photographer Henry Pointer
   C. photographer, Henry Pointer,
   D. photographer; Henry Pointer

4. F. NO CHANGE
   G. a French term meaning
   H. being things called
   J. and naming them

GO ON TO THE NEXT PAGE.

Pointer's first photographs, those without captions, did

not sell well initially, though they have recently been better

appreciated. Pointer made a good deal of money from

his photos because photography equipment was still

relatively rare and expensive for his day. He likely never knew,

however, that his pictures would be the basis for a hugely

popular movement over a century later. ⌑7⌑

By the mid 2000s, though, anyone with a camera and a

computer could create a lolcat image. The only requirement was

a basic fluency in the language of *lolspeak*, a grammatically

incorrect, often misspelled form of English. The most famous

phrase known widely in all of lolspeak is "I can has

cheezburger?", or "Can I have a cheeseburger?"

Additional phrases and the language could be fairly easy to

learn, and lolcats became some of the trendiest images on the

Internet at the time.

As a result of their popularity, lolcats attracted all kinds of

new press. *Time* magazine covered lolcats in a July 2007 issue.

Even the American Dialect Society

5. Given that all the choices are true, which one best conveys
the idea that captions contributed to the humor of Pointer's
photographs?

A. NO CHANGE
B. Pointer would occasionally reuse captions when the
picture could communicate most of what he wanted it to.
C. In fact, he soon understood that the humorous caption
could make even the most mundane cat pictures charm-
ing or funny.
D. Pointer took so many pictures and wrote so many captions that neither required much effort of him.

6. F. NO CHANGE
G. with
H. in
J. of

7. If the writer were to divide this paragraph into two, the most
logical place to begin the new paragraph would be at Point:

A. A.
B. B.
C. C.
D. D.

8. Which of the following alternatives to the underlined portion
would NOT be acceptable?

F. in fact,
G. however,
H. by contrast,
J. on the other hand,

9. A. NO CHANGE
B. phrase
C. phrase that many people know
D. phrase that is pretty popular

10. F. NO CHANGE
G. is being
H. is
J. was

11. A. NO CHANGE
B. Now earning lots of money,
C. With their cameras in hand,
D. Promoting them on the Internet,

GO ON TO THE NEXT PAGE.

named "lolcat" one of the <u>mainly</u> creative coinages of the
¹²
decade. There were financial gains as well: in 2007, the
"I Can Has Cheezburger?" website was purchased by a group of
investors for $2 million and spawned many spinoffs. It seemed
at the time, then, that the lolcat would be here to stay and that
cheeseburger-flavored cat food couldn't be far off. [13]

12.
F. NO CHANGE
G. more
H. most
J. a lot

13. If the writer were to delete the phrase "cheeseburger-flavored"
in the preceding sentence and replace it with "another line
of," the paragraph would primarily lose:

A. a particular detail that ends the essay on a humorous note.
B. a more detailed discussion of the different types of cats
discussed in the essay.
C. a resolution to a difficult problem posed earlier in the
essay.
D. an open question that is left to the reader to decide.

Question 14 asks about the preceding passage as a whole.

14. Suppose the writer's goal had been to write a brief essay
describing a new generation's interest in animal photography.
Would this essay accomplish that goal?

F. Yes, because it shows how important lolcats were to a
broader interest in photography.
G. Yes, because it narrates the simultaneous rise of digital
photography and Internet usage.
H. No, because it details the different types of animal photography popular on the Internet.
J. No, because it focuses on lolcats and their history, not on
photography more generally.

PASSAGE II

My Summer as a Teacher . . . or as a Student?

I was there only for a summer, but the memories I have
of teaching English in Mexico have stayed with me. The
experience didn't start well. I was assigned to a small village—
located a few hours west of <u>Monterrey; in</u> the central north
¹⁵
part of the country, in the state of Durango. The most direct

15.
A. NO CHANGE
B. Monterrey. In
C. Monterrey in
D. Monterrey—in

GO ON TO THE NEXT PAGE.

route was to fly into the large city of Monterrey and then take

a seven-hour bus ride. Once we got out of the city, the ride was

bumpy, and the bus's air conditioning was no match for the

heat of the desert sun burning overhead.
                    _____
                         16

Mexico's climate is warmer than that of the United States
_____
                                                  17
because Mexico is closer to the equator. The adults in the
_____
              17
village, many of whom did not even know I was coming,

welcomed me when they got around to it. More than that, my
            _____
                    18
host family had reserved a room in their house exclusively

for me, so I could have some privacy when I needed it. Even

though I was in a new place, I already felt like I was at home.

The language situation was more difficult than I expected. I

learned very quickly that the good grades I had received in my

Spanish classes would not necessarily translate to success here

where people spoke the Spanish language and no other. Still,
                      _____
                                    19
my host family and others in the village were very patient

with me. Before long, we had held all of our conversations in
                        _____
                           20
Spanish.

The family I was hosting in Mexico asked me about my family
    _____
           21
and encouraged my school interests. They told me about their

16.
F. NO CHANGE
G. burning.
H. scorching.
J. DELETE the underlined portion and end the sentence with a period.

17. Given that all the choices are true, which provides material most relevant to what follows in this paragraph?
A. NO CHANGE
B. I had only been to Mexico one time before, when I went with my parents to the beach.
C. Once I got there, though, I didn't have any of the problems that I had worried about in advance.
D. The heat from the sun was nothing compared to the heat of the spicy food my family liked to cook.

18. Which choice most effectively expresses that the narrator's host family was extremely welcoming?
F. NO CHANGE
G. as if I had lived there my whole life.
H. and asked how long I would be staying.
J. to their town.

19. Which of the following alternatives to the underlined portion would NOT be acceptable?
A. no language other than Spanish.
B. Spanish language others or no.
C. Spanish and no other language.
D. no other language.

20.
F. NO CHANGE
G. hold
H. have held
J. held

21.
A. NO CHANGE
B. family that hosted me
C. family I hosted
D. family, which hosted me,

GO ON TO THE NEXT PAGE.

lives and some of their childrens' previous English teachers. In
<u>22</u>
particular, my host father became a very close friend, and I still
correspond with him today.

I had been sent to this town to teach English to some of
the children and their parents, but I soon realized that I was
learning <u>all about Mexican food and culture.</u> I was learning
<u>23</u>

<u>in circumstances</u> not only how to speak everyday Spanish, but
<u>24</u>

also how to coexist with people who lived unlike my own. ☐25

On my last day of <u>class. I</u> noticed a map of North America
<u>26</u>
on the wall. I realized then what I had sensed all along.

In one sense, I was farther away from home than I'd ever <u>was.</u>
<u>27</u>
However, in another sense, I had simply found a new place that

I could call home. <u>Remembering the details of my trip,</u> I'm
<u>28</u>
more and more convinced that the river that separates

22. **F.** NO CHANGE
 G. childrens's
 H. childrens
 J. children's

23. Which choice most logically contrasts with the first part of
 this sentence?

 A. NO CHANGE
 B. my way around the town.
 C. more than I could ever teach.
 D. about the lives of those in my host family.

24. The best placement for the underlined portion would be:

 F. where it is now.
 G. after the word *speak.*
 H. after the word *Spanish.*
 J. after the word *lived.*

25. At this point, the writer is considering adding the following
 true statement:

 > In Spanish, the word for "coexistence" sounds
 > just like ours: *coexistencia.*

 Should the writer make this addition here?

 A. Yes, because it clarifies the narrator's earlier discussion
  of how welcome he felt with his host family.
 B. Yes, because it supports the paragraph's main idea by
  translating a word into Spanish.
 C. No, because it digresses from the main topic of the
  paragraph.
 D. No, because it shows that the narrator's Spanish was not
  as proficient as he claimed.

26. **F.** NO CHANGE
 G. class, I
 H. class but I
 J. class; I

27. **A.** NO CHANGE
 B. had been.
 C. been.
 D. being.

28. **F.** NO CHANGE
 G. Identified as one of the borderlands,
 H. Showing all the mountains and rivers,
 J. Becoming a new place for me,

GO ON TO THE NEXT PAGE.

Mexico and the United States is actually very small next to all of the wonderful things that bring us together. [29]

29. Which of the following sentences, if added here, would most effectively express one of the main ideas of the essay?

    A. To be honest, though, I was really glad to get home when it was all over.

    B. The main thing I miss about the trip is the opportunity to practice my Spanish.

    C. Ever since that time, I've often thought how alike my two homes really are.

    D. That was my initial reaction, but I don't think I really want to go back.

PASSAGE III

"Haunted" Authors

[1]

In 1915, Maurice E. McLoughlin, a well-known tennis player published an instructional autobiography called *Tennis as I Play It*. Two years earlier, McLoughlin had become the first American finalist at the Wimbledon tournament in England, and tennis fans were excited to uncover the tricks of his success. Anticipation for McLoughlin's story grew even more

in 1914. He was winning a number of major tournaments that year, he was declared the Number 1 tennis player in the world. When *Tennis as I Play It* finally did come out in 1915, no one had any reason to suspect that it might have been written by someone else. However, the author of *Tennis as I Play It* was not McLoughlin at all, but the as-yet unknown novelist Sinclair Lewis, his ghostwriter. Why, then, is *Tennis as I Play It* considered the tennis player's book? [A]

30. **F.** NO CHANGE
    G. McLoughlin a well-known tennis player
    H. McLoughlin, a well-known tennis player,
    J. McLoughlin a well-known tennis player,

31. **A.** NO CHANGE
    B. skills
    C. secrets
    D. abilities

32. **F.** NO CHANGE
    G. Won
    H. He won
    J. Winning

33. **A.** NO CHANGE
    B. for
    C. about
    D. DELETE the underlined portion.

34. **F.** NO CHANGE
    G. athletes'
    H. tennis players
    J. athletes

GO ON TO THE NEXT PAGE.

[2]

A ghostwriter is an author who writes a text that is officially credited to another author, and the history of such practices are lasting longer than we might expect. [36]
₃₅

In other words, *Tennis as I Play It* was not, the first famous
₃₇
ghostwritten book, and it won't be the last. Ghostwriting can

happen for a number of reasons, and although it's merits are
₃₈
debatable, it remains an acceptable practice in the publishing world. [B]

[3]

Today, ghostwriting can take a number of different forms. It is perhaps most prominent in the autobiographies and memoirs of celebrities. How does a celebrity decide to ask a ghostwriter
₃₉
to write his or her book? No, ghostwriting is equally prominent
₃₉
in lesser-known spheres as well. [C] Political speeches, for example, are often credited to the politician who

35. **A.** NO CHANGE
    B. were
    C. are
    D. is

36. At this point, the writer is thinking about adding the following true statement:

    > Some suggest that ghostwriting is as old as authorship itself.

    Should the writer make this addition here?

    F. Yes, because it provides a transition from the previous paragraph to this one.
    G. Yes, because it expands upon a point made in the preceding sentence.
    H. No, because it does not apply to the main subject discussed in this paragraph.
    J. No, because it suggests that most historical texts are ghostwritten.

37. **A.** NO CHANGE
    B. was not the first,
    C. was not the first
    D. was, not the first,

38. **F.** NO CHANGE
    G. its
    H. her
    J. their

39. Which choice provides the most logical and effective transition to the rest of the paragraph?

    A. NO CHANGE
    B. Is the practice restricted to celebrity autobiographies and memoirs?
    C. Why would celebrities want other people to tell their stories?
    D. What makes celebrities think ghostwriters know all the details of their lives?

GO ON TO THE NEXT PAGE.

delivers them, and then that politician just reads the speech
from a teleprompter. [D] In addition, many popular songs
$\underline{\quad}$
40

claim a popular singer or performer as <u>songwriter, although</u>
41
they have been shaped more by a producer than by any of the
credited songwriters.

[4]

　Ghostwriting—whether we approve of it or <u>not</u>—is here
42
to stay. Sometimes, as in the case of Sinclair Lewis,
the ghostwriters will eventually become famous authors in
their own right. [43] Much more often, though,

<u>since</u> we are moved by the writing of authors whose names we
44
will never learn.

40. Given that all the choices are true, which one provides the best support for the statement in an earlier part of this sentence?

　F. NO CHANGE
　G. but the speeches are usually written by a team of speech-writers.
　H. but very few politicians have the oratorical skills of politicians from the last century.
　J. although many politicians like to speak from notes rather than fully written speeches.

41. Which of the following alternatives to the underlined portion would NOT be acceptable?

　A. songwriter, yet
　B. songwriter; therefore,
　C. songwriter, but
　D. songwriter; however,

42. F. NO CHANGE
　G. not
　H. not,
　J. not;

43. The writer is thinking about deleting the preceding sentence. Should this sentence be kept or deleted?

　A. Kept, because it shows the importance of ghostwriting to Sinclair Lewis's career.
　B. Kept, because it provides a contrast to the fact stated in the next sentence.
　C. Deleted, because it discusses a famous novelist in a paragraph about ghostwriters.
　D. Deleted, because Sinclair Lewis is already mentioned in the first paragraph.

44. F. NO CHANGE
　G. because
　H. yet
　J. DELETE the underlined portion.

Question 45 asks about the preceding passage as a whole.

---

45. The writer is considering adding the following sentence to the essay:

> Some in the industry suggest that as many as half of non-fiction books are written with help from ghostwriters.

If the writer were to add this sentence, it would most logically be placed at:

　A. Point A in Paragraph 1
　B. Point B in Paragraph 2
　C. Point C in Paragraph 3
　D. Point D in Paragraph 3

GO ON TO THE NEXT PAGE.

From Broadcasts to Podcasts

In the first half of the twentieth century, Americans couldn't spend their evenings in front of the TV. The television didn't become a regular feature of the American home until well into the 1960s. Instead, the major form of mass entertainment in this period was provided by the radio. The radio had begun its rise to prominence in the 1930s. It was especially popular in the 1940s, when most American households, as many as 91%, had a radio. [46] The residents of many small towns and rural

areas in non-urban parts of the country didn't have access to the newest movies or books, but those residents did have radios.

[1] Throughout the 1930s and 1940s, Americans turned to radio for all that. [2] During World War II, listeners could get more frequent information from their radios than they could from the newspapers. [3] In 1932, U.S. President Franklin Roosevelt, began his series of "fireside chats" over the radio. [4] For those looking for lighter fare, the radio had plenty of mystery

46. The writer is considering deleting the phrase "as many as 91%" from the preceding sentence (adjusting the punctuation accordingly). Should this phrase be kept or deleted?

   F. Kept, because it supports the idea that radio was on the decline after the 1930s.
   G. Kept, because it gives specific evidence of radio's popularity in the 1940s.
   H. Deleted, because it discusses American households in a passage about radio listening.
   J. Deleted, because it doesn't describe the households that had radios.

47. A. NO CHANGE
   B. in parts of the country outside cities
   C. despite their possession of radios
   D. DELETE the underlined portion

48. F. NO CHANGE
   G. their wants and other things that might be perceived as needs, but were more likely wants.
   H. the things they needed to listen to, such as comedy, news, sports, and drama, or other kinds of programs sometimes.
   J. their listening needs.

49. A. NO CHANGE
   B. President Franklin Roosevelt
   C. President, Franklin Roosevelt
   D. President, Franklin Roosevelt,

50. Which of the following alternatives to the underlined portion would NOT be acceptable?

   F. scouring
   G. desiring
   H. wanting
   J. seeking

GO ON TO THE NEXT PAGE.

programs, comedy and variety shows, westerns, and quiz programs. [5] These chats were intended to be as informal as a chat between friends and family members by the fireside, but they tackled some of the most complex political issues of the day:
51

war, depression, and international affairs. 52

By the 1950s, however, radio was losing its dominant position. The main reason for radio's decline was the advent of television. As television's continuing success has shown, Americans would rather *see* their favorite stars mere than *hear*
53

them. Listening (to anything other than music) to appear with
54
a thing of the past.

55 This portable device could hold more music than any record, tape, or CD ever could before. The iPod also brought back forms other than music. New *podcasts* hearkened back to

old-time radio programs called *broadcasts*. Whether funny or
56

serious, whether they're mainstream or they're underground,
57
these podcasts might never reach the heights of old-time radio

---

51. A. NO CHANGE
B. day, these included
C. day,
D. day having been

52. For the sake of the logic and coherence of this paragraph, Sentence 5 should be placed:

F. where it is now.
G. before Sentence 1.
H. after Sentence 2.
J. after Sentence 3.

53. A. NO CHANGE
B. merely then
C. mere then
D. than merely

54. F. NO CHANGE
G. was apparently
H. to appearance was
J. appeared as

55. Given that all the following statements are true, which one, if added here, would most clearly and effectively introduce the main subject of this paragraph?

A. Radio's most popular programs, such as *Gunsmoke*, became popular television hits.
B. At least it seemed like a thing of the past until the iPod came along in 2001.
C. One of the last popular programs, *The Zero Hour*, was on in the early 1970s.
D. The presidential radio address has become a custom ever since Roosevelt's early broadcasts.

56. F. NO CHANGE
G. broadcasts.
H. broadcasts'.
J. broadcast's.

57. A. NO CHANGE
B. being mainstream in the underground,
C. mainstream or underground,
D. if they're so underground they're actually mainstream,

GO ON TO THE NEXT PAGE.

broadcasts, but <u>there basically</u> bringing non-musical listening
₅₈
to a whole new generation. These days, when it can seem
like everyone wants *more* visual culture—IMAX screens, 3D
movies—along comes the podcast to provide a welcome but
not altogether unfamiliar alternative.

58. F. NO CHANGE
    G. they're
    H. it's essentially
    J. their

Question 59 asks about the preceding passage as a whole.

59. Suppose the writer's goal had been to write a brief essay focusing on how contemporary broadcasters have been influenced
by earlier broadcasters. Would this essay fulfill that goal?

    A. Yes, because it makes clear that the podcast would not
be likely to exist without old-time radio.
    B. Yes, because it implies that the podcast has encouraged
listeners to go back to earlier recordings.
    C. No, because it does not offer a contemporary equivalent
for Roosevelt's fireside chats.
    D. No, because it is more focused on sketching the rise in
popularity of the podcast.

PASSAGE V

Vladimir Nabokov, Books, and Butterflies

[1]

Vladimir Nabokov (1899–1977) is best known as a novelist.
His first novels <u>were written</u> in Russia in the 1920s.
₆₀

60. F. NO CHANGE
    G. was written
    H. were wrote
    J. was wrote

However, his <u>novels and books that people seem to like the
₆₁
most</u> were published in the United States and England in the
₆₁
1940s and 1950s. The most notorious of all was *Lolita* (1955), a
novel praised for its skillful construction and beautiful style but
often banned for its lurid descriptions and shocking plot. [62]

61. A. NO CHANGE
    B. most famous works
    C. works that are the most popular among readers
    D. books that are very popular among critics and general
readers alike

62. The writer is considering deleting the parenthetical information (and the parentheses) from the preceding sentence. If
the writer were to make this deletion, the paragraph would
primarily lose:

    F. a detail that helps to place *Lolita* chronologically in
Nabokov's literary career.
    G. the time during which Nabokov stopped writing to con-
duct his entomological research.
    H. a detail needed to understand the historical and literary
significance of *Lolita*.
    J. the number of years that Nabokov spent writing *Lolita*.

GO ON TO THE NEXT PAGE.

Nabokov left Russia to escape persecution from the newly

formed Soviet government. ⁶³

⁶³

[2]

In fact, he made significant contributions to entomology; ⁶⁴

the study of insects. Nabokov's work in charting the structure, ⁶⁵

and migration patterns of butterflies was a major contribution

to science. [A] Moreover, at what might have seemed a high

point in his literary career ⁶⁶ Nabokov accepted a research

fellowship from Harvard University's Museum of Comparative

Zoology. Then, he used this fellowship to conduct his fieldwork ⁶⁷

and to curate the museum's butterfly collection at a time when

he could just as well, of ⁶⁸ been earning a fellowship to work

exclusively on writing.

[3]

Although Nabokov's work was occasionally dismissed by

the scientific community as the ideas of an amateur, recent

findings have supported some of his hypotheses. [B] For

example, Nabokov was the primary one in a long list of scientists ⁶⁹

to suggest that the *Polyammatus blue* species of butterfly came to

North America from Asia in five waves over the Bering Strait.

---

63. Given that all the choices are true, which one most effectively leads the reader from this paragraph into the remainder of the essay?
    A. NO CHANGE
    B. Nabokov's other novels include *Pnin*, *Pale Fire*, and the highly experimental *Ada*.
    C. However, Nabokov was not exclusively a novelist and a man of letters.
    D. *Lolita* is now considered an American classic, despite its original reception.

64. F. NO CHANGE
    G. entomology being
    H. entomology of
    J. entomology,

65. A. NO CHANGE
    B. structure of
    C. structure
    D. structure;

66. F. NO CHANGE
    G. career;
    H. career.
    J. career,

67. A. NO CHANGE
    B. He
    C. Finally, he
    D. Consequently, he

68. F. NO CHANGE
    G. could just as well, have
    H. could, just as well of
    J. could just as well have

69. A. NO CHANGE
    B. first
    C. one before anyone else
    D. scientist that was before others in the field

GO ON TO THE NEXT PAGE.

Moreover, Nabokov was mainly interested in the study of
$\underline{\hspace{1.5cm}}$
70

moths and butterflies but studied some plants. In belated
$\overline{}$
70

recognition of his contributions, a genus of butterfly was

renamed. *Nabokovia* in his honor. [C]
$\overline{71}$

[4]

We can't know whether Nabokov's fiction or his scientific

work was more important, than which pursuit Nabokov found
$\overline{72}$

more enriching. Nabokov the famous novelist could of been
$\overline{73}$

Nabokov the famous entomologist. [D] Who can say? What we

can say is that Nabokov's story is a reminder of the vastness of

human potential. One might say that Nabokov was just

an exceptional person, but isn't it equally possible that these
$\overline{74}$

alternate personalities exist inside of all of us?

70. Given that all the choices are true, which one most effectively concludes the sentence by giving a specific example of Nabokov's contribution to the study of moths and butterflies?
   F. NO CHANGE
   G. aided in his scientific researches by his wife, Vera, who drove Vladimir to his research sites.
   H. the first to describe some species of moth and butterfly, including the Karner blue.
   J. working on his novels at the same time that he made his scientific discoveries.

71. A. NO CHANGE
    B. renamed,
    C. renamed
    D. renamed;

72. F. NO CHANGE
    G. for example
    H. nor
    J. DELETE the underlined portion.

73. A. NO CHANGE
    B. could have
    C. has
    D. have

74. F. NO CHANGE
    G. an exception to
    H. exceptionally a
    J. an exceptionally

Question 75 asks about the preceding passage as a whole.

75. The writer is considering adding the following sentence to the essay:

   The posthumous recognition continued as a number of moth and butterfly species were named after characters in his novels.

   If the writer were to add this sentence, it would most logically be placed at:

   A. Point A in Paragraph 2.
   B. Point B in Paragraph 3.
   C. Point C in Paragraph 3.
   D. Point D in Paragraph 4.

END OF TEST 4
STOP! DO NOT TURN THE PAGE UNTIL TOLD TO DO SO.

Chapter 20
English Practice
Test 4:
Answers and
Explanations

ENGLISH PRACTICE TEST 4 ANSWERS

1.	A	39.	B
2.	J	40.	G
3.	B	41.	B
4.	G	42.	F
5.	C	43.	B
6.	H	44.	J
7.	C	45.	B
8.	F	46.	G
9.	B	47.	D
10.	F	48.	J
11.	A	49.	B
12.	H	50.	F
13.	A	51.	A
14.	J	52.	J
15.	D	53.	D
16.	J	54.	G
17.	C	55.	B
18.	G	56.	G
19.	B	57.	C
20.	J	58.	G
21.	B	59.	D
22.	J	60.	F
23.	C	61.	B
24.	J	62.	F
25.	C	63.	C
26.	G	64.	J
27.	C	65.	C
28.	F	66.	J
29.	C	67.	B
30.	H	68.	J
31.	C	69.	B
32.	J	70.	H
33.	A	71.	C
34.	F	72.	H
35.	D	73.	B
36.	G	74.	F
37.	C	75.	C
38.	G		

SCORE YOUR PRACTICE TEST

Step A
Count the number of correct answers: _____. This is your *raw score*.

Step B
Use the score conversion table below to look up your raw score. The number to the left is your *scale score*: _____.

English Scale Conversion Table

Scale Score	Raw Score	Scale Score	Raw Score	Scale Score	Raw Score
36	72-75	24	53-55	12	23-24
35	70-71	23	51-52	11	19-22
34	68-69	22	48-50	10	16-18
33	67	21	45-47	9	13-15
32	66	20	42-44	8	11-12
31	65	19	40-41	7	9-10
30	64	18	38-39	6	7-8
29	62-63	17	36-37	5	6
28	61	16	33-35	4	4-5
27	60	15	30-32	3	3
26	58-59	14	27-29	2	2
25	56-57	13	25-26	1	0-1

ENGLISH PRACTICE TEST 4 EXPLANATIONS

Passage I

1. **A**   The question *but who knew they also love to eat cheeseburgers?* introduces a unique feature of the cats described in this passage. *Lolcats* are not an actual species, eliminating (B). The essay deals with *lolcats* themselves, not their love of cheeseburgers, eliminating (C). However, their love of cheeseburgers *is* unique, which means that this detail is important, eliminating (D). Only (A) remains.

2. **J**   The verb in this sentence will need to agree with the other verb in the sentence, *take*, which is in the present tense. Only (G) and (J) are in the present tense, eliminating (F) and (H). Of (G) and (J), (J) is better because (G) introduces a participle unnecessarily. Note: Be careful of verbs ending in "-ing." They can often make sentences unnecessarily wordy!

3. **B**   This sentence would be incomplete if the photographer's name were removed. In other words, *In the 1870s, Brighton-based photographer took a series...*would be incomplete. Therefore, the photographer's name should not be set off by commas as it is in (A) and (C), nor should it be set off by a semicolon as in (D). Only (B) correctly indicates that *Henry Pointer* is essential to the meaning of the sentence.

4. **G**   Only (G) contains specific information that is not redundant. Choice (J) cannot work because it does not indicate who is doing the *naming*, and (F) and (H) do not make sense in the given context.

5. **C**   The question asks for an option that shows that *the caption was an essential part of the humor of Pointer's photographs*. Therefore, we will need a choice that suggests the importance of captions. Choices (B) and (D) suggest that captions were not important, so they can be eliminated. Choice (A) does not address the importance of captions, so it, too, can be eliminated. Only (C) remains, and it works because it shows that captions could often be used to enliven otherwise dull pictures.

6. **H**   The idiom *in his day* must be kept intact here, making (H) the best choice. Choices (F) and (J) create a meaning different from the intended one, and (G) creates the phrase *with his day*, which is not used, thus eliminating these choices.

7. **C**   Sentences A and B offer a general description of the *lolcat*. Sentence C changes the focus of the paragraph to the *lolcat's* historical roots. Therefore, because it changes the focus of the paragraph, Sentence C offers a good place to start a new paragraph. Sentence D continues the historical discussion and should therefore be in the same paragraph with Sentence C.

8. **F**   Each answer choice offers a word or phrase of transition. Choices (G), (H), and (J) offer transitions that suggest a contrast, matching the contrasting word *though* in the passage. Choice (F) offers a transition that suggests a continuation. Therefore, (F) is the answer that does NOT work in the given context, meaning that it is the correct answer.

9. **B**   The non-underlined portion of this sentence contains the words *most famous*. These make the words in the following redundant: *known widely* in (A), *that many people know* in (C), and *that is pretty popular* in (D). Only (B) contains no redundant phrasing, and (B) is therefore the correct answer.

10. **F**   The subjects of the underlined verb are *phrases* and *language*. Therefore, the verb will need to agree with a plural subject, eliminating (G), (H), and (J). (F) offers a verb that agrees in number and tense.

11. **A**   The noun being modified by the underlined portion is *lolcats*. Choice (B) cannot work because the *lolcats* were not *earning lots of money*. Choice (C) cannot work because *lolcats* did not have *cameras in hand*, nor can (D) work because *lolcats* were not *promoting*. Only (A) provides an appropriate modifier for the word *lolcats*.

12. **H**   Of all the *creative coinages* of the decade, the *lolcat* was called one of the *most creative*. Choice (G) cannot work because more than two coinages are being compared. Choices (F) and (J) cannot work because they do not offer comparative words in a sentence that requires them. Only (H) can work in the given context.

13. **A**   Choice (B) cannot work because the *cheeseburger* refers to only one type of cat. Choice (C) cannot work because *cheeseburger-flavored* does not solve any problem posed in the essay. Choice (D) cannot work because no question is being posed. Only (A) can work, suggesting that *cheeseburger-flavored* is more detailed than *another line*, and that it is intended for humorous effect.

14. **J**   The passage as a whole discusses the history of the *lolcat*. Though it touches on photography, Internet usage, and types of animals, none of these can be described as the passage's main idea. Only (J) reflects the passage's main idea accurately, while suggesting that the writer has *not* succeeded in writing a passage that discusses *animal photography* more generally.

Passage II

15. **D**   Note the dash in the non-underlined part of the sentence. The answer will need to contain another dash to keep this notation consistent and to set off the unnecessary phrase *located a few hours west of Monterrey*. Only (D) contains a dash. Choice (A) contains a semicolon, which can be used only when you are separating two complete ideas.

16. **J**   The words *burning* and *scorching* mean similar things, and when they are paired with the word *heat* in the non-underlined portion, they become redundant. Therefore, in order to remove this redundant construction, it is best to remove these words—eliminating (F), (G), and (H)—and to delete the underlined portion. Note: Always give "DELETE" or "OMIT" special consideration. They are often correct!

17. **C**   The first paragraph discusses the author's difficult trip to the small town in Mexico, but the second paragraph switches to the pleasant time he had there with his host family. The discussion of the weather does not continue, which eliminates (A). The paragraph does not discuss Mexican cuisine, which eliminates (D). The paragraph does not discuss the author's earlier trip with his parents, which eliminates (B). Only (C) offers the appropriate transition into the new paragraph.

18. **G**   Read the question carefully. It asks for an option that shows that the narrator's host family was *extremely welcoming*. Choices (F), (H), and (J) do not contain any indication that the family was welcoming. Choice (G), however, suggests that the family was as welcoming as they would have been if the narrator had *lived there* [his] *whole life*. Choice (G) is therefore the best answer.

19. **B** This question asks for the alternative that would NOT be acceptable. Choices (A), (C), and (D) rearrange the words, but they are not grammatically or idiomatically incorrect. Choice (B) is unclear, though, in that it makes *Spanish language* modify the word *others*, whereas the sentence requires that *Spanish language* and *others* be separate nouns. Choice (B), therefore, would NOT be acceptable and is the correct answer.

20. **J** Note the other verbs in this paragraph: *were, asked, told, became*. The verb in this sentence must be consistent with these verbs. Therefore, only (J), *held*, is consistent with the simple past tense. Choices (F) and (H) change the type of past tense and the meaning of the sentence, and (G) switches to the present.

21. **B** The sentence as written cannot work because the narrator does not host the family; rather, the family hosts the narrator. Choice (C) makes the same mistake. Then, the words *that/which hosted me* are necessary to the meaning of the sentence: they clarify which *family* the narrator is referring to. Therefore, because this information is necessary, the information should not be set off by commas and should contain the word *that*, as in (B).

22. **J** The sentence describes the *previous English teachers* of the *children* and therefore requires that *children* be made possessive. Choice (H) contains no apostrophe and can therefore be eliminated. Choices (F) and (G) make the word *children* possessive in incorrect ways. Only (J) offers the correct possessive form of *children*. Note: What comes before the apostrophe must be a word. In other words, *childrens'* , as in (F), is incorrect because *childrens* is not a word. The same is true for (G).

23. **C** The first part of the sentence discusses the narrator teaching English. Therefore, in order to contrast with the first part of the sentence, we will need some indication that he is *not* teaching English, or that he is not exclusively teaching English. Choices (A), (B), and (D) are not related to English, nor do they contrast with the idea that the narrator is a teacher. Only (C) offers the appropriate contrast: while the narrator is a teacher, he is also *learning more than [he] could ever teach*.

24. **J** The current placement of the underlined portion cannot work because it does not clarify what the *circumstances* are, eliminating (F). The same is true for (G) and (H). Only (J) clarifies: *circumstances unlike my own*; therefore, (J) is the best answer.

25. **C** When you are asked whether to add a sentence to the given passage, make sure you have a very good reason to do so. In this particular case, the proposed sentence does not contribute meaningfully to the main idea or development of the paragraph or passage, so it should not be added, eliminating (A) and (B). Choice (D) can be eliminated because the passage does not give adequate grounds to assess the narrator's proficiency in Spanish. Only (C) works.

26. **G** The sentence as written cannot work because the phrase *On my last day of class* does not offer a complete idea, meaning that (F) and (J) can be eliminated. Then, the word *but* suggests a contrast where none is present, eliminating (H). Only (G) works, setting *On my last day of class* off as an introductory idea.

27. **C** Separate the contraction *I'd* into its component parts: *I had*. This makes (B) clearly redundant. This also eliminates (A) and (D), which use *had* again incorrectly. Only (C) works in the context created by the non-underlined portion.

28. **F** The word after the underlined portion is *I'm*; therefore, the underlined portion must modify the word *I*. The sentence works as written because *Remembering the details of my trip* refers appropriately to the *I* it is modifying. Choice (G) can be eliminated because *Identified as one of the borderlands* refers to some part of Mexico or the United States. *Showing all the mountains and rivers* refers to the *map*, eliminating (H). Choice (J) can also be eliminated because *Becoming a new place for me* refers to the village.

29. **C** The essay details the author's trip to Mexico, where he goes to teach English and also learns a good deal about the people and himself. The first paragraph suggests that the start was difficult but that the narrator quickly feels at home. There is no indication that (A) and (D) will work in the context because both suggest that the narrator did not enjoy his trip. Choice (B) highlights the importance of Spanish, but it does so too much. Only (C) can work in the context of the paragraph and the essay as a whole.

Passage III

30. **H** This sentence conveys the information that McLoughlin published a book. The phrase *a well-known tennis player* is not essential to conveying this meaning, and therefore that information is not essential to the meaning of the sentence. Because the information is not essential, it must be set off by commas as in (H). Note: On questions that test restrictive and non-restrictive information, the correct answer will typically have two commas, or none, so if you're unsure, eliminate answers with only one comma.

31. **C** Pay close attention to the non-underlined portion of the sentence. The word *uncover* indicates which word will be needed in the underlined portion. One does not uncover *tricks*, *skills*, or *abilities*, eliminating (A), (B), and (D). One does, however, uncover *secrets*, as in (C).

32. **J** The sentence as written creates a comma splice because *He was winning a number of major tennis tournaments that year* and *he was declared the Number 1 tennis player in the world* are both complete ideas. We can't change the comma, so this eliminates (F) and (H). Choice (G) does not make sense in the given context. Only (J) correctly makes the first part of the sentence incomplete by turning it into the modifying phrase *Winning a number of major tournaments that year*.

33. **A** A variety of prepositions can come after the word *written*, but each has a different meaning. *Written for* suggests that the book was written as a gift for someone, or that it was dedicated to that person. This can't work with the *someone else* in this sentence because there is no indication that the book was written *for* anyone in particular. Eliminate (B). The book is *about* McLoughlin, but there is no indication that the book was written *about* someone else, eliminating (C). We cannot delete the underlined portion because *written someone else* does not make sense. Only (A) remains: the book was not written *by* McLoughlin but *by* a ghostwriter.

34. **F** This sentence refers to the *book* belonging to *the tennis player*; therefore, there should be an apostrophe to indicate possession. This eliminates (H) and (J). Choice (G) makes the word *athletes* into a plural possessive when there is only one athlete involved, eliminating (G). Choice (F) gives the correct singular punctuation of *the tennis player*. Note: If you were not sure whether to choose *the tennis player* or *the athlete*, you could still have solved this question by looking at apostrophes and using Process of Elimination.

35. **D** The subject of the underlined verb is *history*, not the prepositional object *practices*. Therefore, the verb in the underlined portion should be singular, eliminating (A), (B), and (C). Only (D) offers a present-tense verb that agrees with a singular subject and has no redundant information.

36. **G** The previous sentence concludes with the idea that *the history of such practices is longer than we might expect*. This suggests the following sentence should make some historical claim or give some historical detail. The proposed addition does this, so it should be added, eliminating (H) and (J). It cannot, however, provide a transition from the previous paragraph because it is not the first sentence of this paragraph, eliminating (F). Only (G) correctly states that this sentence should be added and that it expands upon a point made in the preceding sentence.

37. **C** The answer choices offer different opportunities to insert pauses in the phrase *was not the first*. In the given sentence, though, no pause is necessary, so no commas are necessary, eliminating (A), (B), and (D). Choice (C) gives the best option because it contains no unnecessary commas.

38. **G** The sentence describes the *merits* of *ghostwriting*: in other words, *ghostwriting's merits* or *its* merits. Choice (F), *it's*, is the contraction of *it is*, not a possessive pronoun. Ghostwriting is not a person, so (H) can be eliminated, nor is it a plural, so (J) can be eliminated. Only (G) offers the correct possessive pronoun.

39. **B** The sentence that follows reads, *No, ghostwriting is equally prominent in lesser-known spheres as well.* Therefore, the sentence in this problem should offer some question to which the next sentence could answer *No*, particularly one that deals with ghostwriting in *well-known spheres*. The preceding sentence says that ghostwriting is *most prominent in the autobiographies and memoirs of celebrities*. Only (B) expands upon this idea and sets up the appropriate contrast with the following sentence. Choices (A), (C), and (D) deal exclusively with the details of celebrity ghostwriting.

40. **G** The passage as a whole discusses ghostwriting, and the sentence preceding this one reads *No, ghostwriting is equally prominent in lesser-known spheres as well.* Therefore, the sentence in the underlined portion should address ghostwriting somehow. The sentence will not be concerned with styles of reading, *oratorical skills*, or speech notes, eliminating (F), (H), and (J). Only (G) sets up the contrast that speeches *are often credited to the politician who delivers them* but actually are *written by a team of speechwriters*.

41. **B** The question asks for the punctuation and transition that would NOT be acceptable. The ideas surrounding this punctuation-transition combination are as follows: *In addition, many popular songs claim a popular singer or performer as songwriter* and *they have been shaped more by a producer than by any of the credited songwriters.* As the original sentence shows with the word *although*, these ideas should contrast. Therefore, (A), (C), and (D) WOULD be acceptable and can be eliminated. Only (B) removes this contrast and therefore would NOT be acceptable.

42. **F** Note the dash in the first part of this sentence, which sets off the nonessential phrase *whether we approve of it or not*. The answer will need to include another dash in order to keep this punctuation consistent. The sentence must be correct as written because only (F) contains that dash.

43. **B**   The sentence following this one begins with the words *Much more often, though*. If we remove this sentence, we are left with the question *Much more often* than what? Therefore, the sentence should be kept, offering as it does a description of what happens *sometimes*. Eliminate (C) and (D). Then, eliminate (A) because it does not show the importance of ghostwriting to Sinclair Lewis's career: in fact, the sentence suggests that Lewis became a well-known novelist *even though* he was initially a ghostwriter. Only (B) addresses the fact that this sentence gives the first part of a contrast completed in the next sentence.

44. **J**   As written, this sentence is actually a sentence fragment. The subordinating conjunction *since* makes the sentence incomplete, so eliminate (F). Eliminate (G) for the same reason. The word *yet* in (H) is a coordinating conjunction, but it does not fix the problem. The only viable solution to the problem is to remove the conjunction entirely, as in (J). Note: Give serious consideration to "DELETE" and "OMIT" when you see them. They are often correct!

45. **B**   The new sentence discusses the prevalence of ghostwriting in non-fiction. Paragraph 2 discusses that *Tennis as I Played It* won't be the first or last book to be ghostwritten and that ghostwriting is *acceptable*. The new sentence expands on that idea. It also transitions nicely to Paragraph 3, which introduces ghostwriting in different forms.

Passage IV

46. **G**   The phrase in question appears in the sentence *It was especially popular in the 1940s when most American households, as many as 91%, had a radio*. In this instance, the *91%* statistic gives a specific number of how many *American households* had radios. Therefore, because the information serves a specific purpose in the sentence, it should be kept. Eliminate (H) and (J). Then, eliminate (F) because the statistic does not indicate that radio was on the decline.

47. **D**   The sentence as written is redundant because the non-underlined portion already contains the words *of many small towns and rural areas*. This eliminates (A) and (B) for the same reason. Choice (C) is redundant with a later part of the sentence, *those residents did have radios*. The only viable alternative is to delete the underlined portion entirely, as in (D). Note: Give serious consideration to "DELETE" and "OMIT" when you see them. They are often correct!

48. **J**   The sentence as written does not contain adequate information because it is unclear what *that* refers to. Eliminate (F). Choices (G) and (H), however, go to the opposite extreme by giving way too much information, so eliminate them as well. Choice (J) strikes a happy medium: it is not too long and not too ambiguous.

49. **B**   In order to determine whether the name *Franklin Roosevelt* is essential to the meaning of the sentence, see if the sentence works without it. Without the name, the sentence would read *In 1932, U.S. President began his series of "fireside chats" over the radio*. There's something missing from this sentence, which means that the name *Franklin Roosevelt* is essential to the sentence's meaning. Therefore, the information should not be set off by any commas, and only (B) can work.

50. **F**   The sentence as written is correct: one can be *looking for lighter fare*. This question is asking for an alternative that would NOT be acceptable. One can be *desiring lighter fare*, *wanting lighter fare*, or *seeking lighter fare*, eliminating (G), (H), and (J). One cannot be *scouring lighter fare*, however, which means that (F) would NOT be an acceptable alternative to the underlined portion.

51. **A** *War, depression, and international affairs* are some examples of the *complex political issues* mentioned in the first part of the sentence. The word *day* is not part of this list, eliminating (C). Choice (D) creates an awkward construction, and (B) creates a comma splice by making the second half of the sentence into a complete idea. Only (A) can work: a complete idea comes before the colon, and a list comes after it.

52. **J** The first words of Sentence 5 are *These chats*, which suggest that the sentence that precedes Sentence 5 will clarify what the *chats* are. Only Sentence 3 has any mention of *chats*, in its discussion of Roosevelt's *fireside chats*. Therefore, Sentence 5 must come directly after Sentence 3, as in (J).

53. **D** There are two main parts to this answer. First, the sentence offers a comparison between *seeing* and *hearing*, suggesting that the sentence will need the comparative word *than*, not the time word *then*. Eliminate (B) and (C). Second, the remaining word will modify the verb *hear*. Because the word will modify a verb, the word must be the adverb *merely*, making (D) the best choice.

54. **G** The sentence does not make sense as written, because one cannot *appear with a thing of the past*. Eliminate (F). The same can be said of (H). Choice (J) creates a different meaning from the intended meaning, so it can be eliminated. Only (G) offers an alternative that turns the sentence into the clear expression of an idea.

55. **B** This paragraph discusses the rise to prominence of the iPod, and the attendant rise of podcasting. It does not continue the discussion of specific radio programs, eliminating (A) and (C), nor does it address political speechmaking on the radio, eliminating (D). Only (B) can work because it is the only choice that addresses either podcasting or the iPod.

56. **G** The *broadcasts* mentioned in the sentence are not in possession of anything; therefore, an apostrophe is unnecessary, eliminating (H) and (J). The two remaining choices have essentially the same meaning, but (G) is more concise, which means it is the better answer.

57. **C** The underlined portion is part of a list that includes *funny or serious*. All items in a list must be parallel, and only (C) gives a parallel construction. The other choices break this parallelism and add unnecessary words, so eliminate (A), (B), and (D).

58. **G** The sentence may *sound* correct, but this could be said for a number of the choices. Moreover, the adverb *there* does not apply here because no place or location is being indicated. Eliminate (F). Choice (H) cannot work because the singular *it's* does not agree with its plural antecedent, *podcasts*. We don't need a possessive pronoun in this portion of the sentence, which eliminates (J). Only (G), *they're*, the contraction of the words *they are*, makes this sentence clear and complete.

59. **D** The main idea of the passage is that new *podcasts* are similar to old-time radio *broadcasts*. It does not create a direct line of influence between *contemporary broadcasters* and *earlier broadcasters*. If it had been the writer's goal to discuss this line of influence, then this essay would not fulfill that goal, eliminating (A) and (B). It is true that the essay does not offer a contemporary equivalent for Roosevelt's fireside chats, but the essay is not primarily concerned with these chats. Instead, (D) offers the best reason that the essay has not fulfilled the writer's goal. The essay is more concerned with *podcasts* than with *contemporary broadcasting* generally.

Passage V

60. **F**   This answer will have two main parts. First, the verb must agree with the plural subject *novels*, which only (F) and (H) do. Then, we will need the form of the verb that goes with the helping verb *were*. Because *wrote* needs no helping verb, it can't work as *were wrote*, eliminating (H). Only (F) remains.

61. **B**   Since all the options have essentially the same meaning and are grammatically correct, choose the option that is the most concise. This is clearly (B), which is much shorter than the other choices and does not contain any excessive words.

62. **F**   Most sentences of the first paragraph contain a year or some piece of the chronology of Nabokov's career. Therefore, the parenthetical portion of this sentence, containing the year of publication of the novel *Lolita*, continues to situate Nabokov's life and work historically. The mere mention of a year cannot give *historical and literary significance*, eliminating (H). It would be unreasonable for Nabokov to have spent 1,955 years writing this novel, eliminating (J). Also, because this is the date of publication of a novel, we can't assume that Nabokov stopped writing at this point, eliminating (G). Only (F) makes the appropriately modest claim that the year gives historical context.

63. **C**   The first paragraph discusses Nabokov's fame as a novelist, but the remainder of the essay discusses his significant contributions to entomology. Therefore, a transitional sentence should somehow signify that the remainder of the essay will be about something other than Nabokov's career as a novelist. This eliminates (B) and (D). The essay does not turn to Nabokov's political beliefs, eliminating (A). Only (C) indicates that the remainder of the essay will be about something other than Nabokov's career as a novelist.

64. **J**   Choice (F) can be eliminated because semicolons separate only complete ideas, and *the study of insects* is not a complete idea. Choice (G) introduces the awkward construction of the participle *being*, so it can also be eliminated. *Entomology* is the *study of insects*; therefore, it would not make sense to do the *entomology of entomology*, eliminating (H). Choice (J) indicates appropriately that *the study of insects* is meant as an appositive defining the word *entomology*.

65. **C**   This sentence describes the way that Nabokov charts the *structure and migration patterns of butterflies*. There is no reason to set the word *structure* off from the rest of this phrase, eliminating (A) and (D). The word *of* in (B) is redundant because the word *of* is already contained in the non-underlined portion of the sentence. Therefore, the best answer is (C) because it includes no unnecessary pauses.

66. **J**   The words *Moreover, at what might have seemed a high point in his literary career* do not create a complete idea or a sentence that can stand on its own. Therefore, these words should not end with a period or a semicolon, eliminating (G) and (H). However, they do offer an introductory idea that will lead into the rest of the sentence, so the words should be set off with a comma, eliminating (F) and making (J) the best answer.

67. **B**   Choices (A), (C), and (D) all introduce transition words where no transition word is necessary. Choice (B) is the best choice because it is the most concise while preserving the meaning of the sentence.

68. **J**   Although the two forms may sound identical, the correct verb form is *could have*, not *could of*, eliminating (F) and (H). Then, because the words *could have* are part of a single verb, they should not be separated by a comma, as in (G). Therefore, the correct verb form with the correct lack of unnecessary pauses is shown in (J).

69. **B**   All four answer choices have the same basic meaning, and all are grammatically correct. When this is the case, choose the most concise of the answer choices. In this case, the most concise choice is (B).

70. **H**   Read the question carefully. The correct answer must contain a *specific example of Nabokov's contribution to the study of moths and butterflies*. Choice (F) speaks of his work too generally. Choice (G) discusses Nabokov's wife. Choice (J) returns to a discussion of his novels. None of these gives a *specific example of Nabokov's contribution*. Only (H) does that in giving the name of one of the butterfly species he discovered.

71. **C**   The phrase Nabokovia *in his honor* cannot stand on its own, so it cannot be punctuated with either a semicolon or a period, eliminating (A) and (D). Then, (B) adds an unnecessary pause before the word *Nabokovia*, so it can be eliminated. Only (C) remains, and it correctly omits unnecessary punctuation.

72. **H**   The sentence begins *We can't know*, and the second part of the sentence should continue in this vein, as if to suggest *nor can we know*, making (H) the best answer. The word *than* suggests a comparison where none is present, eliminating (F). The words *for example* are not followed by an example, eliminating (G). Then, deleting the underlined portion suggests that the phrase *which pursuit Nabokov found more enriching* modifies *more important*, which it does not, eliminating (J).

73. **B**   The first paragraph of the passage suggests that Nabokov is most famous as a novelist, but the rest of the passage suggests that he *could have* been a famous entomologist instead. It would not make sense to say that Nabokov *has been* a *famous entomologist*, because he was not, eliminating (C). Choice (D) can also be eliminated for the same reason, as well as for using *have been*, which is not the right verb for a singular subject. Only (B) works because the similar-sounding words *could of* are not used.

74. **F**   Nabokov was a person, but to say that he was *exceptionally a person* doesn't make sense, eliminating (H) and (J). The same is true of calling Nabokov *an exception to a person*, eliminating (G). Only (F) gives the correct form: the noun *person* is modified by the adjective *exceptional*.

75. **C**   The new sentence discusses naming species in order to honor Nabokov, so it should be placed near a sentence discussing a similar idea. The end of the third paragraph says that a genus of butterfly was named *Nabokovia*, making (C) the best answer.

NOTES

NOTES

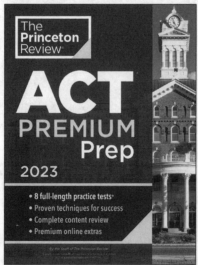
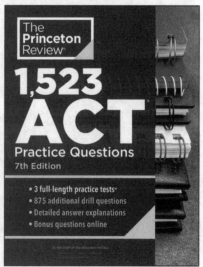